To my darling husband
with lots of love
at xmas 04

INDIAN PETER

By the same author

INDIAN PETER

The Extraordinary Life
and Adventures of
Peter Williamson

Douglas Skelton

MAINSTREAM
PUBLISHING
EDINBURGH AND LONDON

First published in Great Britain in 2004 by
MAINSTREAM PUBLISHING COMPANY (EDINBURGH) LTD
7 Albany Street
Edinburgh EH1 3UG

ISBN 1 84018 839 1

A catalogue record for this book
is available from the British Library

Typeset in Perpetua and Trade Gothic

Printed and bound in Great Britain by
Creative Print and Design, Wales

Acknowledgements

No one, especially me, can tackle a book like this without help from a variety of people. Thanks are due to the following – and anyone I've missed out I hope will forgive me.

To Keith McGregor, of that ilk, for his assistance with the US side of things. I promise I'll never insult the Children of the Mist again.

To Richard McGregor, also of that ilk, for riding to the rescue with some software.

To Gary McLaughlin for the use of his PC when CD-ROMs were not talking to my Mac and also for his help with image-scanning.

To the directors and staff at Mainstream for tolerating my tardiness.

To the staff of both Glasgow's Mitchell Library and Edinburgh Central Library.

To my wife Margaret for the proofreading and steady stream of liquids as I sweated over a hot keyboard.

To John Carroll for all the advice and assistance.

To all at the *Cumnock Chronicle* as well as Graham Turnbull, Mark Sweeney, Elizabeth McLaughlin, Eddie Murphy, Luan Johnston, Allan Eaglesham, Katie Parr, Karin Stewart, Kathy and Alex Allison, who, along with Gary, Margaret and my sisters Katrina and Rosemary, all helped convince me this was a story worth telling.

Contents

Introduction

At the start of the original script for *Butch Cassidy and the Sundance Kid* screenwriter William Goldman wrote the following:

> Not that it matters,
> but most of what follows is true.

The same can be said of what you are about to read.

Peter Williamson was many things in his life. He was a captive, first of merchants in what can only be described as a form of slave trading, then of a Native American tribe. He was a soldier. He was a prisoner of war. He was a writer, showman, businessman, visionary, tavern keeper, serial litigant and cuckold.

I found him by accident. I was writing a book on historical Scottish crimes and was scrolling through a website of famous Scots, looking for something on an eighteenth-century judge, when my eye fell on an entry about an Aberdeen man being the inspiration for *A Man Called Horse*. Being a movie fan – particularly Westerns – I was drawn to this.

I knew the Richard Harris film had been based on fact, but I didn't think it was about a Scotsman (and still don't). However, that was where I first met Peter Williamson. The brief account of his tale I read on that occasion stayed with me for months, and if I was ever certain of one thing, it was that one day I would have to write it down. That day came – and many another after it – and the result you are now holding in your hand.

One of the things that attracted William Goldman to the Butch Cassidy story was the idea of these men being legends in their own land and then going to South America and becoming legends all over again. A similar thing drew me to Peter Williamson's tale. I was fascinated by the way he reinvented himself according to circumstances. He was born into a poor Scottish family and was forced by events beyond his control to begin a new life in the American colonies. He seems to have adapted to his position as an indentured servant and managed to talk his employer/owner into providing him with an education. In order to survive, he resigned himself to being a slave of the Indians. To seek revenge for his life being torn apart, he joined the army. Once back on civvy street – and home in Britain – he became a strolling player, telling and embellishing his story to pay his way north. He set himself up as a writer and commentator on Britain's colonial policy, and as an expert on North American Indians, to whom he remained passionately sympathetic, even though he had apparently revelled in the slaughter of braves. He cajoled and wheedled his way into obtaining an early form of legal aid in order to pursue his court campaign against the Aberdeen merchants. Later, when he was a successful businessman, he pulled off the same trick when divorcing his somewhat energetic wife. He transformed himself into a man of letters – both in the figurative, creative sense and the literal, postal sense. When he found himself frozen out of the printing business, he taught himself the intricacies of the press. He was never a rich man, but his chameleon nature – and, probably, his Masonic contacts – helped ensure he was always reasonably comfortable.

Although his legal and personal adventures in Scotland are well documented, many doubts have been cast on Williamson's account of his American adventures, and it is true that little can be officially corroborated: for example, his marriage to the daughter of a wealthy planter is unconfirmed. We know that he was taken to America on a vessel named the *Planter*. We know that the ship foundered and was wrecked off the Delaware coast. After that, we only have his word for what took place. In his memoirs, he wrote of specific Indian attacks on settlers in the Pennsylvanian back-country. That colonists were slaughtered during this time is true, but the names mentioned by Williamson in his various books do not tally with existing records. In his favour, he was writing some years after the events, and it is always possible he got the names wrong. It is equally possible that he knew or heard reports of such attacks and invented names to make his account more readable. He has been accused of exaggerating scenes of torture to make his work more sensational in order to titillate what an Aberdeen magistrate later called 'the credulously vulgar'. However, the mid-eighteenth century was a brutal, bloody time in the American colonies. Atrocities were committed by both sides, and none of the scenes of torture he described are completely outwith the bounds of possibility. On the other hand, as Williamson's career in Edinburgh later showed, he was never slow to fill a need. If lawyers and litigants in Edinburgh's Parliament House wanted a drink, then he would supply it. If the city wanted a penny-post service, he would establish it. If the reading public wanted tales of blood, guts and horror, he would write them.

White captive-taking by Native Americans was common: it has been estimated that 2,700 prisoners were taken during attacks in Pennsylvania, Virginia and Maryland in the decade following 1755. Peter Williamson said he was one such captive, and his tale was one of the earliest entries in this growing branch of literature. I, for one, believe he did spend time with the Indians. There is a quality in his writing that suggests close personal contact, if only for a limited time. His account is resolutely anti-heroic: he is captured with no resistance. The torture he suffers, although painful, is not as ferocious as that meted out to others. He submits to life in the Indian village without a struggle. Certainly, he seizes his first chance to escape wholeheartedly, but it is without any great example of derring-do. He does not kill any of his captors in a feat of bravery, but merely slips away into the trees and spends a few terrified nights skulking around the forests giving his pursuers the slip. If everything he wrote was fabricated, surely he would have painted himself in a more flattering light? If he made up his tale of abduction, then why not make up details of a more dramatic escape, in which he succeeds in finding a weapon and killing some of the Indian braves before making off? As he wrote his first account years after the events, he almost certainly embellished his tale with odd facts and rural folklore he had picked up on his travels – and some outright fabrications – but the basic elements of his American period are rooted, I believe, in fact.

As to what is true and what is false, I have pointed out what I believe are the more fantastic parts of his tale. I am not a historian, I am a storyteller, and this is a rollicking yarn to which I hope I have done justice. I have, though, placed Williamson's tale against the backdrop of historical fact. In order to provide a better understanding of the social and political life of eighteenth-century colonial America, in particular Pennsylvania, I have sketched in details of the times. Through necessity, these can be little more than brief details explaining what was happening at the time. My sources are listed in the bibliography, but, naturally, any errors are mine. Anyone wishing to fully understand the complexities of the Seven Years War in North America should look no further than Fred Anderson's *Crucible of War*, which manages to be both learned and readable. There are also a variety of websites devoted to the period which give brief summaries of the dramatic events. My description of Peter's involvement in these events is drawn from his own narration. The Scottish sections are drawn from contemporary accounts, witness depositions (which are always written in the third person) and the various articles written about Williamson in the nineteenth and twentieth centuries. One other point is worth noting. I am writing about an age that was not as sensitive as our own. The accepted term today for the indigenous people of North America is 'Native Americans'. In Williamson's day they were 'Indians', and I have used both terms in this book.

This is not a debunking exercise; I will leave that to someone else. As another American screenwriter, this time John Milius, wrote at the opening of the published version of his screenplay *The Life and Times of Judge Roy Bean*:

> If this story is not the way it was
> – then it's the way it should have been
> and furthermore the author does not give a plug damn.

So here it is. The life story of Peter Williamson — servant, soldier, Freemason, entrepreneur, author, liar. How much of it is life, and how much story, remains to be seen.

PROLOGUE

The Grave

The graveyard is old now and unused. For almost 300 years its inhabitants have lain under its turf as the city grows and changes around them. In 1718, Calton was merely a village wedged between the stench of Edinburgh and the saltwater tang of Leith. The famed Leith Walk, now a wide, vehicle-filled arterial route between the city centre and the former port, was then little more than a pathway built on the site of a trench and mound constructed around 1650 as a defensive measure against Oliver Cromwell's invading army. Calton, clustering at the foot of a volcanic hill which nodded across the Nor' Loch (North Loch) to its more commanding castellated cousin, was linked to the port physically, by this walkway, and also spiritually, for until 1718 the villagers buried their dead in the Kirkgate of South Leith. The establishment of Calton Cemetery changed all that.

They no longer inter the dead here. The old burial ground, its monuments scattered around in a gap-toothed death's head grin, is little more than a tourist attraction. The city has it firmly in its grip now. It reached out across bridges towering over the drained Nor'

Loch to establish the New Town, then stretched down Leith Walk itself to grasp the old port. The stink of the Old Town has given way to the stench of modern life; the gentle clip of horses' hooves and the rattle of carriage wheels have become the ever-present rumble of the internal combustion engine. Roads have been established, diverted and closed off. Buildings have sprung up and been knocked down again. People have come and gone.

But the monuments remain – stone-faced memorials to past lives and past deaths. Here is the mausoleum designed in 1777 by Robert Adam for philosopher and historian David Hume. They say his friends mounted a vigil for eight days after his death lest the Devil should come for him to make him pay for his atheism, although it was more likely a defence against those children of the night, the body-snatchers. Beside it is the bronze monument to Abraham Lincoln, standing high above the outstretched arm of a grateful, newly emancipated slave. The eye-catching statue forms part of a memorial to five Scots who died fighting on the Union side during the American Civil War. There is another monument in the graveyard, a tall, dark obelisk, in remembrance of a group of political reformers, including firebrand lawyer Thomas Muir, who wished to 'live free or die'. In 1793, they lost the chance of the former and may have fervently wished for the latter when they were arrested, convicted and sent in chains to the Australian hellhole of Botany Bay.

It is said that Robert Louis Stevenson chanced upon the grave of one John Silver while wandering around these memorials and was so taken with the name that he appropriated it for one of his most memorable creations, the wily pirate and sea cook from *Treasure Island*. Stevenson may also have heard of another man whose final resting place can be found here. He did not use his name, but it is possible that he used part of his early life in his other great work of high adventure, *Kidnapped*. In many ways, during his lifetime this man was as famous, in his adopted city at least, as Stevenson's later fictional heroes. But there is no stone to mark his grave, no monument to recall a life of high adventure and high drama.

What did he think of as he lay dying during the young days of 1799, when his once-strong body betrayed him and his once-sharp wits deserted him? Did his mind roam, as all men's must, over the days of his life? Did he look back with pride, with sadness, with regret? Did he think of lost lives and lost loves? Did he once again find himself back in the lands of his youth? Did he once more smell the pine forests of North America or hear the roar of guns in a lakeside fort? Did the yells of pursuing tribesmen cut through his dreams like a scalping knife? Did he recall the echoing voice of a Scottish judge delivering a victorious verdict?

Or did he find himself back at the first time he felt his life was almost at an end?

ONE

Monsters of Impiety

He could smell the fear.

It rose like a cloud from the bodies of his young companions and flashed like a warning light in their eyes as they listened to the storm howl around them. Crammed together in the hold of the ship, terror flowing from every pore, they could do little as the vessel ploughed through the foaming ocean, no more than a splinter of wood in the vast black mass that swirled around it. They had grown used to the creaking of the timbers over the past three months, but this night the sounds were different. The wooden beams and planks shrieked like souls in torment and, more worryingly, seawater poured from them like blood from open wounds.

The storm had raged out of the south-east eleven weeks into the Atlantic crossing, the wind screaming from the open sea like a vengeful titan, scooping the waves up in its dripping maw and spitting them out at the three-masted vessel bobbing on the surface. The ocean seethed and writhed like a host of angry serpents against a hull that had seemed so robust when the voyage began but now appeared so very,

very fragile as the wind roared through the rigging and whipped around the reefed sails. The ship pitched and tossed in the breath of the gale, its bow dipping and rising in a hissing explosion of spray.

The human cargo hung on to their bunks as the ship bucked around them, fingers curled tightly round wood or clinging to ropes to prevent being thrown to the deck in the wake of each shuddering roll. Trapped with the rats between the decks, they were certain they would never see morning. Never again would they see their homeland. Never again would they embrace their families. Never again would they breathe unsalted air. They would die this night on this little ship as it futilely battled a storm on a vast and unfriendly ocean.

He could hear weeping and praying. He could hear someone crying out for God to help them. But God could not help them, for was this hurricane not part of His creation too? He could hear the lamentation of the young ones, younger even than he, as they called for their mothers. But their mothers were not there to comfort them. Those youngsters were alone, and now they were sure they would die alone without ever seeing the land they had been told flowed with milk and honey.

Suddenly, their wooden world took on a new tone: a scraping rasp from the very bottom of the ship that vibrated through the soaked timbers. And of all the sounds – the banshee wail of the wind above, the boom of the waves breaking around them, the crash of the water hurling itself at the deck – this one was the most terrifying.

And when the ship came to a bone-jarring halt, he knew with fresh certainty that this was when his life would come to an end.

* * *

That life began thirteen years and thousands of miles away in a tiny farmhouse in the north-east of Scotland. It was the year 1730 and, with a slap and a wail, the third son of ploughman James Williamson was brought into the world. Williamson worked the small farm at Hirnley, part of the rich lands of Lord Aboyne on the banks of the River Dee, and was, in the later words of his new son, 'if not rich, yet reputable'. Five years later, the boy was inducted into the local kirk. His baptismal records, written 'under the hand of the Reverend William Fordyce, Minister of Aboyne parish', state that in 'February, the fifteenth day of One Thousand and Seven Hundred and Thirty-Five years, James Williamson in Hirnley had a son baptized in the face of the congregation, called Peter'.

James Williamson would ultimately father five sons and two daughters. By the standards of the day, it was by no means a large family, but times were often hard in rural Scotland, as elsewhere, and scratching a living out of even the most fertile ground could at times be a precarious proposition. Even so, by 1740 Peter had grown into a tall, strong lad with a quick and ready wit, and his father decided it might be best for him to spend some time away from home. There could have been a number of reasons for this. With nine mouths to feed by then, James Williamson may have been finding things difficult, although he had rented more land in another part of the parish in addition to his holding in Hirnley. Years later, a family friend observed that 'he was very capable to maintain and bring up his family and that there were few bairns brought up like them in the parish'. Peter himself wrote that his parents 'supported me in the best manner they could, as long as they had the happiness of having me under their inspection'. It was noted that the boy had a quick intelligence, and it is not unreasonable to assume that Williamson senior wanted the best for his third born – and perhaps believed that town life could offer him a superior education.

Many years later, during one of Peter's numerous court cases, the Reverend William Fordyce and the elders of Aboyne parish certified that:

In the year one thousand seven hundred and forty, when a young boy of ten years of age, he left this place with a fair character and of a promising disposition and that there was no reason known then to us why he might not have met with all proper encouragement and be admitted into any Christian society.

On the morning of his departure, the bright-eyed, strapping boy would have set out filled with eagerness and excitement. All he had ever known in the first decade of his life was the farm and the tiny settlements that were dotted around it. Now he was embarking on a great adventure: a new life in the town of Aberdeen. We do not know how he left his home and his family, whether on foot or perched on a cart, but we can imagine the scene as he waved one last time to his mother as she stood in the doorway of their little house, before he turned away to face the future.

In the twelfth century, King David I of Scotland, who felt the wide mouth of the Dee offered an attractive and safe harbour, established the town of Aberdeen, which would later become known as the Granite City. Perched on the north-eastern coast of the country, over the centuries it had established itself as a fishing and trading centre with a thriving port. Wheat, salt, wool, timber, animal hides and textiles all passed through the increasingly busy docks, helping the northern town become a viable rival to the already thriving port of Leith in the south.

Even though plagues, famines and wars all took their toll, by the 1720s, according to Daniel Defoe in his *Tour through the Whole Island of Great Britain,* the town had the:

> largest and fairest market place in Scotland; the generality of the citizens' houses are built of stone four story high. They have a very good manufacture of linen, and also of worsted

stockings, which they send to England in great quantities, to Holland and into the North and East seas. They have also a particular export of pork, pickled and barreled, which they chiefly sell to the Dutch. They also export corn and meal from the Firth of Moray, or Cromarty, the corn coming from about Inverness.

But there was, as ever, a darker side to this spirit of free enterprise. The plantations of the American colonies were in desperate need of young workers, and there were men in Aberdeen who were only too happy to provide them, whether the youngsters wanted to go or not. The men behind this flesh trade used every means, fair and foul, to entice their young prey onto the ships that would take them half a world away. Recruiting parties piped and drummed their way through towns and villages calling for volunteers to seek a new life in the Americas. Merchants or the ships' captains who were often their partners placed advertisements in newspapers inviting people to sell their indentures to them and seek a new life in the New World. The merchants agreed to feed and even clothe them while they were in their care, often promising high wages at the other end. All they had to do in return was pledge their body for a period of three to seven years. America was the land of promise, and a bright young lad could make his fortune there, if he was willing to work.

Many people, of course, signed up willingly and happily pledged their service, or indenture, before a magistrate, saw the papers duly signed and went off with their benefactors to be transported to their new life. They may have wished to escape crippling poverty, or debts, or even crime. In his autobiography, Benjamin Franklin wrote of Oxford scholar George Webb, whose indentures had been bought from a ship's captain by a Philadelphia printer. Webb, originally from Gloucester, had studied at the famed university for a year before he tired of academic life and headed for London to become an actor, having shown some aptitude for the theatre in his home town. On receiving his quarterly fifteen guinea (just over fifteen pounds) allowance, he left Oxford – and his debts – behind, 'hid his gown in a furze bush and footed it to London'. Once in the metropolis, however, he found an actor's life was not for him. 'He fell into bad company,' wrote Franklin, 'soon spent his guineas, found no means of being introduced among the players, grew necessitous, pawn'd his clothes and wanted bread.'

Starving, ragged and having no idea what he was going to do with himself, the 18-year-old would-be actor was wandering the cold streets of the city one day when he found a crimp's bill thrust into his hand. A 'crimp' was an agent of the merchants who gathered servants for indenture in the Colonies, and the flyer promised 'entertainment and encouragement to such as would bind themselves to serve in America'. Penniless, hungry and not giving a tinker's cuss who at home worried about him, Webb signed up and was soon on a ship bound for Philadelphia.

Webb's story is not unique, although he did have the advantage of taking the decision himself. Others were not so blessed. Fathers would pledge sons and daughters, brothers would sell brothers, and wives would barter husbands (and vice versa) to make a few pennies in times of hardship – or simply because the individuals were troublesome. In lists of accounts from the period, there are entries such as 'To Robert Ross, for his son, one shilling', and 'To Maclean, for listing his brother Donald, one shilling and six pence'. In another, more sinister, entry, a Colonel Horsie received one pound for 'his concubine', suggesting that the officer and gentleman had tired of his lover and decided that parting would be much sweeter sorrow if he made a few shillings out of it.

The subjects themselves, like David Balfour in Stevenson's *Kidnapped*, may have been unwitting or unwilling participants in this enforced emigration scheme, but they were bound for the New World nonetheless. Some, like Webb, were lucky enough to fall into the hands of a respectable master. Not all indentured servants were so fortunate, for they had effectively sold their bodies, albeit only for a period of a few years, and once their papers had been transferred to plantation owners, they became their property, more or less to do with as they saw fit. This was, of course, little different from being apprenticed to a tradesman, but few such apprentices were herded around the town, sometimes for weeks on end, while the rest of the human cargo was gathered, then bundled on board a ship and transported thousands of miles to a foreign land.

Some transportees were tricked into putting their lives into the merchants' hands. The agents employed to gather them exaggerated the benefits of colonial life to lure the prospective workers, but where such salesmanship did not work, other deceitful arts were employed. Victims were invited into a tavern for a drink. One drink led to many, and the unwary young man or woman was steered in the direction of a willing magistrate, who signed off on the indenture. If strong liquor could not tempt them, then perhaps a young man's raging hormones could prove to be his undoing. Prostitutes were employed as seductive bait, and the post-priapic country boy, having dipped his wick and slaked his thirst, found himself dazed and confused in a magistrate's room, and swearing the next seven years of his life away.

Yet even these methods were not enough to furnish the trade with enough of its raw materials. So, the pursuit of profit pushing them ever further, the agents – with or without their masters' knowledge or approval – adopted other means of filling the holds of the ships bobbing at the quaysides. Taking a leaf out of the book of the Royal Navy, they formed press gangs to snatch likely lads and lassies from the street. This practice became so widespread that, as the influential and oft-quoted history of the town *The Book of Bon Accord* states:

> The inhabitants of the neighbourhood dared not send their
> children into the town, and even trembled lest they should be

snatched away from their homes. For in all parts of the country emissaries were abroad, in the dead of night children were taken by force from the beds where they slept; and the remote valleys of the Highlands, fifty miles distant from the city, were infested by ruffians who hunted their prey as beasts of the chase.

The official line was that each person, when appearing before a magistrate, was asked whether he or she was signing the indentures willingly or if any force or compulsion had been brought to bear. If the person raised any complaint, then the magistrate was duty-bound to declare the contract null and void. It was said that an indenture not attested to by a magistrate was 'not worth two pence in America'.

But what if the magistrates were also merchants? And what if those merchants were behind the scheme? Where were the legal checks and balances then?

It was this atmosphere of fear, suspicion and corruption that Peter Williamson entered some time in 1740. For the next few years the trade was to flourish in Aberdeen and the north-east, with agents making regular forays to the country's interior for fresh supplies. It is estimated that 600 boys and girls were abducted and sent abroad between 1740 and 1746. How many returned cannot be said.

On his arrival in Aberdeen, Peter went to stay with an aunt, and it is possible that she may have warned him of the dangers in the streets. But, even in the eighteenth century, boys would be boys. The town would have held unimaginable promise for a child of Peter's nature. The streets, many paved and lit by oil lamps, which were novelties in themselves for a country boy, were thronged with people: the merchants, the traders, the hawkers and the travellers. The harbour was packed with ships large and small from all over the world, and these would have drawn the curious boy like a compass point to magnetic north. During the following three years in Aberdeen, he would have heard a multitude of different accents and witnessed the rolling gait of mariners in whose hands and faces he saw the promise of many a tale, both tall and true. The air would have been pungent with the smell of fish and spices and tar. And above it all would have been the sound of hammering and sawing as carpenters and shipwrights made vessels ready to sail. The sights, the sounds and the smells would have distilled into an intoxicating brew for the youngster – and perhaps made him easy prey for the men out scouting for potential servants.

He would have been an obvious target. By January 1743, he had grown into what he described as a 'stout and robust boy', making him an ideal candidate for the tough passage and potentially even tougher work ahead. The fact that he was, at only thirteen years of age, too young to even consent to selling his indentures would have mattered little to the men he later branded 'monsters of impiety'. He was a strapping lad, and they needed strapping lads to fill the hold of the ship. Williamson admitted that he took little persuasion to go with the men – what inducements they offered can only be guessed at – and he whiled away the days before the ship was to sail 'in childish amusements with my fellow sufferers'. Sooner or later, though, he would have wanted to leave – and that would have been when the iron fist burst from the velvet glove. He and other young people, some as young as eight or ten, were penned up in a barn on the Aberdeen Green where they were fed, watered and entertained by pipers and card games. But they were still prisoners, and the presence of guards armed with clubs and whips attested to this. If any one of them tried to escape, they were brought back by force.

The fact that boys and girls destined for the Americas were being held in this barn was well known to the townsfolk, and, with little attempt being made to hide the trade, the building even became something of a tourist attraction. Robert Reid, a rural lad visiting his sister in Aberdeen in 1740, said she suggested that they 'go and see the country boys who were going to Philadelphia in a barn'. He said they went to the Green and heard loud music and 'a great noise', but he refused to actually go inside and see them, for he had heard 'in his own country' that many boys had been 'decoyed by particular artifices of merchants'.

In a deposition some years later, Robert Thomson, Aberdeen Town Clerk, claimed he knew nothing about the trade, but he did recall that he was 'once . . . in the street called the Green and saw a parcel of people in a barn, and heard them merry and a piper along with them'. Mr Thomson said he asked who the people were and 'was told they were indentured servants for America'. However, he disputed that any of them were being held there against their will, for 'the doors of the barn were open, and people standing in them'.

Peter Williamson's father and brother found the opposite. Naturally, Peter's aunt sent word that the lad had gone missing, and the worried farmer and his son Alexander arrived in Aberdeen to search for him. They scoured the streets and docks but could find neither hide nor hair of the boy. We can only imagine the anguish felt by the worried farmer as he hunted through the town, asking strangers if they had seen a youngster 'upwards of twelve years of age, a rough, ragged, hummle-headed, long, stowie [stout], clever boy' (as Peter was then described). We can only imagine the pain he felt as heads were shaken and doors were closed. Eventually, Alexander heard talk of the boys in the barn and went off to investigate. Once there, he watched carefully for a sign of his brother and finally caught sight of Peter among the dozens inside. But the guards refused to let Alexander speak to him. Alexander Williamson tried to press the point but was forced to retreat when he was threatened with being taken hostage himself.

He returned to his father, who had by this time been compelled to go back to the farm, for he had work to do and other children to feed. On hearing the news of Peter, the older Williamson dropped what he was doing and went back to Aberdeen to seek the release of his son.

By this time, however, the birds had flown. The barn was empty.

James Williamson assumed that the traders panicked when Alexander found them, and moved their cargo elsewhere. According to later court papers, he and his son applied to local magistrates for some redress but failed to find a sympathetic ear. They then left Aberdeen and found a rural Justice of the Peace who was willing to sign a warrant allowing them to search for young Peter and secure his release. But by the time they obtained the warrant and returned to Aberdeen, Peter was gone. John Wilson, a family friend, said that, 'James Williamson lamented the loss of . . . his son, and that he could not find him out and that his lamentation was very sore and grievous.' The heartbroken father never again laid eyes on his third son.

Whether the traders would have panicked is open to question for one very good reason: they had protection at the very highest levels. This could explain the lack of support the Williamsons found among the Aberdeen magistrates, for many members of the local judiciary and town worthies were heavily involved in the trade. Just how involved some of them were would only be made clear many years later.

Another case of kidnapping and transportation around this time echoes the treatment dished out to Peter's father and supports the allegation that threats were made to Alexander. Details are contained in a deposition by a man called William Jamieson. Jamieson lived with his family in Old Meldrum, a village about eighteen miles north-west of Aberdeen. He had a son named John who, in the spring of 1741 when he was about ten or eleven years old, vanished from the house. Neighbours told Jamieson that they had seen a servant of Aberdeen merchant John Burnet, known locally as 'Bonnie John', heading towards Aberdeen with two boys, one of whom was Mr Jamieson's son. It was known that Burnet was involved in the indentured servant trade, and Jamieson realised then that his boy was destined for the plantations – unless he could get him back first. So he went to Aberdeen and sought out Bonnie John, who confirmed he had several lads under contract but claimed he did not know if John Jamieson was among them. However, Burnet warned, even if young John was among them, the father would not get him back 'because he was engaged with him'. For Burnet, obviously, a bond was a bond, and even the fact that the Jamieson boy was 'under the age of pupillarity', and so could not legally consent to the contract, was no deterrent. Perhaps Bonnie John was not so bonnie after all.

The anxious father heard in the streets that the boys being stored for transportation were often taken to the shore for air and exercise. He made his way there and found 'about sixty boys diverting themselves' under the stern eye of a man employed by Burnet as a guard. The man took his job very seriously, for he wielded a horsewhip to keep the boys in line and prevent them from straying. Jamieson saw his son among the crowd and called out to him. The boy trotted over and told him he would willingly come away if he was allowed. The guard, though, was having none of it. Jamieson later said he 'came up and gave the boy a lash with his whip and took him by the shoulder and carried him among the rest'. He then rounded up his charges and, with the lash snapping over their heads and occasionally slicing the flesh from their backs, drove them like sheep through the streets.

Jamieson trailed along behind the flock, begging the guard to allow him to speak to his son. The man said 'that he should get leave to speak with him bye and bye, when they were come to the barn'. But when they got to the barn, possibly the same one in which Peter Williamson would be caged two years later, the guard locked the door, pocketed the key and refused the distraught father access.

Like James Williamson later, William Jamieson unsuccessfully sought legal help in the town. He was told that he would 'be in vain to apply to the magistrates to get his son liberate, because some of the magistrates had a hand in those doings as well as the said John Burnet'. He said that anyone who complained was told that 'if they were not pleased they would be sent away themselves'.

Jamieson heard rumours, or was 'informed by the voice of the country', that his son was put aboard a ship bound for Maryland about two weeks after he had found him on the shore.

But he did not let it lie there. He wanted justice, and if Aberdeen would not provide it, he would find somewhere that would. The following summer he went to Edinburgh and obtained a summons against John Burnet. However, not one of the Aberdeen magistrates would execute the summons, again showing their partiality to the merchants – and perhaps even a deeper involvement in the trade. A messenger had to be hired from Old Meldrum to serve the paper and Burnet responded by speaking with Lord Aberdeen, who owned the land farmed by William Jamieson's father. Jamieson senior and his troublesome son were ordered to an audience with the nobleman at his home, Haddo House, and when they arrived, they found John Burnet sitting with his Lordship. During the meeting, it was agreed that the merchant would give Jamieson 'his bond to restore his son to him within the space of a twelvemonth under the penalty of fifty pounds sterling'. But the son was never restored and the bond was never paid.

Lord Aberdeen assured his tenants that he would force Burnet to honour the agreement but unfortunately died before any moves could be made. By this time, William Jamieson had enlisted in the army and was posted to Flanders, where Britain was involved in fighting the French. While he was away, Prince Charles Edward Stuart landed at Arisaig, raised his standard at Glenfinnan, led his army south to victory and retreated north again to bitter defeat on a blood-soaked moor known to history as Culloden. Jamieson did not return from Flanders until after the Bonnie Prince had fled to the safety of France. By that time, John Burnet had been bankrupted and had also left the country.

In a deposition given almost twenty years later, Jamieson, by then living in Edinburgh, said he 'did not know whether his son John is alive

31

or dead, having never heard from him since he was carried from Aberdeen'.

James Williamson, of course, knew nothing of Jamieson's experiences two years before as he continued his frenzied search for Peter, who had been taken from the barn with the others and herded through the streets to their next resting place. The boy had been a hostage for some weeks, and now he was taken to a place more fitting for his prisoner status.

Peter Williamson was going to jail.

TWO

Eat Sugar and Drink Wine

Spending much of an icy Aberdeen winter in a barn would have been hard, but life in the town's tollbooth was a freezing hell. Built over one hundred years earlier, and known as the Wardhouse, the imposing building was the town's remand home and prison combined. Accused persons were kept there until their appearance in the adjacent courthouse and then returned when found guilty, so the young people found themselves sharing space with thieves, rapists and murderers, as well as debtors, gypsies and vagrants. That the town's jail was used to house some of the newly indentured is yet another confirmation of the involvement of the local magistrates. Young Peter, freshly moved from the barn, was placed for a time in the cramped cells and punishment quarters of the steepled structure on Castle Street.

As the cargo list grew, so did the need for storage space. The merchants used their influence to obtain room in the town's workhouse, which was supposed to provide employment for the poor and indigent, but in this case helped increase the profits of the rich and powerful. Peter was not among the workhouse lodgers, but, following his sojourn in the tollbooth, he was moved to a house nearby, where a woman named Helen Law cared for him and other boys. He had no way of knowing it, but it would not be his last experience of the Aberdeen tollbooth. He would be back in the cold stone rooms among the dark, scowling faces of the men, both innocent and guilty. But before then he had some living to do and death to face many times.

Speaking almost twenty years later, Helen Law remembered a boy named Peter McWilliam or Williamson being boarded with her who was, in her opinion, 'beyond twelve years of age'. He was, she recalled in a deposition, 'ragged and had very bad cloaths until he got new ones after he was boarded with her'. The boy was 'of such a big stature and size that she has known several lads of fifteen or sixteen years of age of a less size and stature than he'. Naturally, since she was part of the trade, she insisted she knew of no illegal methods employed to entice servants to the trade. However, she did point out that she could remember 'particularly that there were several of those boarders much younger than the boy called Peter McWilliam or Williamson'. Clearly, though, promises had been made by the agents selling the notion of a life in servitude in the Colonies, for she said that 'her boarders often told her that they were going to a country to eat sugar and drink wine'.

Not all of her young charges were as keen to emigrate, however, and as their new owners were aware of this, they placed two men in the house to watch over them. Their presence did nothing to deter escape bids. Mrs Law said that some of the boys lodged in the workhouse broke through a wall to escape and ended up in her house. She fed them and sent word to the merchants' agent, an Aberdeen saddler by the name of James Smith, to come and fetch them. Four or five of the strongest lads, she said, were put in the tollbooth for their trouble. One, named James Byres, fell ill, and Mrs Law claimed she put a case to Mr Smith requesting that the boy be placed in her care. But the hard-headed Smith believed the boy was not as ill as he was making out and was intent on having him locked up in the tollbooth until Mrs Law offered her own son as surety for Byres' good behaviour. The offer was accepted, and the youngster stayed in her house for five or six days until his fever abated. It was, however, little more than a reprieve, for as soon as his temperature subsided he was carted off to enjoy the cold comforts of the tollbooth. Mrs Law, who had a kindly side despite being involved in the slave trade, felt the Byres boy had been harshly treated. She observed that he 'had not recovered his strength, nor was he so well as before he fell sick when he was taken back to the Tollbooth, or when he went on board ship, which was about a month after'.

Despite Smith's tough attitude to James Byres' illness, and her own reservations, Mrs Law was adamant that the man had not offered any false inducements to the young people and had certainly not kidnapped them. 'On the contrary,' she said, 'they had all willingly consented to their engagements and indentures with them, and considered and looked upon such . . . to be a lucky thing for them because they were going to a much better country than their own.'

Although she admitted that many boys had deserted – hence the need for guards – she said that anyone who asked could be 'dispensed with', or freed, on repayment of the original indenture fee plus any further funds the merchants had laid out for their room and board. Her own son, in fact, had contracted with merchant James Abernathie to go to America. Her son was, she said, 'of a great growth and about fifteen years of age, and rather bigger than the boy Peter McWilliam or Williamson'. When she heard what he had done, she approached Mr Abernathie and asked if he could be dispensed with. Terms were agreed and the boy released, but so determined was he to make his fortune in the Americas that he promptly signed up again and sailed westwards.

Peter Williamson told a different version. He said that she 'poured out a great many curses upon the said James Abernathie, for decoying young boys and sending them to America, and particularly her own son'. As Mrs Law was speaking many years after the event, and in a court of law, it was of course unlikely that she would admit to knowledge of any wrongdoing.

The boys remained with Mrs Law for a number of weeks before being moved again, this time to Torry, a harbour directly opposite Aberdeen's docks on the River Dee. It was now April or May 1743. The spring sunshine had defrosted the cold winter; Peter Williamson had been in custody for between three and four months, and during that time he had been kept in a barn, in a prison and in a private house. Now he was to find himself in a new home, at least until they made landfall on the other side of the world. Although the boys were not staying with her this time, they did not leave their house-mother Helen Law behind, for she took up residence in a house specially rented for her on the dockside, from where she would 'prepare their victuals'.

The three-masted ship the *Planter* had been bought in London in February 1743 by Captain Robert Ragg, a local seaman with connections through marriage and commerce to some of the city's more powerful businessmen. These men had entered into partnership with him to buy the vessel in order to claim their share of the healthy profits being made from the tobacco trade. The plan was to sail to America, take on a load of the valuable cargo and bring it back to Scotland. However, in order to defray the expenses of the outward-bound journey, it was decided among the owners, as one of them later testified, that 'servants be indented and engaged to go to America, and their indentures properly attested, as was usual in most of the sea ports of Scotland at that time'.

Aberdeen stabler James Robertson was hired by James Smith to oversee the men, women and children on board ship and 'to ensure that they did not desert'. Such fears aside, Robertson claimed that the servants were 'at liberty to go out and play and divert themselves through the town of Torry and upon the sands or among the shrouds of the ship and very often would have taken a long boat and gone out thereon and taken their diversion in the harbour'.

The contradiction here is evident. If the servants were prone to defrauding the merchants of their legal profits by deserting, prompting the use of guards, why were they given the freedom of the harbour and even a boat? The answer is that most of the servants whose indentures had been legally attested by the magistrates, the ones who believed they were going 'to a much better country than their own', were probably given such liberties, but the more dubious cases – such as Peter Williamson – were subject to stricter security. Robertson himself remembered a boy he believed was named McWilliam on board ship, but said he 'could not be under 16 years of age'. Again, Robertson was speaking many years afterwards when the entire trade was under legal scrutiny, so, like Helen Law, he was unlikely to implicate himself in any way – especially after Peter accused him of being one of the men who had kidnapped him in the first place. Robertson, naturally, denied this.

Although the merchants involved in the trade later tried to deny that he was ever on board, it is evident that Peter Williamson was indeed present on the *Planter*. To begin with, Helen Law confirmed he was lodged in her house, although she could not be certain he did not run away, for by the time she got to Torry, 'there was a great many more there than when in Aberdeen' so keeping track of faces would have been difficult. She knew that, after their arrival at the harbour, some of her former boarders did break out and that one of them, a Robert McKay, was found hiding in the roof timbers of a house. James Robertson confirms Williamson's presence actually on board, although again he was hazy as to whether he was among a crowd of youths who made their escape just before the ship sailed. Twenty years later, Aberdeen woman Margaret Brown spoke to Williamson about her sister, who had consented to sail on the *Planter* when she was eighteen years of age. According to Margaret Brown's later deposition, her unnamed sister's treatment was somewhat different from that of Williamson and others. She said that she went to Torry 'once or thrice' to speak with her and not only was granted ready access but was also allowed to take her sister on shore 'to the house of William Coutts, who then kept and still keeps a publick house there'. Williamson remembered the sister, who later died on the Caribbean island of St Croix, as 'a black complectioned woman' and said he had attended her wedding in the Colonies. From what he told Margaret Brown, she was satisfied he had been with her on board ship.

Peter Kemp was another young boy who sold his indentures to Smith and his masters, in his case willingly. Although Helen Law said he was one of her boarders, Kemp himself denied this, claiming he 'staid in the house of the said James Smith where he got his victuals and was under no confinement'. He confirmed there was one boy 'of the name Peter Williamson on the voyage towards America' and that the lad was in fact 'messed to eat his victuals' with him.

But it is sailor William Wilson who gives the best account of some of the incidents on the *Planter* and of the presence of a lad named Williamson on board. First Mate Alexander Young hired Wilson along with six or eight other crewmen for the voyage, with a second mate and a carpenter making up the full ship's complement. Seaman Wilson was actually on board when the human cargo was brought alongside in a boat. Some of the young boys were aged between fourteen and eighteen, but others, he said, appeared 'not to exceed ten or twelve years of age'. As soon as they were brought aboard, the young people were stowed away below decks along with a load of tables and chairs that were, like the young people, destined for sale in America. Wilson said the 'hatches of the ship were put down and locked every night, both while the ship continued in the harbour of Aberdeen and afterwards when she was at sea'.

They were guarded at all times. Wilson said Aberdeen porters arrived with them on the boat to keep watch all night and every night until the ship sailed. During the day, these guard duties fell to the ship's crew, half taking care of the regular tasks required on a ship in port preparing to make way, the other half keeping a watchful eye on their young charges. Even so, he said, two of the servants managed to escape.

The *Planter* set sail on 12 or 13 May 1743. Its departure was a matter of great celebration for its owners. After all, this was the vessel's maiden voyage under their ownership, and it was hoped their new enterprise – the export of servants, tables and chairs, and the import of tobacco – would bring them all considerable profit. According to Helen Law, there was 'a treat or entertainment on board of Captain Ragg's ship before she sailed from Torry, to which a great many people were invited and whom she saw at the entertainment when she came on board ship with supper to those boarded with her'. She also went below to collect some blankets she had given her boarders and to deliver special treats of gingerbread and tobacco, which she distributed to her former lodgers. According to her, they begged her 'to go along with them to America and cook their victuals'. The woman gently told them it was not possible and left the young people behind.

Peter Williamson said that there were sixty-nine youngsters on board, but it is not clear if that total included the legitimately indentured servants, so there may have been more. James Robertson stayed with them while the vessel left Torry harbour, but once it was in the bay and heading for the open sea, he returned to the mainland on the pilot boat. That left up to eleven crew members, including mates and master, at least sixty-nine souls below decks and a cargo of wooden furniture all off to Philadelphia on the morning tide. Their course more than likely hugged the Scottish coastline northwards, crossed the Moray Firth and squeezed through the Pentland Firth between the mainland and the Orkney Islands before veering west. It was the beginning of summer so they would have missed the worst of the storms that can wrack the far north of Scotland. They may have turned south-west at Cape Wrath and, keeping their homeland on their port side, crossed the North Minch into the Little Minch until they reached the end of the chain of islands that stretch out from the southernmost tip of Barra. At some point after that they would have left the various firths and sounds behind. From then on, they were sailing the wide Atlantic.

In his writings, Peter Williamson was dismissive of the voyage. In his book *French and Indian Cruelty*, he wrote:

> The treatment we met with, and the trifling incidents which happened during the voyage, I hope I may be excused from relating, as not being at that time of an age sufficiently to remark anything more than what must occur to every one on such an occasion.

What occurred on the voyage may not have been unusual, but the treatment and at least one incident were far from trifling.

Seaman William Wilson first took note of the boy after they had set sail. Putting the Scottish coastline behind them, Captain Ragg would have felt able to give some of his prisoners the freedom of the decks, no doubt reasoning that it was unlikely that any of them would launch themselves over the side in a bid to swim to freedom. Peter was, according to Wilson, 'then a stout, well-set boy and appeared . . . to be about twelve years of age and not exceeding thirteen'. He said he took particular notice of him 'because he appeared to be an active, clever boy, for [Wilson] had seen him run up the ship's shrouds and come down the ship's stays'. (The ship's shrouds were the part of the rigging that supported the main mast. The stays were ropes that stretched to other masts or spars.)

During the next few weeks, Wilson got to know Williamson and some of the other boys who were, as he put it, 'very foul and nasty', as he was ordered to take care of keeping them clean. The boys' heads were shaven, which may have been an attempt to combat the plague of lice that would have infested them below decks and also to reduce the risk of typhus.

Life on board ship was difficult for experienced and weathered seamen. It would be doubly so for young 'landlubbers'. Seasickness would be the least of their problems, although there would be a great deal of it to contend with as huge waves and ferocious winds pummelled the vessel. Some provision would certainly have been made for their welfare – they were, after all, trade goods, and the merchants would have wished as many as possible to reach the Colonies in sufficiently good condition to be sold at a profit. However, rations on board even the best of ships at this time were renowned for their sparseness. Hot food would have been available but may have been something of a rarity, certainly for the passengers, and what meat there was, pork or beef, was heavily salted and would eventually become so hard that sailors could carve figures out of it. The salt created great thirst, and in the early stages of the voyage, there would be water to slake it, but as the weeks wore on, that supply would dwindle and turn brackish, unless they pulled in somewhere for fresh supplies. There was wine aboard, but that was reserved for Captain Ragg's use – and William Wilson noted the captain's anger when some vanished. There can be little doubt that the missing bottles ended up in the crew's quarters and not the hold.

There may also have been a supply of cheese, but that would prove to be home to a long red worm. The famed ship's biscuit – a very hard cake better known as hardtack – could be gnawed on even when it was infested by maggots (one sailor described eating them as being like chewing calf's-foot jelly). However, when the weevils began to feast on it, even the hard biscuit crumbled and lost what little allure it had. Hardtack could be ground into porridge, but it was often best to wait until dark to eat it so as not to see the maggots squirming in it. If things got really desperate during a long voyage, the ever-present ship's rats could be trapped and roasted, although on a ship such as the *Planter* that particular delicacy would be kept for the captain and crew.

Bundled into steerage and allowed out on deck for minimal periods during the voyage, the servants shared their space with those rats and their constant companions, fleas. Body lice would have been prolific – one man stated that during a voyage in 1750 from Holland to Philadelphia, 'the lice abound so frightfully, especially on sick people, that they can be scraped off the body'.

Hygiene was not a word often associated with such voyages and, although the human cargo was generally a hardy lot and not used to the luxuries of life even at home, they would be ill-prepared for the conditions in which they were forced to wallow on board ship. Dysentery was endemic, and the liquid result of it would have slopped around on the deck, along with the vomit. Certainly this would have been swabbed away on occasion, but the residue would seep through the cracks in the floors and end up festering in the bilge water that splashed about at the bottom of the hull. The stench would have been overpowering. Toilet facilities on board were virtually non-existent, and the crew and passengers urinated and defecated into buckets or over the sides, if they got that far.

Scurvy, the scourge of the sea, caused by a complete lack of vitamin C, would not have been much of a problem. It takes a few months without fresh fruit and vegetables for signs of the disease to manifest themselves, and long though the Atlantic crossing would have felt, it was perhaps not quite long enough for the first symptoms to appear. However, ship's fever – typhus – would have been a major concern. This disease is associated with cramped and unhygienic conditions, and could be passed on by rat fleas or head and body lice. It is extremely contagious and would have ripped through the crew and passengers swiftly had it broken out on board the *Planter*.

Luckily, no such epidemic raged through the *Planter*, but the young women, and possibly some of the boys, faced another danger.

According to a contemporary account of the voyage, one of the passengers was 'a lusty young woman'. He may have meant she was healthy or attractive, or he may have been referring to her enjoyment of male company. Whatever it implied, she had caught the eye of the sailors on board.

On a merchant ship, the crew's quarters were in the fo'c'sle (the forecastle – the term dates back to when this part of the ship looked like a castle's walls), and that was where she was when she died. The transatlantic voyage was a long one, and the minds of some of those hardy men of the sea would naturally have turned to sex. The female presence on board would have been too good an opportunity to miss, and it is impossible to say how many were invited, cajoled or simply forced into the fo'c'sle. The woman, possibly a Highlander, is unnamed in the records, and the cause of her death is unknown. Both Peter Kemp and William Wilson mention her only briefly in depositions, so we can only imagine the scene. The body would have been carried out of the crew's quarters and laid on the deck, where it is known one of the indentured men, also a Highlander, knelt beside her and muttered a few prayers 'in the Irish language [Gaelic]' before wrapping the corpse in his plaid. Ropes would have been wrapped around the body and the men would have hefted it over the side. Perhaps the passengers, those who knew her, joined in the prayers. Perhaps, as the body was lowered into the waves, they sang a plaintive Gaelic lament. Perhaps someone cried as the woman's body was consigned to the deep, never to reach her destination, never to return home.

Sudden and unexplained deaths aside, the greatest fear for those on board would have been that of sinking, as the North Atlantic gales battered the tiny ship, lifting waves one hundred feet high and sending them crashing down on the deck. The cargo would have been tossed around in the enclosed space below decks, spewing out the contents of their stomachs over each other. Disease, thirst, starvation, discomfort and terror combined to debilitate the young Scots until they longed to reach their destination, wherever it might be. Perhaps they had heard the word Pennsylvania, but it would not have meant much to them, even those who could speak more than Gaelic.

They had been at sea for almost three months when they were caught in the gale that sprang up from the south-east and launched itself out of the darkness at the *Planter*. After being battered and tossed around for some time, the ship ran aground on a sandbank, much to the surprise of Captain Ragg, who appeared to have no idea how close he was to land. As it turned out, they were near an island off Cape May, on the southern tip of New Jersey as it dips into Delaware Bay. As the vessel twisted and shook in the teeth of the snarling storm, the masts snapped one by one and flew off into the violent night. With the ship in serious danger of breaking up, the thoughts of Captain Ragg and his crew turned to self-preservation. The longboat was hoisted into the turbulent ocean, with the men all claiming their place. They took some of the women passengers – perhaps their favourites – but ignored the pleas of the other passengers. 'When any of the indented servants offered to come in to the longboat,' said Peter Kemp, 'they were not allowed to come in but were left to their shifts on board the ship and were obliged to take all methods for saving themselves from the water.'

Peter Williamson put it more dramatically when he wrote, 'The cries, the shrieks and tears of a parcel of infants had no effect on, or caused the least remorse in the breasts of these merciless wretches.'

As the seamen rowed through the biting wind to the safety of the nearby island, the ship's hull finally ruptured and, in Williamson's words, 'to the great terror and affright of the ship's company, in a small time was almost full of water'.

Locked below battened hatches, abandoned by their overseers,

under siege by wind and water, the young Scots believed they were
going to die. Some had been snatched from everything they had ever
known and been moved from pillar to post over three months. Some
had been lured away with promises of a better life in a better land.
They had all travelled thousands of miles in a cramped and stinking
hold. Now they were facing what they thought was certain death in the
chill waters of an ocean of which few of them had ever heard.

The little *Planter,* though, was tougher than they thought, for she
refused to succumb to the elements that raged and foamed around her.
Perhaps her position on the sandbank saved her, but, come daylight,
she was still in one piece. Her masts were gone and she was still taking
in water, but she was above the waves. The storm had blown itself out,
and Captain Ragg sent his men back in the longboat to salvage what
they could – including the precious cargo that he had been more than
happy to leave to its fate during the hours of darkness and shrieking
wind. After eleven hellish weeks at sea, the youngsters planted their
feet once more on dry land, albeit an island in the wide mouth of an
unknown river in a land some of them had never wanted to see.

Dutchman Cornelius Jacobsen Mey, who had been sent to the
Delaware Bay area by the Dutch East India Company, had named the
cape in the 1620s. He called the point on the south of the bay Cape
Cornelius and, as if such egotism was not enough, dubbed the
corresponding north promontory Cape Mey. Years later, the southern
point was renamed Cape Henlopen, but the northern one, which
Peter Williamson could see from his new island home, retained the
Dutchman's name, although the spelling was altered by English
settlers.

These islands and inlets running the length of the American eastern
seaboard were long a haven for pirates, who would raid the fat ships
plying the Caribbean and then retreat here for repairs and relaxation.
It had only been twenty-five years earlier that the buccaneering career
of arguably the most famous and feared pirate of all, Edward

'Blackbeard' Teach, came to a sudden end with two strokes of a Highland sailor's broadsword. His final battle had taken place only a few hundred miles to the south of Cape May, off Ocracoke Island. The British officer in charge, First Lieutenant Robert Maynard, sailed home with the pirate's head swinging from the bowsprit (a spar jutting out from the front) of his sloop as a grisly message to anyone who dared follow in Teach's bootsteps.

Peter and his young fellow passengers would not have known of all this, and even if they had, they would probably not have been afraid. They had already been to hell and back. They had already cheated what they believed was certain death on the beleaguered *Planter*. Although now safe on dry land, they knew it was only a matter of time before they were sold into servitude. The prospect of being taken now by pirates, who would no doubt subject them to the same fate, would have held few terrors for them. The crew, on the other hand, would certainly have known about the area's bloody reputation. Seamen were a superstitious lot, and even though the so-called golden age of piracy was almost over when Blackbeard's headless body was pitched overboard off North Carolina, there were still bands of lesser-known but no less ruthless cut-throats roaming these waters. One gang was known as the Moon-Cussers, and they operated from the mainland, sending a line of horsemen riding out at night with lanterns to lure unwary ships too close to the shore. As they could only use this strategy when there was no moon, they tended to curse when there was a bright night sky, hence their name.

And then there were the privateers to consider. England was then at war with France and each side had merchantmen who had turned sea raiders, their freebooting permitted by letters of marque from their government. They lurked in the same inlets that the pirate brotherhood had used and swept down on enemy traders, splitting the booty between them but always keeping a commission for whichever Crown they had pledged their allegiance to. With these threats in mind, it would have been an extremely nervous group of men who set up camp on the uninhabited island. Passing privateers would not have thought twice about slitting their gizzards and taking the human cargo for themselves. After all, money was money, whether it be gold, jewellery, doubloons – or a group of young Scots whose destiny was the slave block in Philadelphia.

According to Peter's own account, the sailors built a makeshift camp on the beach, using the sails and whatever else they could salvage from the ship, and there they waited, eking out what little stores they had. Captain Ragg and some of the crew set out in the longboat to make for Philadelphia via the Delaware Bay and River, promising the crewmen left behind extra pay. During their three weeks of living a castaway life, some of the servants escaped. How they did so is not explained in any of the papers; they may have tried to swim the four miles to the mainland, or perhaps the term 'escaped' was a euphemism for died in the wreck. However, the remainder got through the three weeks without incident until, finally, the sail of a sloop was spotted heading towards them from the west. Captain Ragg had reached his destination and hired the vessel to come and pick up his cargo.

Once again, Peter and the other young people found themselves penned in a ship's hold. They were now only days away from Philadelphia, the City of Brotherly Love.

THREE

A Humane, Worthy, Honest Man

Philadelphia was a city built on a dream.

Its founder, William Penn, was a Quaker and, as such, believed in religious freedom, democracy and justice. Founded in England in 1657 by minister George Fox, the Society of Friends, known as 'Quakers' because they were said to 'tremble at the word of God', believed the Bible was not a means for direct communication with the Almighty but rather with one's own conscience. The sect did not need a preacher to guide them but sat at their meetings silently unless one of their number felt the Holy Spirit move them to speak. They liked plain dress and a plain life. They were also, significantly, pacifists. They were, in short, a menace to a government that sought to control its people through organised religion and which now aimed at stamping the Quakers out. Attending Quaker meetings was banned by law, and in 1667, the twenty-three-year-old William Penn, after a chequered educational history due to his increasingly rebellious religious beliefs, found himself arrested. During his time in jail, he began to write about those beliefs and, worryingly for the authorities, plead for religious freedom. These writings gained great currency among his fellow Friends, but one of his works, *The Sandy Foundation Shaken*, outraged the established Protestant Church, and he found himself once again under lock and key, this time in the infamous Tower of London. He spent seven months in the riverside fortress, refusing devoutly to recant his beliefs. 'My prison shall be my grave before I will budge a jot,' he wrote, 'for I owe my conscience to no mortal man.' During his time in the Tower, he wrote what is often regarded as his defining work, *No Cross, No Crown,* an emotive plea for religious tolerance. But even as he was calling for 'No pain, no palm; no thorns, no throne; no gall, no glory; no cross, no crown', Charles II and his advisors were pushing ahead with plans to impose religious conformity on all his subjects. And the Quakers, among others, would either be swept along in the rush towards that uniformity of devotion, or be brushed out of the way. The move ultimately benefited the fledgling Colonies across the Atlantic, but a lot of blood had to be spilled in the process.

King Charles I had tried to standardise religious worship across his domain by declaring that all churches should be Episcopal in nature, complete with bishops answerable to the Crown. The Civil War of 1642–6 put a stop to that, but, following the Restoration of the Stuart line in 1660, Charles II enforced even harsher disciplines in a bid to bring non-conformist groups like the Quakers and Scottish Presbyterians under the Royal thumb. They found themselves banned by law from attending meetings. When discovered, these meetings – or conventicles – were broken up forcibly by soldiers and the worshippers imprisoned, or even shot on the spot. Those taken into custody received only a cursory trial and were either executed or transported. Thousands of men and women were sent abroad during this period, some eventually to prosper, a few to return home, but others to die of fever or exhaustion in the tropical heat of the West Indies, under the lash in the American colonies or at the hands of native tribes. Some did not make it across the Atlantic at all. Over 250

Presbyterian Covenanters captured in battle at Bothwell Brig in 1679 were sentenced to be sold into slavery in Barbados, but their ship, the *Crown of London*, foundered on rocks near Orkney and 209 of them perished.

William Penn was among those who defied the conventicle ban, organising a mass meeting in London in August 1670. He was duly arrested, and, in a landmark legal case, Penn, a trained lawyer, defended himself and won a momentous victory. However, he was now certain he would never change things in England. His longed-for religious utopia could never thrive in a country so deeply entrenched in dogma and prejudice. Somewhere there must be a new land, a happy land, a promised land.

His late father, Admiral Sir William Penn, had been a Royal favourite, and through this family connection the young William had access to the King and his brother, the Roman Catholic Duke of York (eventually to become James II). In return for the cancellation of a debt to the Penn family (said to be £16,000 of back pay), Charles agreed to sign over to William land west of the Delaware River and north of Maryland in the Colonies. The land would be called Pennsylvania, 'forests of Penn', in honour of the late lamented Admiral. Penn's plan was to establish a haven for religious dissidents of whatever faith. Charles's idea was to rid himself of a troublesome menace and establish an English colony on land at that time home to Germans, Dutch, Swedes and, of course, Indians. Hopefully, Penn would take all the Quakers with him and let Charles get on with the business of absolute monarchy. According to the terms of the agreement, the King would also receive two beaver skins every year, plus one-fifth of any precious metals found. A short time later, Penn convinced the Duke of York, who, being a Catholic, knew something about religious bigotry, to grant him further lands in Delaware itself.

On 8 November 1682, Penn, by then thirty-seven years old, along with a handful of fellow Friends, arrived in the New World on the ship

Welcome. On a site between the Delaware and Schuylkill rivers, they founded a city to be named Philadelphia, the Greek for 'city of brotherly love', for that was the image that Penn wanted to project to the rest of the world, whether they be Europeans or Native Americans. Africans, though, were a different matter, for in those early years, Quakers were also slave-owners.

Later, Peter Williamson wrote, 'The city would have been a capital fit for an empire had it been built and inhabited according to the proprietor's plan.' Originally, it was to cover 10,000 acres, but this was deemed impractical so it covered at first only 1,200 acres between the two rivers. If the city's philosophy was to be one of enlightenment, then so was its design: the streets were well spaced, and each house was to have a garden. Penn and his designers sought to leave behind the unhygienic and cramped slums of the Old World and create a fresh kind of open-plan, green city in the New. Philadelphia's grid street system was then ahead of its time but is now commonplace. Meanwhile, its emphasis on parklands was a reaction to the ferocious outbreak of plague in London in 1665, which Penn had survived, and the inferno of the Great Fire of 1666, which helped wipe out the last of the infection but also nearly destroyed the city.

To Williamson, Philadelphia was 'the finest city in America and one of the best laid out in the world'. Naturally, it has grown considerably since Peter first saw it, when it had just eight long streets, each two miles in length, running between the two rivers that bounded the city. To the east lay the Delaware and its access to the sea, to the west the Schuylkill, the waterway that put the rich interior of the colony within reach of the settlers. Each of the eight roads were traversed at right angles by sixteen smaller roads of one mile in length, forming the grid pattern later to be adopted by cities such as New York. The streets took their names from timber found in the Pennsylvanian colony – names like Mulberry, Chestnut, Beech and Cedar. The spacious city centre boasted a courthouse, town hall, schoolhouse and, of course, a prison.

Penn, given the title of proprietor of the new colony, spent only three and a half years altogether in his new home, although he did build a magnificent mansion to the north of his city. From the start, he was involved in a border dispute with Lord Baltimore, who was the proprietor of the largely Roman Catholic Maryland colony to the south. Two years after his arrival in the colony, Penn returned to London to engage in protracted negotiations over the extent of his 'holy experiment'. He managed to prevent Lord Baltimore from taking possession of the disputed lands – which included the site of his dream city, Philadelphia – but the war of words raged long after his death. The row continued until the astronomer Charles Mason and surveyor Jeremiah Dixon established the famous Mason–Dixon line in 1763, thereby settling the argument.

While in England, Penn's troubles worsened with the hurried departure of James II in 1688, the year of the 'Glorious Revolution'. James's Roman Catholicism had doomed his reign from the start, and he quit the country, leaving the throne to his sister Mary and her husband, the staunchly Protestant William of Orange. Penn, caught in the middle of this religious family squabble, was under suspicion by the new regime, despite the fact that he disagreed strongly with the former monarch's policies. Once again, he was a marked man, and it took some years to prove he was no Jacobite. During this period, his wife, Gulielma, died, and he married again, to a Quaker woman twenty-five years his junior named Hannah.

In December 1699, he was back again in Philadelphia. It had grown in his fifteen-year absence and was now a lively trading port, exporting tobacco, fur, hemp, iron and lumber. Again, he was not allowed to stay long, for pressure from the mother country to bring the colony under full control of the Crown forced him to return to England. He left in November 1701, never to see his dream land again. On 30 July 1718, William Penn, Quaker, lawyer and visionary, died aged seventy-three.

He left behind a colony built on the ideals of liberty, equality and fraternity. He had helped establish an elected provincial assembly, which did not rely totally on the power of the governor to introduce legislation, although that individual could veto bills. Laws were passed to protect the rights of the people to follow their religious beliefs. In England, there were some 200 crimes that carried with them sentence of death. In Pennsylvania, during the early days, only two crimes carried the ultimate penalty: murder and treason. That, though, would change.

Even before his death, Penn's land of peace had inevitably transformed. All sorts of people were flooding into the colony from Europe – and not all had the lofty ideals of William Penn or the pacifist principles of the Quakers in general. However, in keeping with the anti-war sentiments of the founding sect, the colony had no militia to defend it – a state of affairs that would cost its citizens dear in the coming years.

It was not, as has already been pointed out, a land of liberty and justice for all. Slavery was big business in America, and the Quakers were not above trading in the black gold themselves. Even William Penn owned slaves. A British ship, the *Isabella,* docked the colony's first batch of 150 African workers in 1684. After that, Philadelphia became a centre for the traffic in African servants. In 1754, the London Coffee House was built to give the local merchants somewhere to go to talk business and buy and sell human beings at auction. Certainly, Quaker thinking on the matter later changed: they were at the forefront of the anti-slavery movement so that by 1779, Pennsylvania was the first of the fledgling United States of America to order the emancipation of its slaves. But in 1743, when Peter Williamson and the other Scots sailed into the port on the hired sloop, Philadelphia was still a slave centre. And the young Scots were about to find themselves on the block.

Once again, Peter Williamson was imprisoned in a barn and under guard.

The sloop had weighed anchor in Philadelphia's busy harbour, and the cargo was transferred to this wooden holding cell while, in the words of fellow servant Peter Kemp, advertisements were published 'through the town of Philadelphia and the country adjacent that their indentures were to be sold and disposed of'. Kemp, who later became a sailor, explained, 'The custom there is their indentures are transferred and made over from one master to another as oft as they please during the whole space and term of years specified in their indentures.'

Seaman William Wilson confirmed that Peter Williamson was among the young people locked in the barn awaiting sale. He, however, was not involved in guarding them, as Captain Ragg had hired local labour for that duty. Wilson lingered in Philadelphia for one good reason – he had not received his wages for the voyage. On arrival in the city, Ragg told the crew that they would not receive their dues until after the servants were sold. Wilson's deposition reads, 'sometime thereafter, he did receive his wages, from whence he presumes that the captain by that time had got all the servants off his hands and Peter Williamson, of course, among them'. He had no idea who bought the lad, although he did recall seeing people 'taking the boys away like a parcel of sheep by taking up their indentures'. He also noted that one girl was kept by the ship's first mate, Alexander Young; for what purpose is unknown.

Williamson wrote that Ragg sold the servants for around sixteen pounds a head. He said fellow Scotsman Hugh Wilson bought his services. It was the first piece of luck the young boy had experienced since he was picked up on the Aberdeen quayside, for Wilson, whom he describes as 'a north Briton', had himself been abducted as a servant from the streets of St Johns Town, as Perth was once known.

'Happy was my lot in falling into my countryman's power,' wrote Peter Williamson, 'as he was, contrary to many others of his calling, a humane, worthy, honest man.'

We know that Wilson bought Williamson's services for the full period of seven years, although we are not told where in Pennsylvania his farm or plantation was. His master seemed to take the boy under his wing; he had no children of his own and, according to Peter, treated him very much like the son he never had. Recognising that the boy was much weakened by his ordeal, Wilson first set him about 'little trifles' until he was strong enough to take on harder work. It was while he was building that strength that Williamson noticed that many of his fellow servants could read and write.

'It incited in me an inclination to learn, which I intimated to my master,' wrote Williamson, 'telling him, I should be very willing to serve a year longer than the contract by which I was bound, if he would indulge me in going to school.'

Wilson agreed but suggested the boy wait until winter before he began his schooling, as it was then summertime and there was work to be done. Williamson filled the intervening period by obtaining a primer, an elementary book for teaching children to read, and learning what he could at the hands of his fellow servants. Clearly, he had fallen on his feet on his arrival in the New World. Other young Scots were not so fortunate, he learned. Boys, he later wrote, were 'commonly very harshly used by their masters and kept upon a very coarse diet, so that they [were] often forced to desperate measures and to make away with themselves'.

Owners, and the authorities, took a very dim view of indentured servants running away, and the newspapers of the day were filled with notices about runaway servants. Williamson heard of two brothers – William and James Sheds, aged fifteen and six respectively – who were bought by a John Graham of Quantico Creek in Virginia. William was indentured for five years while his young brother was to serve until he reached twenty-one years of age. One former servant said that those who behaved themselves were 'well used and treated' but 'those who behaved ill were as ill treated'. Peter Kemp, although insisting he himself was 'well used', did admit that 'the common treatment given those indented servants upon their indentures being sold is as if they were convicts'. The younger Sheds boy, James, learned just how vicious the authorities could be. After being sold to another planter who ill-treated him, he ran off, but was soon caught and flogged for punishment. He deserted again, this time remaining at large for a month before he was brought back. On being recaptured, he found himself punished in a different way, for the owners had developed a tariff for runaways which saw time being added on to their indenture period. As Williamson wrote, 'for every day they have been absent they are compelled to serve a week, for every week a month, and for every month a year. They are obliged to pay the cost of advertising, apprehending and bringing them back; which often protracts their slavery four or five years longer.' James Sheds had to serve a further year on his indentures, which means that by the time he was a free man, he had served for more than sixteen years.

While these were hard times, life had improved considerably since the early days of colonisation. In one case in Virginia in 1642, a servant had his ears nailed to a pillory for four days and was publicly whipped for 'openly and impudently abusing his (master's) house, in sight both of Master and Mistress, through wantonnes with a woman servant of theirs, a widdowe, but also for falsely accusing him to the Governor both of Drunkennes and Thefte, and besides for bringing all his fellow servants to testifie on his side, wherein they justly failed him'.

A century later, indentured servants were, however, still regarded as property, and the law was often on the side of the property owners – especially as local magistrates and judges were friends of theirs and generally property owners themselves. Of course, as Hugh Wilson's example shows, not all masters were inhuman monsters, and there is some disagreement amongst historians and economists over just how exploitative the system was. It is true that the merchants and ships' captains who penned their cargo up in the holds of ships or in barns while awaiting the completion of sale cared little about the calibre of person to whom they were selling these men, women and children. The family unit meant nothing to the merchants, each individual being viewed as a saleable item. Sons and daughters could be sold separately from mothers and fathers, brothers and sisters separated and handed over to different masters. As Williamson said, 'if the Devil himself came in the shape of a man to purchase us, with money enough in his pocket, it would have been as readily accepted as of . . . the most humane man in the world'. Williamson, despite his own good fortune in being taken up by such a decent man, held a poor opinion of the men who bought indentures. 'The planters themselves,' he wrote, 'are generally of an idle, indolent disposition, not caring to fatigue themselves with work.' Hence the need for indentured servants and, after 1619, outright slaves.

It was in August of that year that a Dutch ship landed at Jamestown in Virginia and unloaded twenty black people, fourteen men and six women, in exchange for food. That cargo of twenty slaves, uprooted from their homes in Guinea, was the first to be sold in the American colonies, and they and their later counterparts laboured in the fields and houses of the planters and farmers alongside their fellow forced labourers, the Indian tribespeople. They also worked side by side with white indentured servants. There is some debate as to whether the early black slaves were indentured for a period of time like their white co-workers; later, however, African slaves became property for life. Their children also became their owner's chattels, to do with as he pleased. So, although the system of indentured servitude, with its punishments and charges which saw the period of time under contract extended, is to modern minds abhorrent, it can in no way be seen as being as exploitative or reprehensible as the slave economy that grew alongside it and ultimately replaced it.

Peter Williamson grew into a tall, strong youth. Hugh Wilson was as good as his word and sent him to school, where, over years of winter study, the boy learned his letters with 'tolerable proficiency'. That 'tolerable proficiency' was honed over the following years of his life and would later stand him in good stead. His time as a servant also helped him learn the ways and customs of his new land, putting him at a distinct advantage over many of the voluntary migrants who were left to make their own way amid the harsh realities of frontier and colonial life.

He would also have become familiar with the city of Philadelphia, as he would likely have been sent by his employer to the market there. Aberdeen had been his first experience of a more cosmopolitan life, but Philadelphia was a real melting pot. Settlers were streaming into the colony from Europe, and on the teeming streets of the city he would have heard not just English voices but also French, German, Irish and, of course, Scots. Then there were the strange, dark-skinned men and women dressed in deerskins and blankets, whom he discovered were the native peoples of this land, and the even darker forced immigrants who also sweated alongside him in the fields. Aberdeen was busy, but Philadelphia bustled. The streets were filled with tradesmen and shopkeepers, advertising their wares with signs and symbols, for many of their customers were illiterate or had limited English. There was the huge horseshoe of the blacksmith or the oversized boot of the cobbler; here was a giant tooth proclaiming the services of a dentist or the large scissors of the tailor. And on market days, the farmers would stream in from the frontier country in their large Conestoga wagons, named after the West Pennsylvania Valley where they were developed. These were the forerunners of the so-called 'prairie schooner' that would take the settlers ever further west. They rattled through the streets to bring their goods for sale, churning dust into the bright summer sunshine and forcing the townspeople and visitors to dodge both them and their strong horses. The streets were clogged with the wagons and the city's own carriages, and when the shopkeepers threw water on the paving stones, it was as much to wash away the horse droppings from under customers' feet as it was to cool the ground from the baking sun. At the market, Williamson would have seen people of many languages, faiths and colours haggling and trading in fruits, vegetables, cereals and furs. He would have seen the Native Americans with their deadly tomahawks at their waists and the buckskin-clad frontiersmen with their equally deadly long rifles couched under their arms. He would have seen and sensed the mistrust and hatred between the two groups that had so often boiled over into bloodshed and would do so again. And then, as the market closed and every deal had been done, the great horses were hitched again to the Conestoga wagons, and the convoys of farmers headed home to their log cabins and their fields.

Williamson had been contracted to serve seven years with Wilson. Adding a further one year in return for his education, he would not have been due to leave his service until he was twenty-one years old. After that, the young Scot could expect to be given a lump sum of cash and possibly some land to farm as a freedman. However, when he was seventeen, his 'good master' died and 'as a reward for my faithful service, he left me $200 currency, which was then about £150 sterling, his best horse, saddle and all his wearing apparel'.

Williamson, now a free man of means, decided to see something of his adopted land. 'I employed myself in jobbing about the country,' he said, 'working for anyone that would employ me.' He did this for seven years until, aged twenty-four, he decided it was time to settle down. He claims to have met the daughter of a wealthy Pennsylvania planter and fallen in love. He found his proposal of marriage 'was not unacceptable to her or her father, so that matters were soon concluded upon, and we married'. Unfortunately, Williamson omits to mention the name of his first love, or that of her father, although *Chambers Miscellany*, written decades later, states that her name was Rose and her father owned a plantation at a place called Mount Hiram in Chester County (although this cannot be substantiated). Peter did say that his new father-in-law made the happy couple the gift of land near the Forks of the Delaware, in what is now Northampton County. Thirty of the two hundred acres, Williamson said, 'were well cleared, and fit for immediate use, whereon was a good house and barn'. Rose, although unhappy to be leaving her father and family, was looking forward to her new life as a wife and, they hoped, a mother.

It was on a bright spring morning that the young couple set out for their new home. Williamson's whip cracked briskly over the heads of the horses and the wagon, filled with furniture and supplies, lurched forward. They spent their first night at the farm of Rose's uncle, who presented them with a wedding gift of a young cow. The following morning they set off again with the cow tied to the rear of the wagon. The next two nights were spent in the homes of settlers along the way, for frontier life was nothing if not hospitable, but after that the number of farms and cabins thinned out, and they had to camp out under the stars, preferably near water. The horses would be unyoked from the wagon, their reins staked to the ground to prevent them from straying. Small trees would have been cut down and built into a makeshift defensive palisade, for there were dangers, both human and animal, abroad in the wilderness country. Game could be hunted, roasted and eaten with cakes made of Indian corn. They may even have met up along the way with others with whom they could travel towards their own land, for there was a certain safety in numbers.

Williamson was happy with that land and settled down to the life of a farmer, spending most of his savings on stock, furnishing his new home and tools for the further clearing of the land for farming. Eleven years before he had been a 'rough, ragged' youth playing on the streets of Aberdeen. Now he was a full-grown man, with a wife and property. He had put his past travails behind him and was 'happy in a good wife' and looking forward to a new and prosperous future.

Fate, though, had something different in store. For even while he was settling in with Rose, thoughts of hearth and home uppermost in his mind, a new sound was throbbing across the land. It rumbled in the mountains of the north and west, and was carried on the wind down the valleys to echo through the trees of the great forests and pulse on the swift waters of the Susquehanna, the Juniata, the Delaware, the Hudson and the Mohawk.

The drums of war were beating again in the Colonies, and by the time they had stilled, life would never be the same again for white settlers and Native Americans alike.

FOUR

Down That River I Will Go

England, that old warhorse, was always arguing with someone, whether it be Scotland, Wales or Ireland at home, or France, Holland or Spain abroad. In the first half of the eighteenth century, this tiny but outward-reaching country had been at war almost continuously. After 1746, when the Jacobite cause met a chilly end on Drummossie Moor, better known as Culloden, things at home were settled, if tense in the northern lands where a bloody government pacification programme was doing its best to wipe out the Highland way of life. Abroad, the 1748 Treaty of Aix-la-Chapelle created an uneasy peace with France and her allies after the eight-year-long War of the Austrian Succession. The same year saw the final shots fired in King George's War, a battle for dominion between Britain and France in North America. But that four-year struggle was nothing compared to what was coming in the Colonies. Again, the cause of the conflict would be the empire-building ambitions of the two great superpowers of the age; caught in the middle would be the white settlers and the Native Americans.

It was a dam-building, buck-toothed little creature that was indirectly to cause the carnage. While the beaver was busy doing what it does best, namely erecting its intricate water palaces and making little beavers, humans were eyeing it and other forest creatures for their pelts. It was the pursuit of fur and the insatiable hunger for the land that was the creatures' home that ultimately led to the sound of cannon and musket fire erupting in the great silent forests of the north.

When, in 1609, Sir Henry Hudson sailed past the capes of Delaware northwards and found the river behind the island of Manhattan, he opened up a major waterway that would enable Europeans to float inland on this huge continent in search of new financial adventures. The principal source of profit was at first fur, and it was the Dutch, then kings of the sea, who originally capitalised on the new trade routes. But over the next century and a half, Britain and France began to stick their noses in the trough. As the slave trade grew in the south, the fur trade boomed in the north, for from beaver skins came felt, and felt was much sought-after for hats in Europe. There was also a strong market for deerskins, bear hides and the pelts of anything that walked or crawled in the great wilderness. Alliances were forged with local Indian tribes who had been hunting the lands for generations. Companies were formed to control what was becoming a hugely profitable industry. And a new breed of adventurer, the fur trapper, came into being.

It was the French who led the way in this new enterprise, moving inland from Montreal to trap and to trade with tribes from the Great Lakes to the Mississippi Valley. Later came the British with the Hudson's Bay Company, creating a competitive spirit on which the Indian tribes capitalised to gain the best deals for themselves, bartering furs for trinkets such as mirrors, beads and combs, as well as more useful items such as knives, guns and ammunition. While most tribes welcomed the trade, they could have had no idea of the effect it would have on their culture. It brought fierce and destructive inter-tribal wars, for as the increase in hunting wiped out supplies of animals, tribes which had become dependent on trade links with the white man began to look to other territories for pelts. The Five Nations of the Iroquois confederacy, which first began trading with the Dutch and then the English, moved against the peoples in the west and north who were working with the French traders. These wars were bitter, bloody and destructive. Entire tribes were wiped out. And in the end, the Iroquois were among the last men standing.

In the latter half of the seventeenth century and the early part of the eighteenth, France and England and their various Indian allies had often come to blows over territory. In 1689, there was King William's War, which raged on until 1697 and gave birth to Queen Anne's War, between 1701 and 1713, and the aforementioned King George's War. Each side made gains and lost ground in these indecisive struggles. But it was King George's War that planted the seeds of the last great battle for empire in the northern colonies.

Britain's naval power was immense, and during the 1744–8 struggle, her blockading navy easily prevented French ships from supplying traders with the means to barter with their Indian suppliers, who had become dependent on the white man's goods, having left behind their traditional way of life long before. France duly forged a link between its northern holdings, its Mississippi trading posts and the burgeoning port of New Orleans by staking a claim to the Ohio Valley beyond the Allegheny Mountains. The Virginia colony, however, also claimed this rich land, and the British government had granted the Ohio Land Company, formed in 1747, the rights to half a million acres on which to base settlers. As if inter-country rivalry was not enough, inter-colonial rivalry also reared its head, for Peter Williamson's new home, Pennsylvania, also claimed sovereignty over the territory.

Irish-born George Croghan, a hard-nosed trader from Pennsylvania's frontier country, crossed the mountains and set up a trading post-cum-fort to traffic with the Miami Indians at

Pickawillany, on the site now occupied by Piqua, north of Dayton, Ohio. The French, naturally, could not ignore this flagrant invasion, for they knew that a trading post was only the beginning and soon thousands of immigrants would be streaming over the mountains in search of land to plough, plant and irrigate. The French generally had limited interest in colonisation, seeing the New World as little more than a repository of furs and precious metals that was crying out to be stripped. However, this land was their land, and the settling on it of immigrants from any other country was not to be countenanced. Action had to be taken and taken fast, so a group of French trappers and their Ottawa and Ojibwa allies attacked the new post on 21 June 1752. They came upon the Miami Indians as they worked in their cornfields. The white traders ran for the safety of the stockade, but there were too many French and Indians for their small force to fight, so after some bartering, they agreed to surrender. One of the white traders, badly wounded in the stomach, was killed by the Ottawa, who then gouged out his heart and ate it. Croghan's post was destroyed, and Memeskia, the Miami chief who had sided with the Pennsylvanians and was known as 'Old Briton' by the English and 'La Demoiselle' by the French, was boiled and eaten. The victory, small though it was, sent out a clear message to both British settlers and local Indians: the French were here to stay. Many, but not all, traders and settlers quickly scuttled back over the mountains while the Miami Indians, realising that no help would be forthcoming from the British, swiftly returned to the French fold.

After the Pickawillany attack, the new French governor, the Marquis de Duquesne, decided that the only way to prevent any further incursions into France's territory was to build a series of forts. The final one he named after himself, Fort Duquesne; it was built in 1754 on the site of a British trading post.

Britain – as well as Pennsylvania and Virginia – realised that this chain of forts would cut them off from the lucrative wilderness beyond the mountains. There was still plenty of territory to be settled on the eastern side, but immigrants were constantly arriving, and the lure of the vast interior was strong. There was land out there for the tilling and animals for the skinning. There was profit in the earth and the great forests. There was an empire waiting to be built, and they were determined it would be Protestant and English-speaking, not Roman Catholic and French-accented.

Both sides had been tuning up for war for years and both knew that the secret to winning any future conflict in the northern colonies lay in alliances with the Native Americans. The overture was heard at Pickawillany. The symphony was about to begin.

Peter Williamson, farming his 200 Pennsylvania acres, knew all about the rumblings of war across the Appalachians. He, of course, put the blame for the bloodletting squarely on the shoulders of the French. He properly identified the need for firm friendships with the Indian tribes, although he was painfully aware of how they had been treated by the British, writing:

> Those French who were sent to dispossess us in that part of the world, being indefatigable in their duty, and continually contriving, and using all manner of ways and means to win the Indians to their interest, many of whom had been too negligent, and sometimes, I may say, cruelly treated by those who pretend to be their protectors and friends, found it no very difficult matter to get over to their interest . . .

Although Williamson was writing some years after the momentous events, the man who would become the American republic's first president had earlier shared his views, although to a limited degree. Virginia's lieutenant-governor, Glasgow-born Robert Dinwiddie, recognised the threat posed by the French moves in the Ohio Valley.

He had personal business interests in the expansion of the fur trade and land speculation, as well as a desire to further the interests of his colony and Crown. In 1753, he sent a twenty-one-year-old Virginia surveyor and militia officer named George Washington over the mountains to dissuade the French from their fort-building programme. The French, of course, refused, with one officer telling Washington, 'It is our absolute design to take possession of the Ohio – and by God, we will do it!' Washington reported this back to his superiors in Virginia – and also that he believed that success in any future hostilities in the area would depend on the support of the tribes then living there. The most powerful group of Indians was the League of the Hodenosaunee, originally made up of five nations: the Mohawks, Senecas, Onondagas, Oneidas and Cayugas. Better known as the Iroquois, and later expanding into a confederation of six nations with the joining of the Tuscaroras, the League also laid claim to the lands of the Ohio. They had already suggested to the French that all white men give up their interests in the area and let the Iroquois have dominion. The French delegate to the talks responded by snapping, 'I am not afraid of flies or mosquitoes, for the Indians are such as those. I tell you, down that river I will go. If the river is blocked up, I have the forces to burst it open and tread under my feet all who oppose me.'

Such attitudes helped make the Iroquois, in general, better disposed to British interests, although not completely so. Washington had the typical white man's disregard for the Indian, but he knew that the tribal elders wanted little part of any war between the whites and recognised the need for Britain to woo them over to its side. The French were already winning other bands and tribes to their flag and, as the tall Virginian officer told Dinwiddie, 'Without Indians to oppose Indians, we shall have little hope for success.'

Tanacharison was the chief who had been insulted by the French officer. Also known as the Half King, he did form a loose alliance with the British in April 1754 when Washington returned from Virginia with a small force of militia. Washington had been ordered to oversee the construction of Fort Pitt, on the future site of Fort Duquesne. Work had already begun on the stockade, but a larger force of French and Indians seized the site before Washington arrived. Together, Washington and Tanacharison attacked a French detachment, killing its commanding officer and a handful of men. Tanacharison himself buried his hatchet in the skull of the wounded French leader, then proceeded to wash his hands in the man's brains. There were differing accounts as to how this engagement began: Washington insisted that they were fired on first and that the Indians committed the massacre; an Indian source said that the Indians took little part in the fighting and moved to prevent the atrocities; while the French claimed that the attack was little more than an act of terrorism. Whatever the truth, the massacre did not reflect well on Washington's early career, although things were about to get a lot worse.

Washington next elected to build a fort on a site known as Great Meadows, near present-day Uniontown, Pennsylvania. Tanacharison advised him against erecting a defensive position there, but Washington proceeded nonetheless. Little more than a palisaded earth rampart, the fort was, as Washington said, 'not a design of engineering art but of frontier necessity, so I gave it the name Fort Necessity'. Tanacharison, who had left the fort when it was clear that no other Indian bands would join the hated British, was right. The site chosen was not a good one, as the future president would soon learn.

Meanwhile, the French commander of Fort Duquesne, Captain Claude-Pierre Pécaudy, told his Indian allies, 'The English have murdered my children [by his "children", he meant the soldiers killed in the massacre]; my heart is sick; tomorrow I shall send French soldiers to take revenge.' He invited the assembled tribes, which included Hurons, Abenakis, Iroquois, Nipissings, Algonquins, Ottawas and Delawares, to join his forces. 'I invite you all by this belt of *wampum* [a beaded belt often used for recording treaties] to join your French father and help him crush the assassins,' he urged. 'Take the hatchet, and with it two barrels of wine for a feast.'

The French and their Indian allies launched an all-out attack on the new fort on 3 July 1754. The two sides battled against each other all day in the midst of a torrential downpour, French marksmen and Indians sniping down at the palisades from the shelter of tree-lined ridges, their gunfire falling like the rain. The defenders, having been exposed to the deluge all night and all day, found their ammunition soaked and unusable. All around, men were dropping as the dry French musket balls found their mark. The land around the small fort was filled with flashes of gunfire, and the smoke that puffed from the muskets gathered close to the ground like a mist. Finally, as a new day dawned, the besieging French forces offered Washington terms for surrender. Realising he could not defend his poorly chosen site much longer, he agreed, and as the rain continued to batter down, he and his bedraggled, defeated force made their way home. This was the first notable 4 July in Washington's life – and the one he would rather have forgotten.

As the smoke from the flaming Fort Necessity drifted up into the grey skies, it was clear that after months of skirmishing, both physical and verbal, the French and Indian War had begun in earnest. And Peter Williamson was about to be drawn into it.

FIVE

Torments and Miseries

There were twelve of them, slipping easily through the night-shrouded forest. A dozen warriors, their heads shaved but for a single greased lock like a scar on their scalps. The white man called this style a Mohawk, but these warriors were not Mohawk. The white man had first encountered their forefathers in the early days of colonisation, when a sea captain sailing from the Virginian colony of Jamestown in 1610 named the large bay to the north Delaware, after the colony's first governor, Sir Thomas West, the third Lord De La Warr. The name was adopted not just for the bay, but also for the river – and the indigenous people who had lived there for centuries. But they did not think of themselves as Delawares. They were *Lenape,* which means either 'Original People' or simply 'the People'.

They moved effortlessly through the forest, their feet in their deerskin moccasins treading softly in the undergrowth, their legs moving easily in the blue cloth stockings that reached from their ankles to their thighs. Around their waists were two pieces of linen, dangling front and back, but their upper bodies were bare, apart from a few tattoos. They seemed to belong to the land, a force that was part of nature rather than working against it, unlike the pale-skinned men and women who lived on it now. This land had once been their home and hunting ground, but now the *swannuken*, the saltwater people, had washed over it like a tide, forcing them ever westwards. The Lenape had generally tried to find a peaceful way to resolve matters – not for nothing were they known as the mediators of the Algonquin-speaking nations – but the white man's greed and iniquity had wrenched their patience from them. They had never understood the immigrant's need to grasp the land and call it his own, for they believed that only one being owned the earth and everything on it, and that was the Creator. But the swannuken thought differently. The swannuken believed the land was theirs for the taking, and the people who had lived off it for centuries were to be ignored, dismissed or wiped out.

The Lenape's northern branch first had a taste of what the incomers were like in 1524 when Giovanni da Verrazano encountered them in what is now New York. The Italian explorer, who was working for the French, showed them what dealing with the white man meant when he tried to kidnap some of them as slaves. Slavery was not an unknown concept among the Native American tribes, for they often captured members of enemy nations and used them for forced labour but, to them, attempting to enslave those who had shown nothing but hospitality was barbaric. For years after that, the slave-traders raided the villages of tribes down the eastern seaboard, and the captives laboured in the fields and farms to the south alongside the white servants and the new black workers who would eventually replace them.

And as the trickle of white faces became a deluge, the Lenape at home saw their position on the land eroded. Worse, the white man brought a more insidious invader, one that no tomahawk, knife or even musket could fend off: diseases against which they had no resistance arrived from Europe. Measles, typhus and smallpox all disembarked from the immigrant ships and proceeded to decimate the tribes. This and wars with other nations saw Lenape numbers falling and their territories shrinking. It was a Lenape chief named Tamanend, among other leaders, who supposedly met with William Penn in 1682 under some elm trees at Shackamaxon. Penn was aware that the people he knew as Delawares had never been defeated in battle by the Dutch or Swedish settlers who had preceded him. Besides, as a committed Quaker, he believed the only way he could hope to win from them the lands that would become Pennsylvania was by negotiation and fair treaty. Penn gave the Lenape £1,200 for the land on which he would build his city of dreams. The Lenape, however, forgot to mention that some of the land they had ceded was not theirs to give and so Penn was forced to commit to a number of other treaties over the next few years. Voltaire said that the Shackamaxon accord was 'the one treaty with the Indians that the whites never broke'. It is said that Penn's dealings with the native tribes were always fair and honest. Unfortunately, his son was not as honourable.

In 1737, Thomas Penn miraculously produced a deed that purported to cede further lands around the Delaware River 'as far as a man can go in one day and a half'. The original, near legendary, treaty between Penn and Tamanend and other tribal leaders may never have been written down – or if it was, it was lost or destroyed for political reasons. This new agreement, said to have been reached in 1686, was news to the Lenape leadership. However, faced with the constant flood of settlers, they decided that it should be honoured. After all, they reasoned, how far could one man walk in a day and a half? However, Thomas Penn and his fellow colonists had a trick up their sleeve. A hunt was launched for the fittest three men they could find in the colony. The athletic trio was walked over the route they would follow, which was cleared of any obstructions to make the going easier. On 25 August 1737, the so-called Walking Purchase began, but there was not a lot of walking. The three white men tended to run, despite calls from watching tribesmen for them to walk. Only one of the runners survived the day and a half, but by the time he collapsed he had covered sixty-four miles. Curiously, the original fifty-year-old deed cited by Thomas Penn mysteriously disappeared soon after. But the damage had been done. The Pennsylvania colony had a further 1,200 square miles of land to exploit – and the Lenape tribes were forced to move west once more.

The twelve-strong warrior band easing like shadows through the dense forests of western Pennsylvania remembered the rage and shame of that land-grab. They remembered other slights and insults by the swannuken. They remembered being treated like women by the powerful Iroquois.

By the time the French and Indian War started, the Lenape had lost pretty much all of their traditional lands. They had fallen under the control of the Iroquois League of the Hodenosaunee but were not one of the Six Nations. The League had its own empire-building reasons for siding with the white man, so when the Lenape protested over the corrupt Walking Purchase, an Iroquois leader silenced them, saying, 'We conquered you. You are women, we made women of you. Give up claims to your old lands and move west. Never attempt to sell land again. Now get out.'

As the war began, many tribes, including the various branches of the Lenape, intended to remain neutral, believing that the French and British were just two thieves squabbling over the same stolen property. However, some bands of disaffected warriors could not forget the injustices meted out to their people by the British. They had stolen their land and they had stolen their pride, and as the two white tribes prepared to go to war, some Native Americans saw a way to exact a just revenge. They did not trust the French any more than they did the British, but war often makes for uneasy alliances. So the tomahawk was taken up, and the bands of Lenape and other tribes followed the warrior path.

It was the settlers on the frontiers of Pennsylvania who felt the force of the years of pent-up bitterness and hatred. Bands of screaming braves would burst from the cover of the forests that still blanketed much of the province and swoop down on the isolated farms and settlements. The log cabins, one of the contributions to North American culture by Scandinavian settlers, were easily put to the flame, while cattle could be slaughtered or driven off. And the white people fared little better than the beasts. They might be killed, their scalps taken and shown to the French commanders who would pay the warrior in trade goods for each one. Or they might be taken and worked as slaves, just as the white man had enslaved Indians decades before, or ransomed at a later date. Some, especially children and women, might be adopted into the tribe to bolster dwindling populations. Others would be tortured, as a test of courage or manhood, or ritually put to death and even eaten as a means of symbolically consuming their strength.

The twelve Lenape warriors who padded through the forest in October 1754 had aligned themselves with the French. They carried their weapons easily, the tomahawk and the scalping knife and the war club and, thanks to the white traders, the musket. They had raided their way eastward, burning and looting and killing. Now they had reached a farm near the Forks of the Delaware. There was a log farmhouse and a new barn from which they could hear the sounds of animals. They had been watching the house and knew there was only one white man here. This was their next target. They prepared themselves for attack.

> I that was now in an easy state of life, blessed with an affectionate and tender wife, who was possessed of all amiable qualities, to enable me to go through the world with that peace and serenity of mind which every Christian wishes to possess, became on a sudden one of the most unhappy and deplorable of mankind.

So wrote Peter Williamson in *French and Indian Cruelty*. 'Scarce can I sustain the shock which forever recoils on me, at thinking on the last time of seeing that good woman.'

Three months after Washington's defeat at Fort Necessity, the frontier was buzzing with news of Indian incursions. Every day brought fresh tales of slaughter and barbarity. 'Scarce did a day pass but some unhappy family or other fell victim to French chicanery, and savage cruelty,' wrote Williamson, once again putting the blame for the depredations squarely on Gallic shoulders. He was to suffer that savage cruelty at first hand.

It was 2 October 1754, and his wife was away from their farm visiting relatives. According to Peter's account, he was alone in the house and had stayed up later than usual to await her return. It was around eleven o'clock when he became aware of a new sound in the night air. It was the war whoop of a group of Lenape warriors as they surged from the darkness to converge on his house. He seized his musket and opened a small window to see twelve warriors beating at his door. He asked them what they wanted, but they made no answer, simply continuing to make their bloodcurdling war cries, and to hammer and hack at the wooden door with their tomahawks. He yelled down to them that he would shoot, but he knew in his heart that he was doomed. He was one man with one musket. They were twelve seasoned warriors, armed to the teeth and out for blood. One of the Lenape could speak a little English, and he shouted that if the white man did not come out of the house, they would burn him alive. Tales of slaughter had been circulating throughout the frontier for months, and Williamson knew that they meant what they said. However, he suspected that if he came out peacefully, he would be murdered anyway. But the English-speaking warrior then held out an olive branch. He said they were no friends of the English, which Williamson had already guessed, but promised they would not kill him if he came out and surrendered to them.

Williamson had a choice: he could face certain death if his house was torched, or he could rely on the possibility that the 'savages' would stick to their word. He had no idea if they were men of honour or not, but he 'chose to rely on the uncertainty of their fallacious promises'. He unbolted the door and stepped outside into the night, still with his gun in his hand. The warriors rushed him, and he was knocked to the ground, his musket snatched from his fingers. Then he was hauled to his feet and bundled to the nearest tree, to which he was bound, and forced to watch as the raiders plundered his farm. They seized what they thought was of value, then set fire to the rest. Williamson watched with tears in his eyes as the flames consumed his new home, the heat searing his face, the smoke invading his nostrils. The barn was next, and he heard the terrified, agonised cries of his stock of half a dozen cows, four horses and five sheep as they were burned alive inside.

With the night sky ablaze, the war party returned their attention to Williamson. They knew the nearest neighbour was many miles away, and it would take some time for help to arrive. The secret of their raids was to hit fast, hit hard and melt away into the night. This white man was young and strong; they had much booty to take back to their village, and he could carry it for them. One came to him brandishing a tomahawk and promised a slow and painful death unless he agreed to be their prisoner. Williamson agreed, and, no doubt after a few blows were struck to reinforce their message that a far worse fate was in store if he did not cooperate, he was loaded down with their spoils. Then they poked and prodded him into motion, and he stumbled off into the darkness, leaving his old life and his happiness burning and smouldering behind.

Once again, Peter Williamson was a captive.

They walked through the night, moving swiftly back west. As the sun began to lighten the sky, Williamson told, his new captors ordered him to put down his load and stand against a tree. They tied his arms behind him, forcing 'the blood out of my finger ends'. There was, however, worse to come. They kindled a fire nearby, and Williamson thought they meant to burn him alive. They then leaped and danced around him 'with various odd motions and antic gestures, whooping, halloeing, and crying in a frightful manner, as it is their custom'. When their dance ended, they came closer, snatching burning branches from their fire and burning his face, hands and feet with them, singeing hair and stinging flesh. Williamson wanted to cry out, to scream, to swear, but he was warned that if he made the slightest noise, they would set him on fire. 'Thus tortured as I was, almost to death, I suffered their brutal pleasure without being allowed to vent my inexpressible anguish, otherwise than by shedding silent tears.'

The warriors, on seeing those tears flooding his cheeks, said that his face was wet and they would dry it. According to Williamson, they took up more burning twigs and pushed the flaming ends under his eyes. The scorching of his flesh was agonising, but still he could not scream or cry out, for he knew that if he showed such weakness, they would kill him. This was a test of strength and of courage. They wanted to see how well this white man withstood the ordeal, to see if he was man enough to walk with warriors, even as a slave.

Finally, the Lenape tired of tormenting their captive and settled down to feast on some of the meat they had taken from his house. They roasted it on the fire, untied his hands and gave him some of the food. He had obviously passed the test. After he had eaten, and for some reason hidden some of it under the bark of the tree, they bound his hands to the trunk again and left him alone while they slept. Clearly, they planned to travel by night and hide by day, for, as the sun began to sink, the fire was stamped out and leaves thrown over the ashes to cover any sign of their having been there. Then, forcing him to shoulder his load once again, they moved on through the gathering darkness. Williamson had no idea where they were taking him or even if he would survive the journey. Perhaps the next time they decided to torture him they would finish the job. But, as he later observed, 'What I underwent was but trifling, in comparison to the torments and miseries which I was afterwards an eye-witness of being inflicted on others of my unhappy fellow creatures.' For, according to his account, he was about to witness the slaughter of an entire family.

They pushed on through the colony until they reached the Susquehanna River and then forged north to the Blue Mountains. After a brief stop to hide their plunder under some logs, they and their human packhorse moved on to a nearby farmhouse owned by a man Williamson named as Joseph Snider. Williamson said he was forced to watch as the Lenape warriors forced their way into the house and slaughtered Snider, his wife and their five children. He was horrified by the massacre, describing how 'without the least remorse and with more than brutal cruelty, [they] scalped the tender parents and unhappy children'.

On the origins of the custom, a French soldier of the period noted that:

> This horrible custom was practised by these savages alone, and sprang from their own barbarism, for it seems never to have existed in any other nation, not even among nations, who, like them, have never received any idea of civilized life.

However, there have been isolated cases in European history, and the taking of heads was a well-known practice in the Old World. By lifting the scalp of his enemy, the Native American warrior had not only a war trophy, but also the means of symbolically taking on the strength and courage of his dead foe. The whites had no such spiritual reason for promoting the scalping of Indians. To them, it was merely a way of proving just how many 'savages' had been killed. As the colonists sought first to subdue and then, it has to be said, wipe out the Native

Americans, bounties were paid for each Indian scalp lifted. In 1755, Massachusetts governor Sir William Shirley levied a bounty of £40 for the scalp of an Indian man and £20 for that of a woman. In Pennsylvania, the rewards rose to £130 and £50. Certainly, these fees were paid in time of war, when the Indian raids were nigh on unstoppable, but such bounties had also been paid out in earlier years by both Dutch and English governors. Scalping was not new, but the encouragement of the European colonial rulers raised it to epidemic levels.

The body, usually either completely senseless or dead, was rolled over and the scalping knife plucked from the warrior's belt. The victim's head was then jerked back, a swift circular incision made around the skull from front to back. Then, with one foot placed on the back, the scalp was seized in both hands and wrenched from the skull. The entire operation took only a minute or two before the bloody trophy was held aloft. Depending on how much time he had, he might pause to scrape some of the blood and flesh from his prize before it was fixed to his belt, and he went in search of a new victim.

The warriors attacked the Snider farmhouse, screeching and firing their rifles before falling on their victims with their tomahawks, smashing skulls with the blades. Williamson could do nothing but watch as the family was shot, battered and scalped. Then, with the bodies piled inside, the farmhouse was set alight, the Indians 'rejoicing and echoing back in their diabolical manner' as the flames touched the night sky. They also put the barn and stables to the flame, just as they had done on Peter's farm, and once again the air was filled with the screams of animals being burned alive.

There was one survivor. The Sniders had a serving lad who the raiding party reckoned would, like Peter, make a good slave. So after they had seized everything that was of value to them and burned the rest, they loaded the two white men with plunder and marched them back towards the Blue Mountains, where the war party retrieved the goods they had earlier stashed. Then they bullied and battered the two men onwards.

Williamson later wrote:

> My fellow-sufferer could not long bear the cruel treatment which we were both obliged to suffer, and complaining bitterly to me of his being unable to proceed any farther, I endeavoured to condole him as much as lay in my power, to bear up under his afflictions, and wait with patience till by the divine assistance, we should be delivered out of their cruel clutches.

But the lad was not made of Williamson's stern stuff. He continued to gripe and moan until one of the Lenape could take his tears no longer. The boy was felled with a swift blow from a tomahawk and his hair efficiently lifted. Despite having witnessed the massacre of an entire family only hours before, Williamson was stunned by the ferocity and suddenness of this attack and for some time was frozen in horror. Finally, expecting at any time to feel the weight of a tomahawk crushing his skull, he stumbled forward again, leaving the body of the unnamed servant where it had fallen. He recalled:

> But still, such was the terror that I was under, that for some time I scarce knew the days of the week, or what I did, so that at this period, life indeed became a burden to me, and I regretted being saved from my first persecutors, the sailors.

This, however, was just the beginning.

The next victim's name was John Adams, and he was forced to watch his wife and four children beaten and scalped before he was taken prisoner. The warrior band had descended on his small farm in the shadow of the Blue Mountains without warning, and he had no time to mount even the slightest defence. This time, however, according to Williamson, the warriors did not stop at killing and scalping. John Adams had to stand by, his arms pinned, a knife at his throat, while some of the Lenape mutilated his wife's body, ignoring his cries for mercy. As they butchered the woman's remains, John Adams begged them to kill him too, but they had other plans for him. They had already lost one pack animal, and with this new raid they had fresh provisions and goods to carry. He would join the younger man as a slave.

Williamson described the man as being old, feeble and weak. It is perhaps for that reason that their captors decided to have some sport with him. According to Williamson's account, they travelled to a place he called the Great Swamp, where they rested for eight or nine days. To fill the time, the warriors abused the older man, 'diverting themselves in exercising the atrocious and barbarous cruelties on their unhappy victim'.

'Sometimes,' said Williamson, 'they would strip him naked, and paint him all over with various sorts of colours, which they extracted, or made from herbs and roots.' The body painting would have been humiliating for the European, while the pulling of the white hairs from his head would have been painful, although not unbearably so. As they did the latter, they told him that 'he was a fool for living so long, and that they would show him kindness in putting him out of the world'. However, it seems the Indians had worse in store for the old man. Sometimes they would tie him to a tree and whip him. Other times they scorched his cheeks with red hot coals, as they had done with Williamson. They also burned his legs 'quite to the knees'.

'To all of which,' Williamson said, 'the poor creature could but vent his sighs, his tears, his moans, and entreaties, that, to my affrightened imagination, were enough to penetrate a heart of adamant, and soften the most obdurate savage.'

But the 'savages' proved most obdurate indeed. Their people had

suffered greatly at the hands of the white man. They had generations
of abuses to avenge, and these white men were the personification of
those abuses. No amount of pleading or praying on the part of the old
man would stop them from playing their cruel games. And John Adams
did pray and plead. He 'incessantly offered up his prayers to the
Almighty, with the most fervent thanksgivings for his former mercies,
and hoping the flames, then surrounding and burning his aged limbs,
would soon send him to the blissful mansions of the just, to be a
partaker of the blessings there'. John Adams survived his torment,
although for how long cannot be known, for he now disappears from
Williamson's narrative. At this point the twelve Lenape were joined by
another raiding party bearing twenty white scalps and three live
prisoners. The captives were of Scots-Irish stock, hardy settlers whose
bloodline reached back to the central lowlands of Scotland by way of
Ulster. Their forefathers had left their Scottish homes in the early part
of the seventeenth century under a scheme instigated by James VI to
create a buffer of loyal Protestants against the rebellious Roman
Catholics in that troubled land. By the early to mid-eighteenth
century, they were moving westward again, this time to the Colonies,
escaping religious persecution or simply in search of a better life. They
were a tough bunch, and many were drawn to the untamed lands of
the frontier, where once again they acted as a barrier against a
dispossessed people, this time the Native Americans. Although most of
them had been born in Ulster, they thought of themselves as Scots, and
they brought their hardnosed Presbyterian ideals with them. They
were soon in conflict with the indigenous tribes and dealt with them
as harshly as their ancestors had dealt with the Catholic families of
Ulster one hundred years before.

The three prisoners had been taken at a place Williamson called
Cannocojigge, which he said was a small town near the Susquehanna.
It may have been the Conococheague Valley in Northern Maryland. In
hushed tones, the newcomers told Williamson of attacks on

homesteads and farms in their territory, each one similar to the raids on their own homes. According to Williamson, one family suffered more than the others who were simply killed and scalped. He named the patriarch as George Folke and stated that he, his wife and their nine children were 'inhumanely scalped, then cut to pieces, and given to the swine, which devoured them'. Pigs will play an important role in Williamson's tale more than once.

The Scots-Irish newcomers, again not named, went on to tell their horrified comrades in captivity another grisly story of Indian barbarity, this time involving a trader who was ambushed, roasted and eaten, his head being turned into an Indian pudding. (An 'Indian pudding' was a dessert made of baked cornmeal, fruit and molasses. What these braves were supposed to have done with the trader's head is unexplained.)

The three captives were not in Williamson's company long, as he recorded that they managed to make good their escape. Their freedom was short-lived, however, for they were swiftly recaptured and dragged back. Williamson graphically describes their punishment:

> The poor creatures, almost famished for want of sustenance, having had none during the time of their elopement, were no sooner in the clutches of the barbarians, than two of them were tied to a tree, and a great fire made around them, where they remained till they were terribly scorched and burnt; when one of the villains, with his scalping knife, ript open their bellies, took out their entrails, and burnt them before their eyes, whilst the others were cutting, piercing, and tearing the flesh from their breasts, hands, arms and legs with red hot irons, until they were dead.

The third victim was kept alive longer, he claimed. A hole was dug deep enough for him to stand upright in and the earth crammed around him until only his head remained above the surface. He was scalped but kept alive in great agony for three or four hours. Then a fire was lit nearby:

> causing him to suffer the most excruciating torments imaginable, whilst the poor creature could only cry for mercy in killing him immediately, for his brains were boiling in his head: inexorable to all his plaints, they continued the fire, whilst, shocking to behold, his eyes gushed out of their sockets.

The man suffered for almost two hours until he died and the Indians cut off his head and tossed it towards Williamson, who was to bury what remained of the bodies.

With winter now beginning to bite, his captors turned their thoughts to home, so he was marched a further 200 miles to reach Alamingo, a Lenape village on the Susquehanna.

SIX

The Most Implacably Vindictive People upon the Earth

As the warrior band entered the village, the women and children came out of the wigwams, singing, dancing and cheering their menfolk back from the raiding expedition. Williamson, naturally, became an object of great interest, not to mention derision. He was stripped naked of his ragged clothing and given a blanket to wrap around himself, a yard of coarse cloth to cover his modesty and a pair of *mogganes* (moccasins) for his feet. Over the following months, he claimed, he was able to observe much of the tribe's way of life.

They called their huts wigwams, and these consisted of deerskins wrapped around three or four wooden stakes thrust into the ground. He said they warmed themselves in winter with white blankets, often with designs painted on them. In time of war, these designs might be of leaves, in order to blend in with the forest background. However, it is also known that they fashioned clothes from deerskin and decorated them with porcupine quills, feathers and beads. Their moccasins were also made of deer hide and sometimes adorned with beads or ribbons.

Williamson went on to say that their legs were covered in blue cloth stockings and their midriffs by loincloths. He observed that:

> The better sort have shirts of the finest linen they can get, and to these some wear ruffles; but these they never put on till they have painted them of various colours which they get from Pecone root, and bark of trees, and never pull them off to wash, but wear them till they fall to pieces.

For decoration, he said, they wore silver bangles round their wrists, but we know that the Lenape also favoured copper, which they obtained in trade with other tribes. In addition to forging ornaments with the metal, they used it for arrowheads and pipes. They also wore belts known as wampum, decorated with shell beads, while some sported noserings and earrings, often made of silver. The men, Williamson noted, were beardless 'to prevent which they use certain instruments and tricks as soon as it begins to grow'. They kept their heads shaved or plucked, apart from the greased scalp lock. Older men let their hair grow long, while the women twisted their locks down their backs. Although Williamson did not mention it, the women also stained their skin red with ochre, while the *sachems,* medicine men or tribe leaders, decorated their hair with eagle feathers.

'The females are very chaste and constant to their husbands,' Williamson said, 'and if any young maiden should happen to have a child before marriage, she is never esteemed afterwards.' The fact was there was no formal system of marriage, but when a Lenape man and woman came together, they tended to remain so for life.

The main food was Indian corn, maize, 'soaked, then bruised and boiled over a gentle fire for ten or twelve hours'. They also grew squash, sweet potatoes and beans. They supplemented this with game, which was boiled or roasted. Bread, said Williamson, was made of wild oats or sunflower seeds.

He may well have suffered at their hands, but Williamson never wavered in his admiration of the Indian warriors. He said that in time of war all they carried with them was their 'gun, tomahawk [which he said was about two feet long and likened to a plasterer's hammer], scalping knife, powder and shot'. They seldom used bows and arrows, he said – one of the many changes to the tribal way of life brought about by the white man. Although the tribes eagerly learned to use new weapons, as both the French and English were soon to discover to their cost, the Indian way of fighting was not one of set-piece battles in which, as was the European custom, the warring parties lined themselves up as easy targets. Williamson explained:

> They industriously avoid all open engagements, and besides ambuscades, their principal way is bush-fighting, in the exercise of which they are very dextrous: for the back country being one continued wood, except some few spots cleared for the purpose of husbandry by our back settlers, the Indians squat themselves down behind the trees, and fire their muskets at the enemy; if the enemy advances, then they retreat behind other trees, and fire in the same manner; and as they are good marksmen, they never fire in vain, whereas their pursuers seldom hit.

He went on:

> No people have a greater love of liberty, or affection to their neighbours; but are the most implacably vindictive people upon the earth; for they revenge the death of any relation, or any great affront, whenever occasion presents, let the distance of time or place be ever so remote.

Although he thought the Native Americans 'inhumanely cruel', Williamson believed that European armies, riven with class divisions and plagued by nepotism, would do well to copy them in making 'wise conduct, courage and personal strength, the chief recommendations for war captains, or *werowances,* as they call them'.

They had one particular weakness, however, and it was one that white traders played on. The Lenape, like other tribes, did not have a head for liquor. According to Williamson, they grew 'very dangerous and troublesome' when drunk – a trait they shared with many white men:

> The traders availed themselves of this weakness; instead of carrying our clothes to cover the naked savages, they carried them rum, and thereby debauched their manners, weakened their constitutions, introduced disorders unknown to them before, and in short corrupted and ruined them.

However, he noted with some pleasure that the traders who plied – and cheated – the tribes with rum often found themselves on the wrong end of a tomahawk. 'A just reward for their wicked designs,' he wrote with a barely suppressed cackle.

They were very quick to punish wrongdoing. Hanging was not a favoured method of execution, but burning was, although, he observed with some distaste, the condemned often did not die immediately, but 'sometimes remain roasting in the middle of the flames for two or three days before they are dead'. They also, he claimed, practised a form of euthanasia, which he said he witnessed during his stay:

> [An old man] being through age, feeble and weak, and his eyes failing him, so that he was unable to get his living either by hunting or shooting, was summoned to appear before several of the leading ones, who were to be his judges. [They] very formally, and with a seeming degree of compassion, passed sentence on him to be put to death.

The old man was tied to a tree, and his executioner, a young boy, stood by with a tomahawk. However, the youngster was not tall enough to lift the hatchet high enough to strike the fatal blow, so he had to be lifted up. 'Then, though the young devil laid on him with all his strength, he was not for some time able to fracture the old man's skull, so that it was near an hour before he was dead.' The old man was then buried in a shallow grave, his gun in his hand, a powder horn and bag of shot over one shoulder and a wampum belt around his neck. In his right hand, according to Williamson, they put a little purse with some money inside.

Williamson said he witnessed all this and made his anthropological observations during a two-month stay in Alamingo. He was allowed to build his own wigwam, covering it with tree bark and earth, and keeping a fire going near the door to deter the winter chill. He was, he observed, free to come and go very much as he pleased. He had long since realised he was too far away from home for escape to be practical, while the memory of what had befallen the three Scots-Irish captives would be fresh in his mind. His captors knew all this and so left him alone. Sometimes they would allow him a little meat, but mostly he survived on corn. He was submissive, obedient and filled with despair over ever regaining his freedom – or seeing his wife again. He would have thought of her often during those long, cold nights as he huddled beside his little fire, listening to Lenape voices all around him – men talking to women, laughing, fighting, making love. And as the weeks turned into months, he must have known that she would have been forced to presume him dead and return to her father's farm. At least there she would be safe from harm – or so he hoped.

He survived the winter by following this policy of compliancy, he said, but as the temperature rose, the camp began to fill with warriors from other villages, including a number from Fort Duquesne, the main French outpost in the Ohio Valley. They had been well supplied with powder and ball by the French army and were ready, with the melting of the snows, to strike out once more against the British settlers. The war party this time numbered 150, a 'terrible and formidable body', Williamson said, and, again acting as a packhorse, he was loaded down with supplies — but never a weapon of any kind. Beaten and submissive he may have been, but the warriors were no fools — they were not going to give any white man the chance to fight back.

Williamson had no intention of fighting back. He had already come through torture — relatively minor though it was — and been accepted to a limited degree by the warriors. Fighting was not part of his plan. Escape, however, was a different matter. Although he had seen what happened to captives who attempted to flee, he was still intent on gaining his freedom at the first opportunity. It was not something he could plan, certainly not now that he was on the move, but he was resolved he would seize the first chance that presented itself — and, with luck, remain at large long enough to reach his own people.

The large war party marched eastward from Alamingo for several uneventful days. They took only what they needed and the only food they carried was some corn, which Williamson said he was 'glad to eat dry'. The warriors themselves shot game in the early days of the expedition, but as they neared the white man's territory, they, too, were on reduced rations. They did not want to fire their guns and alert the settlers to their coming.

Although the snow was melting, the air was still bright with frost, and at night they clustered round a series of fires, ten or twelve men to each blaze, their feet towards the flames with only a blanket each to ward off the night air. When they reached the Blue Mountains, a council of war was convened, and the Indians decided to split into parties of around twenty men in order to spread their raids over a wider area. Williamson, naturally, was to stay with the warriors who had taken him from his farm. He was not, however, to go on any of the raids, as his captors thought it unwise to allow him anywhere near a settlement or plantation.

For months he had dreamed of escape. He would soon have his chance.

As they marched closer to the most remote of the settlements, the woodlands began to look familiar to the white captive. In years past, he had often hunted in these woods with friends; but he was careful not to let his guards know that he was beginning to recognise his surroundings. After lingering in the foothills for three days, the hungry Indians decided to slip into the mountains where they could safely hunt for food. However, they knew that Williamson would be something of a hindrance on the hunting trip, for they could not keep a sharp lookout for game while keeping at least one eye on him, so he was tied to a tree and left. When he thought it safe, he tested his bonds, but he found he was securely trussed so he settled down to wait for the Lenape to return, which they did as darkness began to fall, carrying with them a brace of dead polecats.

'We all sat down together to supper,' he wrote, 'and soon after (being greatly fatigued with their day's excursion) they composed themselves to rest as usual.' This time, though, they forgot to bind him. An idea began to take shape in Williamson's mind. Perhaps here, at last, was the window of opportunity for which he had been praying. He waited until he 'observed them to be in that somniferous state' and then began to move around, to test just how deep their sleep was. He even touched one or two of their feet.

Not one of the Indians stirred.

'My heart then exalted with joy at seeing a time come that I might in all probability be delivered from my captivity,' he wrote. That joy, though, was short-lived, for he was overtaken by a dread of being caught, either by his guards or by another band of raiders who could at that moment be making their way back to this base camp. However, this was much too good a chance to miss, and he was determined to seize it. He reasoned that if he could somehow get hold of one of the muskets, he would at least have the means to defend himself should the need arise or 'to die in my defence rather than be taken'. He crept closer to the sleeping group, bathed in the red glow of the snapping fire at their feet, and gingerly tried to ease a rifle from under the head of the nearest Indian. He would not have pulled too hard, for he knew any sudden or sharp movement would snap the Lenape warrior into wakefulness.

But the rifle would not move.

Time was passing, and Williamson knew that the men could wake up at any minute. He did not try to steal another weapon as each of the braves had them secured in a similar fashion:

> Frustrated in this my first essay towards regaining my liberty, I dreaded the thought of carrying out my design into execution: yet after a little consideration, and trusting myself to the divine protection, I set forward naked and defenceless as I was.

He moved slowly at first, each step of his moccasin-clad feet carefully chosen lest he should stand on a twig, and he stopped every two or three yards to glance back at the sleeping braves. But with each stride further away his pace quickened and his desire, his *need*, to escape grew. Those first few hesitant treads became a brisk walk, then a lope, then a trot until, when he was around 200 yards away from the group, he broke into a full run. He pushed through bushes and leaped over tree roots in a desperate attempt to put as much distance between him and the warriors as possible, for he knew they would not sleep forever; sooner rather than later, one would awaken and find him gone. So he kept moving, arms batting branches out of his path as he ran.

Then he heard it and he was 'struck with the greatest terror'.

It sounded like '*Jo Hau, Jo Hau*' and it could have been a bird or an animal howling in the night. But he knew it was no forest beast. It was the wood cry of the Lenape floating through the trees behind him, and he realised his guards had awakened to find him missing and were in pursuit. 'The bellowing of lions, the shrieks of hyenas, or the roaring of tigers would have been music to my ears, in comparison to the sounds that then saluted them,' he said. They would separate and swoop through the forest in search of him – and if they caught him, the best he could hope for was a swift death. It would, though, be a vain hope. Terror rising in his throat, he quickened his pace, 'and scarce knowing where I trod, drove through the woods with the utmost precipitation'.

He burst through bushes and ducked under low branches, thin twigs whipping at his face, stumbling on occasion and 'falling and bruising myself, cutting my feet and legs against the stones in a miserable manner'. But each time, he pulled himself upright again and pressed on, the sounds of the pursuing Indians forcing him to ignore his pain, for worse awaited him if he was captured again. All through the night he ran, until above him the sky began to lighten. Exhausted, he looked for somewhere to rest and found a hollow tree into which he climbed, and there he nibbled on some of the corn he had carried with him in a bag. 'I lay very snug and returned my prayers and thanks to the Divine Being that had thus far favoured my escape.' He could not continue without some rest, and so, every nerve jumping with each fresh sound outside what he called his 'circular asylum', he at last allowed his eyes to flutter and close.

The sound of the voices knifed through his fitful sleep and he jerked instantly awake. He would not have been able to tell at first how close they were to his hiding-place, but he would have known they were heading his way. His every instinct would have been screaming that he should run, but he knew that would have been foolhardy. His body rigid inside his tree trunk, his breath freezing in his lungs, he listened to the men talking among themselves as they passed. He had an idea what they were saying, although he did not fully understand the language. Enraged at their slave for escaping – and no doubt at themselves for giving him the chance – they were muttering about what dire revenge they would have on his body when they found him. Williamson did not need to speak their tongue to sense their anger, and their tone only served to increase both his terror and his determination not to be recaptured.

Finally, as the voices passed to leave only the calling of the birds and the sigh of the breeze through the trees, Williamson breathed again and his muscles unclenched slightly. The danger might have passed, but it was still out there. To travel in daylight was too risky, so he resolved to move only by night. He had no gun and no knife with which to defend himself if the time came. His only defence was darkness, and he would exploit it to the fullest. But terror was always with him. 'At night I ventured forwards again,' he said, 'frightened and trembling at every bush I past, thinking each twig that touched me to be a savage.' He kept off the trails, forcing his way through parts of the dense woodlands that perhaps no man had ever travelled. Although he had a hazy idea of the direction he was taking, this indirect route added miles to his journey, and he said it was 'more painful and irksome than I can express'. He could not risk bumping into any of the searching Indians or their raiding comrades, who would no doubt have begun to filter back by this time. But if the darkness helped conceal him from their eyes, then it also hid them from his – and on the fourth night he almost stumbled over a group of raiders sleeping round a small fire. Cursing himself for not detecting the aromatic tang of wood smoke or even seeing the glow among the tree trunks, he veered off.

But he was a farmer, not a hunter and had not perfected the art of moving soundlessly through the forest. The rustling he made in the undergrowth alerted the war party and they leaped up, guns at the ready. Williamson froze again in the dark as they fanned out from their campfire and crept into the woods to investigate. Tired, terrified and hungry, Williamson was at a loss as to his next move. If he pressed forward, they would surely hear him and take up a howling pursuit. If he stayed where he was, there was the strong chance they would stumble across him. He crouched in the bushes, listening to the stealthy approach of the warriors, his heart drumming in his chest, his nerves singing a song of blind panic. They would find him now, he knew it. They would find him now and he would die here in this uncaring forest, his body ripped apart by bloodthirsty savages, never again to see his wife, never again to hold her close, never again to smell the soap in her hair and feel the touch of her hand on his skin. He could not run and he could not fight. It was over.

But just as he resigned himself to his fate, a new sound rustled through the forest. It was not the Indians, for it was too unmindful of who heard its progress. It was not white hunters, for it was too haphazard. He twisted round as the sound grew nearer and saw a parcel of wild pigs trotting through the undergrowth towards the suspicious Indians. The animals snorted past him, moving towards the war party, and from his hiding-place he saw the men relax. Thinking it was the hogs they had heard earlier, they laughed, put up their weapons and returned to their fire. He watched as they wrapped themselves in their blankets, laid their heads on their rifles again and went back to sleep.

Thanking God for creating wild pigs, Williamson pressed on, slowly this time for fear that he would either make another noise that would bring the braves raging out of the forest behind him, or inadvertently blunder into another band in front. At daybreak, he slid under a felled tree, covered himself with leaves and tried to get some rest. He had been at large for four days now, eating only what little corn he had in his pouch and sipping water from streams. Hunger, fatigue and sleep deprivation all combined to weaken his already weary body. If he did not reach a safe haven soon, he would die in the wilderness or, worse, fall captive again to the Lenape. Travelling by night, and his circuitous route, meant he had only the faintest sense of direction, so he decided to risk being spotted in daylight in order to get his bearings. He slept all morning and as the sun reached its zenith, crawled out from under his log and began to climb the nearest hill in order to get the lie of the land. He arrived at the summit 'with great difficulty' and, his chest heaving and legs trembling with fatigue, looked out over the sea of trees that swayed around him. To his 'unutterable joy' he saw a patch of cleared land about ten miles distant.

He walked the rest of the day and, breaking with his routine, slept by night. The following morning he continued on his journey and finally arrived at the farmhouse at about four o'clock in the afternoon. He staggered out of the tree line and made for the front door of the log cabin. He recognised this farm as one belonging to a man he named as John Bell, and he believed he would receive a warm welcome. In fact, he was almost shot. He had forgotten the picture he presented. He was naked, apart from his Indian blanket and the loincloth. He wore a pair of moccasins. His flesh was caked with filth and dried blood from the myriad of scratches and cuts he had received over the months and during his headlong flight through the forest. He looked more Lenape than white man and he was mistaken for such by Mrs Bell, who answered the door. On seeing the vision before her she 'flew from me like lightning,' he recalled, 'screaming into the house'. Mr Bell and his sons snatched up their rifles and levelled them at the creature in the doorway, for with the troubles setting the frontier ablaze it was policy to shoot first and think about asking questions later. Williamson held out his arms and told them who he was. John Bell edged forward, his gun still cocked and ready, until he recognised the man he once knew in the emaciated, mangled figure before him. He laid his weapon to one side and turned back in time to catch Williamson as he collapsed with relief and weariness.

Peter Williamson said he stayed with the Bell family for two or three days, during which 'they affectionately supplied me with all the necessaries'. After his collapse, they gave him some food, but not too much, for they realised that in his 'weak and famished condition' his system was unlikely to cope. During his stay, he said, they 'carefully attended to me until my spirits and limbs were pretty well recruited [recovered]'.

They had been shocked to discover that the battered and naked wretch standing in their doorway that day was Williamson because they had heard he had been murdered by Indians months before. Although he must have inquired after his wife, they were unable, or as it turned out perhaps unwilling, to give him news of her. So when he felt well enough to ride, he borrowed a horse and some clothes and, bidding a fond farewell to the family who had given him succour when he had most needed it, set out on the 140-mile journey to his father-in-law's home in Chester County. There a shock awaited him.

He arrived on 4 January 1755. He had been missing for three months. His wife had been dead for two.

Williamson does not say in his writing what claimed Rose. All he wrote was that 'this fatal news, as every humane reader must imagine, greatly lessened the joy and rapture I otherwise should have felt at my deliverance from the dreadful state of captivity I had been in'.

It is probable that the late Mrs Williamson had been buried near her father's home at Mount Hiram and so it is likely that Williamson made a pilgrimage to her grave. It was still deep winter and if there was no snow, then the ground would still be hard with frost. Peter was only in his mid-twenties. He had lost his family in Scotland. He had lost a kind master. He had lost his farm. And now he had lost the woman he loved. As he stood by that silent grave in the bleak mid-winter, with the naked trees around him etched starkly against the grey skies, he realised that throughout his short life things had been taken from him: by conniving businessmen; by the vagaries of fate; by marauding Indians.

No more, though. Now it was his turn.

SEVEN

The Only Good Indian Is a Dead Indian

News of Peter Williamson's deliverance from the hands of the savage Indians swiftly spread through the county and soon his father-in-law's plantation was invaded by neighbours and those who had travelled further, eager to hear about his adventures. How much the tales grew in the telling cannot be said for certain, but Williamson did say that he satisfied them all with his account. He was also called to see the colony's governor, Robert Morris, whom he described as 'a worthy gentleman', who wanted details of his time in the Indians' custody. He particularly wanted to know whether the raiding party which had first abducted him were sympathetic to the French or if they were a renegade band from a tribe friendly with Britain.

> I assured His Excellency that they were of those who professed themselves to be friends of the former; and informed him of the many barbarous and inhuman actions I had been witness to among them, on the frontiers of the province; and also that

they were daily increasing, by others of our pretended friends joining them; that they were all well supplied by the French with arms and ammunition, and greatly encouraged by them in their continual excursions and barbarities, not only in having extraordinary premiums for such scalps as they should take and carry home with them at their return; but great presents of all kinds, besides rum, powder, ball &c. before they sallied forth.

Williamson said Governor Morris seemed satisfied with what he had told him; he claimed to have sworn to the contents of an affidavit which was then forwarded to the Colonial Assembly sitting at the Philadelphia State House.

The Indian raids on the frontier were, naturally, a great cause for alarm, not only in Pennsylvania but also in the other twelve English colonies. Although the hostilities that became known as the French and Indian War had obviously already begun, Britain would not formally declare war on France until May 1756. That declaration marked the official commencement of the Seven Years War, of which the struggle in the northern colonies was but one, albeit highly important, campaign. There was only a nominal British Army presence in the Provinces and the defence of the colonies very much fell to the individual assemblies. In 1754, Pennsylvanian printer and politician Benjamin Franklin, with the League of the Hodenosaunee in mind, put forward a plan for the union of the colonies. The idea was that the Thirteen Colonies would band together under one government, as Franklin put it, 'so far as might be necessary for defence, and other important general purposes'. The proposal, put forward at a congress in Albany, was that a president general, backed by the Crown, be appointed and a Grand Council elected by the people's representatives in each colonial assembly. The plan was placed before the Board of Trade in London as well as the individual assemblies. Its fate, Franklin later wrote, 'was singular'.

The assemblies rejected it, he said, because there 'was too much prerogative in it'; in other words, the Crown had too much say. Also, the colonies had never been known to act in accord, but tended to favour their own interests first – the situation in the Ohio territory, where the lands were claimed by both Virginia and Pennsylvania (not to mention the Iroquois), being an example. Meanwhile, the Board of Trade turned the plan down because it was 'too democratic' – the Crown had always viewed the independent streak of some of the colonies with suspicion. So London put forward another idea – that the governors of the colonies and some members of their assemblies meet to order the raising of forces and building of defensive forts, and to draw on the Treasury for the expense, which in turn would levy a tax. Benjamin Franklin was in no doubt that this was a bad decision all round. He wrote:

> The Colonies so united [under the rejected scheme] would have been sufficiently strong to defend themselves, there would have been no need for troops from England; of course the subsequent pretense for taxing America, and the bloody contest it occasioned, would have been avoided.

That bloody contest was the War of American Independence, which would erupt in 1776. Its causes were rooted firmly in the events of the past – and the French and Indian War in particular. For while Britain subjected the Colonies to increased taxation, it also eventually forged a treaty with the Indians that no colonists would push further into their territory to exploit the vast riches that lay on the far side of the Appalachians. The land speculators, the merchants and the would-be settlers wanted that territory and resolved to ignore the British law. The American Revolution may have had freedom somewhere on the agenda, but financial gain was also behind the Declaration of Independence.

Money was also one of the reasons Pennsylvania, at least, was slow to defend itself. It was steeped in Quaker pacifist ideology but that was not the only reason why no militia was raised in 1754 and 1755. The Pennsylvanian proprietors, the heirs of the original founding family, continually used their influence to veto any attempt to raise taxes to finance the colonial forces. It was not that the proprietors were against the idea of defending the frontier, it was just that they felt they and their estates should be excluded from paying anything towards that defence. The assembly, of course, took a differing view and for years the argument raged back and forth across the floor of the Assembly House. As the rich man sought to protect his riches, the poor man saw his farm being ravaged and burned, his livestock slaughtered and his family left homeless, or worse. 'It caused great confusion among the people to see the country so destroyed, and no preparations making for its defence,' said Williamson. As this confusion mounted, raids became more frequent, and soon settlers were abandoning their farms and heading back towards the relative safety of the cities.

Williamson wrote that on receiving his affidavit from Governor Morris, the assembly sent for him. Although still weak, he claimed, he made the journey to Philadelphia and gave evidence over a two-day period before he was allowed to return to his father-in-law's farm. He was unwilling to return to his own farm, even though he recognised it as being 'an exceedingly good one'. He and his father-in-law both saw the desirability of some sort of employment, and Williamson said that, with the need for men to be raised 'to check those barbarians in their raving depredations', he duly enlisted 'with the greatest alacrity and most determined resolution, to exert the utmost of my power, in being revenged on the hellish authors of my ruin'.

Finally, some agreement had been made about financing a defensive force, although in Pennsylvania's case not without some considerable political derring-do. Benjamin Franklin formulated a financial plan to provide £10,000 worth of provisions without first having to gain the support of the proprietors through their puppet, Governor Morris. General William Shirley, governor of New England, was to revive two provincial regiments, the 50th and 51st, to take the fight to the enemy. They were to head for the frontier lands to the north and west, seek out raiding Indian bands and destroy enemy forts. Williamson said he enlisted with Shirley's regiment for three years. However, before he was to join the troops in Boston, he had to spend a further two months in his father-in-law's care in order to regain his strength. By the spring of 1755, Williamson felt recovered enough to travel to the Puritan city in the north-east along with other young Pennsylvania men who had joined up to fight the French and their Indian allies. They crossed the Delaware River into New Jersey and struck out for Boston by way of New York, Middletown and Mendon in Connecticut.

The founding fathers of New England had none of the Quaker scruples regarding the Native Americans shown by William Penn. The local tribe, the Wampanoag, had, like many other tribes, suffered horribly at the hands of the white settlers and their diseases. In December 1620, the *Mayflower* set 120 Pilgrim settlers ashore at a site the Europeans named Plymouth Harbour. Like the Quakers later, they were fleeing religious persecution at home. They did not know that the land on which they had settled had previously been home to the Patuxet tribe, which had been decimated by fevers introduced by European slavers and fishermen who worked the waters of the North Atlantic. The newcomers did not thrive until they received aid from Samoset, an Abenaki Indian who, to their amazement, could speak English, which he had learned from the same fishermen who had helped, inadvertently, destroy the Patuxet. The colonists received with delight news that the indigenous people of this land were no more. Almost gleefully, colonist William Bradford wrote, 'There is neither man, woman nor child remaining, as indeed we have found none, so that there is none to hinder our possession or lay claim unto it.'

There was, in fact, one surviving Patuxet, a warrior named Tisquantum who had been kidnapped by English slavers in 1614 and sold in Malaga, Spain. He was taken away by Spanish monks before he escaped his servitude and made it to England, where he befriended a kindly merchant who taught him English and arranged for his return to North America. Tisquantum, also known as Squanto, was desolate to find his people dead of the plague and since his return he had been living with the local Wampanoags, whose sachem was named Massasoit. The Wampanoag leader listened intently to Tisquantum's tales of the white men across the water who numbered more than the flakes of snow in the winter and the leaves on the trees in summer. When he heard of the arrival of the settlers, Massasoit decided to greet them using Tisquantum as interpreter. Treaties were reached by which each side would support the other if either side were attacked. Massasoit had an ulterior motive in assisting the white man, for he was under threat from the Narragansett tribe, which had escaped the worst of the epidemics and was flexing its muscles, seizing land from neighbouring tribes. With Tisquantum taking the lead, the Indians showed the colonists how best to clear the land of trees, how to plant it with maize and the best waters in which to fish. The two cultures managed to exist side by side in relative peace for forty years. Naturally, given the white man's greed and arrogance, it would not last.

'They received the English upon their first arrival with open arms, treated them kindly, and showed earnest desire that they should settle and live with them,' wrote Williamson:

> They freely parted with some of their lands to their new-come brethren, and cheerfully entered into a league of friendship with them. As the English were in immediate want of the assistance of the Indians, they, on their part, endeavoured to make their coming agreeable. Thus they lived for some years

in the mutual exchange of friendly offices . . . But by their different way of living, the English soon acquired property, while the Indians continued in their former indigence; hence the former found they could live easily without the latter, and therefore became less anxious about preserving their friendship.

Relations had soured considerably by 1663. Massasoit had died the year before, still clinging to his treaty with the increasingly rapacious settlers, who, while seeking religious freedom when fleeing England forty years before, were now often intent on denying such freedom to the native peoples of the New World. Hunting on the sabbath was punished severely, while any Indian who refused to embrace Christianity could face the death penalty. Massasoit's son Wamsutta was not so keen on the English. However, while he was imprisoned at Plymouth by the Puritans, he mysteriously died; whether it was of fever or poison depended on the colour of skin of the person telling the story. His brother Metacom, also known as King Philip, took over as sachem. Over the following years, he carefully built up a confederacy of other New England tribes who had also suffered at the white man's hands. King Philip's War erupted in 1675, eventually sucking in the Wampanoags' traditional enemies, the Narragansetts, who were forced to abandon their neutrality after English settlers attacked one of their townships and slaughtered over 600 men, women and children.

Despite early successes and the union of the tribes, Metacom's forces were hopelessly outnumbered. Some braves lost heart and surrendered, only to find themselves sold as slaves to the plantations of the West Indies. In April 1676, the Narragansett warlord Canonchet was captured and placed before a firing squad. 'I like it well,' he said at the end. 'I shall die before my heart is soft or I have said anything unworthy of myself.'

An Indian in the pay of the English forces shot Metacom in August 1676. His wife and nine-year-old son had already been captured and sold as slaves. In the year-long struggle, 3,000 Native Americans had lost their lives. Entire tribes had been wiped out and the once-powerful Wampanoags and Narragansetts were reduced to a few hundred people.

New England's first governor, John Winthrop, had selected land on the coast of Massachusetts Bay to build what would be the colony's seat of government, Boston. The city, like Philadelphia, was built on trade. To the chagrin of old-style Puritans, one of the city's greatest exports was rum, although they were less outraged at the import of slaves. Indeed, although the Puritan Church still kept a firm grip on the morals of the city, with a rapidly growing population of immigrants, their austere ideal of a holy, God-fearing, single-religion society was placed under severe strain. As the port grew, so did the prevalence of taverns and prostitutes. The city fathers tried desperately to control these twin evils, but, thirst and lust being what they are, they were fighting a losing battle.

According to Williamson, by the time he arrived in 1755, Boston had 24,000 inhabitants and the town itself lay 'in the form of a half-moon, round the harbour, and consisting of about 4,000 houses'. The result, in his eyes, was 'an agreeable prospect; the surrounding shore being kept high, the streets long, and the buildings beautiful. The pavement is kept in good order, that to gallop a horse on it is 3 s. 4 d. forfeit.'

The main street of the town, Williamson said, came down to the head of the pier. On this street was situated:

> the Town House, or Exchange, a fine building, containing, besides the walk for merchants, the Council Chamber, the House of Commons, and a spacious room for the Courts of Justice. The Exchange is surrounded with booksellers' shops

that have a good trade – here being five printing houses, and
the presses generally full of work, which is in great measure
owing to the colleges and schools in New England; and
likewise at New York and Philadelphia, there are several
printing houses lately erected, and booksellers constantly
employed, as well as at Virginia, Maryland, South Carolina,
Barbados, and the Sugar Islands.

Williamson's fascination with booksellers and printers may seem
strange, but it has to be remembered that he had a keen interest in
improving himself and would no doubt have read everything he could
lay his hands on. On the frontier, books and newspapers would have
been in short supply, so it is understandable that he would have been
irresistibly drawn to such shops while in a big city. This fascination was
to be put to profitable use later in his life.

Williamson and his fellow volunteers spent the spring of 1755 in the
city, being taught the intricacies of army discipline – never an easy task
with colonial fighters, as more than one British commander would
discover in the course of this war. Meanwhile, they waited for their
military and political masters to reach some sort of decision regarding
how best to proceed. Plans had been formulated for an attack on the
French stronghold at Niagara, as well as one on Fort St Frédéric at
Crown Point in northern New York. However, Williamson reported that
the latter proposal was delayed by dithering politicians. And so the
colonial troops bided their time in Boston, thirsting for action.

According to Williamson, some of them saw that action earlier than
expected.

Williamson wrote that a 'gentleman of large fortune in these parts'
named Joseph Long had once been 'a great warrior among the Indians,
and frequently joined in expeditions with those in our interest, against
the others'. However, Williamson claimed, it was his notoriety that

proved to be his undoing. He reported that, 'His many exploits and great influence among several of the nations were too well known to pass unrevenged by the savages against whom he had exerted his abilities.'

According to Williamson, Joseph Long had a plantation about thirty miles from Boston, and in April 1755, a party of Indians friendly to the French attacked his home and killed Long, his wife and their nine servants, scalping and mutilating the bodies. Long's son and daughter they spared and, after the customary torching of the house, barn, outbuildings and livestock, they were marched off into captivity.

News of the massacre swiftly reached Boston and the ears of Captain James Crawford, the fiancé of the captured Miss Long. 'Distracted, raving and shocked as he was,' wrote Williamson, 'he lost no time, but instantly raised 100 resolute and bold young fellows, to go in quest of the villains.' It seems one of those resolute and bold young fellows was Williamson himself. Not that he volunteered to go on the rescue mission; he was, he said, nominated to join them as one who had experience of the 'savages'. However, he was more than willing to go along. 'Never did I go on any enterprise with half that alacrity and cheerfulness I now went with this party,' he stated. 'My wrongs and sufferings were too recent in my memory to suffer me to hesitate a moment in taking an opportunity of being revenged to the utmost of my power.'

With Captain Crawford at its head, the one hundred-strong rescue party set out from Boston, arriving at the ruins of the Long plantation, Williamson stated, on 2 May 1755. They had hoped to cross paths with the raiding party on their march towards the plantation, but saw no trace of them. When they arrived at the Long property, some of the men were sent to the top of a nearby hill to scour the horizon for signs of the Indians. They were rewarded with the sight of a thick column of smoke billowing from the tree canopy some miles away. Presuming this to indicate the whereabouts of the raiders, Captain Crawford led the vengeful white men through the forest.

Their scouts would have told them that it was indeed the war party. There were about fifty of them, and the scouts could see Miss Long among them. Of her brother, though, there was no sign. Crawford split his men into two divisions and surrounded the camp. Williamson made no mention of the Indians posting lookouts but it has to be presumed that they did and that these were overcome by the creeping militia. They waited until nightfall before launching their attack, for which the young captain gave the signal by firing his gun. The night was then filled with a cacophony of gunfire as the hundred men fired their pieces at once, the dark illuminated by muzzle flashes sparking from behind trees and bushes, the air alive with the singing of lead bullets and the soft thud of impact as they found their mark. The Indians, roused from sleep, would have tried to resist but were apparently no match for the deadly bayonet charge that followed the initial volley of gunfire, as the attackers surged from their hiding-places to slice and hack their way through the campsite. It was all over in minutes. Every Indian lay dead and no white casualties were reported.

'Great as our joy, and flushed with success as we were at this sudden victory, no heart among us but was ready to burst at the sight of the unhappy young lady,' said Williamson. 'What must the thoughts, torments and sensations of our brave captain then be, if even we, who knew her not, were so sensibly affected.'

According to Williamson, Miss Long was quite a beauty, 'which rendered her the envy of her own sex and the delight of ours'. She was naked, he said:

> encircling with her alabaster arms and hands, a cold rough tree, whereto she was bound, with cords so straitly pulled, that the blood trickled from her finger ends! Her lovely tender body, and delicate limbs, cut, bruised and torn with stones, and boughs of trees, as she had been dragged along, and all besmeared with blood!

The girl collapsed when her bonds were cut, and one of the men ran off to search for her clothes, which were found among the dead Indians. Her fiancé 'for a long time could do nothing but gaze upon and clasp her to his bosom, crying, raving, and tearing his hair like one bereft of his senses'. When her clothes were brought, Williamson reports, Captain Crawford gently wrapped them around her and held her close until she came to and, 'eagerly fixing her eyes on her dear deliverer', rewarded him with a smile.

The men, meanwhile, turned their attention to the bodies of the dead Indians – and were about to prove they were as savage as the tribes they hated. The fifty braves were scalped and their bodies hacked into pieces. With one hundred hate-filled white men all intent on avenging some past outrage, disputes arose over who was to have the honour of mutilating the enemy, 'there not being enough for every man to have one wherewith to satiate himself'. Captain Crawford, still cradling his fiancée, heard the arguments and ordered that lots should be cast for 'this bloody, though agreeable piece of work'. The lots were cast, and the winners, 'with the utmost cheerfulness and activity, pursued their revenge, in scalping, and otherwise treating their dead bodies as the most inveterate hatred and detestation could suggest'. The losers, meanwhile, looked on 'with half-pleased countenances': although they enjoyed the sight of the Indians being hacked to pieces, they would have mourned the loss of the bounty on the scalps.

Having slaked their bloodlust, Williamson said, the rescue party built a makeshift sedan chair for the much weakened Miss Long and, taking it in turns, four men at a time, to carry her, began the trek back to Captain Crawford's home. As they travelled, she gave them a blood-curdling account of what had happened after the raid.

She and her brother were dragged about four or five miles after the burning of the land before they stopped and the braves ripped off her clothes and 'treated her in a shocking manner'. Her brother was suffering a similar fate, his naked body being whipped rather than sexually abused. After this, they were dragged further into the forest until they reached the campsite that was to become the Indians' grave. According to Williamson's account, it was here that they decided to stop to torture the unfortunate twenty-two-year-old Mr Long. Had they pushed on with their captives, the rescue party would likely never have caught up with them, and Miss Long might have become one of the many white women who were subsumed into tribal life.

Williamson said the raiding party:

> butchered her beloved brother in the following execrable and cruel manner: they first scalped him alive, and after mocking his agonising groans and torments, for some hours, ripped open his belly, into which they put splinters and chips of pine trees, and set fire thereto; the same (on account of the turpentine wherewith these trees abound) burnt with great quickness and fury for a little time, during which he remained in a manner alive, as she could sometimes perceive him to move his head, and groan. They then piled a great quantity of wood all around his body, and consumed it to ashes.

According to *French and Indian Cruelty,* the young man's sister would have suffered a similar fate the following day had her beloved Captain Crawford and his band of merry men not arrived when they did. This, however, seems unlikely. Female captives were much prized by Indian tribes as breeding stock and any raiding party would plan to carry her home with them. Also, why the Indians remained so close to their recent attack site is a puzzle. If the Long plantation was only thirty miles from Boston, as Williamson claimed, a force such as Captain Crawford's would arrive very quickly — and the Indians knew it. They were more likely to raid and run, taking what little they could carry in the way of booty and captives. Williamson's account of the Long raid, at worst, may well be a piece of fiction inserted to juice up his narrative; at best it could be an amalgam of other raids, again inserted to give his readers another atrocity to savour.

Nevertheless, he went on to claim that Captain Crawford and Miss Long were soon married and the entire company invited to the wedding, although 'no riotous or noisy mirth was allowed, the young lady we may well imagine being still under great affliction, and in a weak state of health'.

What is important about Williamson's story is what it tells us about the attitude of white settlers to the Indians at this point, one which often extended even to friendly natives. As the raids on the frontier gathered pace, so did hatred for the Native American peoples, regardless of their loyalties. The attitude was, in the words of the later American general Philip Sherman, that 'the only good Indian is a dead Indian', and even the friendly tribes were viewed with mixed feelings. On the one hand, the colonists knew they could not hope to win this war without them; on the other, they did not trust them. Historically, the white settlers had done much to foster the Indians' mistrust. They had lied, cheated and stolen. They had killed, maimed and slaughtered. Much of what the tribes were now doing was in response to generations of ill-treatment. Williamson's account shows how the white settlers could gleefully commit atrocities, citing the atrocities committed on them as justification. But, as the cliché goes, two wrongs do not make a right, and while the torture and violence perpetrated by the Indians cannot be condoned, neither can the previous and subsequent treatment of Native Americans by white settlers.

However, whether this particular expedition to punish the Indians happened or not, Williamson said that by the end of May he was back in Boston, where he now had orders to march with his regiment. They were heading west, to the very frontier with the French territories of Canada. They were marching off to war, to a place called Oswego.

But while they marched, another British force was to meet death in the thick forests of Pennsylvania.

EIGHT

They Behaved Like Men and Died Like Soldiers

Major General Edward Braddock sailed from Cork on 14 January 1755 to take command of His Majesty's forces in North America. He brought with him two regiments of foot, the 44th and 48th, although their muster-rolls would have to be supplemented by colonials. The crossing took just over a month and on 20 February, the new commander landed at Alexandria in Virginia. At a meeting with the governors of Virginia, Pennsylvania, Massachusetts Bay, New York and Maryland two months later, Braddock decided on four expeditions against the French and their allies. One was Governor William Shirley's march to the British fort and trading post at Oswego on Lake Ontario, prior to launching an attack on both Niagara, to the west, and Frontenac, a French fort fifty miles north. Another was the assault on Fort St Frédéric at Crown Point, New York, to be led by Irish trader and Indian expert William Johnson, who had been given the rank of Major-General. A third, under the command of Brigadier General Robert Monckton, was a raid on French forces entrenched on the isthmus that connected British-held Nova Scotia with Canada before launching an attack on French-held Cape Breton Island. The fourth was a second attempt to take Fort Duquesne, to be led by Braddock himself.

Braddock was a difficult man. He had little time for the colonial leaders or their fighting men and no time at all for Britain's few Indian allies. Although he ostensibly recognised the need for their help in the coming fight, he insulted one group of Mingo warriors who had agreed to fight with him by banishing their wives and families from the camp. An attempt to recruit the Lenape failed when he told Shingas, their war chief, in no uncertain terms that only the British would be allowed to live on the lands taken from the French. Shingas had already shown his willingness to support the British by smuggling out a detailed plan of Fort Duquesne. Incensed that they expected his warriors to fight and die for them but not share the spoils, he took his Lenape band over to the French. The Shawnee and Mingo chiefs followed suit. That left the British with only eight native warriors in their camp, including Scarouady, an Oneida chief who had succeeded Tanacharison as the representative of the League of the Hodenosaunee after the latter died in mysterious circumstances the previous October.

Benjamin Franklin met with Braddock at Frederick, Maryland, and cautioned him against alienating the Indian forces, as well as reiterating the dangers of Indian attack. Braddock dismissed the words of warning, saying, 'These savages may indeed be a formidable enemy to your raw American Militia; but upon the King's regular and disciplined troops, sir, it is impossible they should make any impression.'

Certainly, there was a lack in the colonial and Indian fighters of the rigid discipline that kept the British regular soldier in line and ready to face the enemy. The Indians were interested in glory and plunder, be it property, scalps or captives. After an engagement, they were prone to taking their spoils and returning home to their villages. The colonial forces in particular bucked against the often brutal regimen of the regular army, with its reliance on flogging and hanging even for minor offences. They also generally signed on for perhaps a single campaign and expected to be allowed to return to their homes when it was over. However, Braddock was wrong to dismiss their effectiveness. Both were seasoned in the particular kind of warfare that the North American continent bred: the natives through centuries of tribal struggles and the white settlers through decades of wresting the land from those same tribes. Many white settlers dressed in deerskins just like their Indian foes or friends and, more importantly, had become just as adept as the Indians in the ways of the backwoods.

The colonial fighters were also deadly shots with their long rifles, which became known as the Kentucky rifle, even though it owed its birth to German gunsmiths in Pennsylvania. They took the barrels of imported firearms and lengthened them to as much as four feet to aid accuracy, as well as reducing the bore so that a smaller amount of precious lead and powder was needed. These single-shot weapons were devastating in the hands of an experienced marksman, and years of hunting game and Indians ensured there was no shortage of such men. Loading and firing might seem a long, laborious process, but the backwoods people had it down to a fine art. Powder was poured down the muzzle from the cow horn that hung from the rifleman's shoulder. A greased patch of cloth was placed over the muzzle and the lead ball placed in the centre. Both were pushed carefully down the long barrel with a ramrod made of hard hickory. The firing pin – holding a flint – was then cocked and some priming powder poured from a second, smaller cow horn, onto what was known as the pan. The pan was then covered again and the weapon was ready to fire. The firing pin snapped forward when the trigger was pulled, and the flint struck a steel battery, simultaneously pushing it back to reopen the pan and creating a spark to ignite the priming powder, which in turn touched off the gunpowder. It has been said that a skilled shooter, whether white or

Indian, could bring a deer – or a man – down at 200 yards. Their skills and their uniquely designed weaponry were ideally suited to the kind of warfare that lay ahead, while the British infantry's notoriously inaccurate Brown Bess musket was designed for the traditional line-and-volley European style of fighting.

Braddock, however, was resolutely unimpressed by these claims. Williamson stated:

> He was a man (as it is now too well known and believed) by no means of quick apprehension, and could not conceive that such a people could instruct him . . . and, of course, no care was taken to instruct the men, to resist their [the Indians'] particular manner of fighting.

It was that attitude that would lead to the regular British Army's first devastating defeat in North America – and Braddock's own death. They were about to encounter a new form of warfare, one in which stealth and surprise was of more importance than discipline and strength of numbers.

With the aid of Benjamin Franklin, the army gathered the 150 wagons, 600 horses to pull them, and 150 saddle horses it needed for the expedition through the forests and over the hills to the Ohio country. In June 1755, the regimental bands struck up a triumphant tune as the column snaked out of Fort Cumberland and began to trudge north-west. The sound of the drums and flutes was punctuated by the tramp of the men, the clip of the horses' hooves, the clink of metal and the rumble of the wagon wheels. The dust the column kicked up rose like a cloud in the hot summer sun, clogging nostrils and clinging to the thick red material of the uniforms. At the rear came the wives and camp-followers. The line stretched for three miles and employed three hundred axemen at its head to hew a way through the dense woods.

'After taking Fort Duquesne,' Braddock had told Benjamin Franklin, 'I am to proceed to Niagara and having taken that, to Frontenac, if the season will allow time; and I suppose it will, for Duquesne can hardly detain me above three or four days.'

One of the general's aides-de-camp was the young Virginia militia officer George Washington, whose experience during the earlier campaign Braddock felt was important. It was Washington who suggested that Braddock take 1,500 men forward, leaving the wagons and heavy artillery to follow behind. On 9 July 1755, this smaller, more lightweight detail had reached the banks of the Monongahela River near its junction with Turtle Creek. They were only eight miles from their destination.

Such a large body of men was bound to attract attention, and the French commander at Duquesne was forewarned of their arrival. A combined squad of French regulars, Canadian militia and over 600 Indians were sent to engage the British. This would be no set-piece battle such as the British commander was used to; this was to be war American-style. However, Scarouady and his advance guard spotted the French force and the alarm was raised. The British troops at the head of the column quickly fell into disciplined ranks and fired off a handful of volleys, killing the French commander almost immediately. The French and Canadian troops, their ambush plan ravaged by the musket fire, were thrown into disarray. Only the Indian warriors, who had been cajoled into joining the expedition by the French in the first place, kept their heads. This was their country and their style of battle. They quickly spread through the forest and found vantage points – behind trees and logs and rocks – from which to lay down a murderous barrage of musket fire. The French and Canadians rallied and followed suit. The British soldiers, gathered together in their tightly held lines, made easy targets. But still they fought. As men around them fell, bursts of scarlet erupting from the red uniforms, the soldiers relied on discipline and long-practised routine to get them through the day. They followed the same methodical process as the backwoods gunmen – powder, ball, ram, aim, fire. Some of them prayed as they did so: powder, ball, ram, aim, fire – please God, don't let me be hit – powder, ball, ram, aim, fire – please God, don't let me be next – powder, ball, ram, aim, fire – please God, let me live through this day.

But many of them did not live through that day. The British line was a powerful weapon in open warfare, but here in the forests, it failed to make a dent in the enemy forces. The soldiers could not see what they were fighting and were firing blind through the smoke that rose from the muskets. The most they could do was pinpoint the location of a muzzle flash and fire at it, but often the marksman had already moved on and was little more than a shadow among the trees, flitting from trunk to trunk, stopping only to fire and claim another target. After a few minutes of carnage, the British broke and ran. Braddock, leading the second detachment, met the retreating troops as they streamed back down an incline. Sensing panic in the air, he tried to rally his red-coated men into the traditional columns, but the hidden muskets continued to pour out death from the trees around them, and they toppled in the summer sunshine. Braddock and his officers, galloping around on their horses with their swords drawn, screamed orders at their men in an attempt to restore discipline, but the die had been cast. The men, conditioned by incessant drilling, tried to follow those orders, but enemy muskets continued to pick them off. Singing bullets plucked officers from their saddles, while their horses shrieked as musket balls ploughed into their flesh. Everywhere there were the screams of wounded men and the groans of the dying. And above it all was the rattle of the rifles from the woods and the piercing yells of the unseen Indians.

The provincial forces, however, did not wait on the road to be cut down, but took to the woods themselves and, using the backwoods experience and lore of which Braddock was so dismissive, attempted to mount some sort of a defence. The general, though, called them out and ordered them to fight like British soldiers, in formation, and they too were cut down like the regulars around them. Some of the Virginians managed to fight their way to the top of the slope where they could get a better idea of the positions of the Indian forces. They fired down on the enemy but were themselves cut to pieces when the British soldiers below thought they were a new detachment of French and laid into them with their muskets. Over fifty of the American colonials were killed in this incidence of friendly fire. 'They behaved like men,' wrote George Washington to Governor Robert Dinwiddie, 'and died like soldiers.'

George Washington later admitted he barely got out of the battle alive. 'I luckily escaped without a wound,' he wrote, 'though I had four bullets through my coat and two horses shot under me.' Major General Braddock was not so fortunate. He had five horses killed beneath him and was himself seriously wounded in the arm and lungs. Once word that their General had been hit leaked out, it was all over for the British troops. They turned and fled, pursued by scalp-hungry Indians.

Over nine hundred British and American soldiers were killed or taken prisoner in what became known as the Battle of the Wilderness. Of Braddock's eighty-six officers, sixty-three were left on that blood-spattered road. The French suffered a mere sixty casualties. Braddock himself survived for another four days and died saying, 'We shall know better how to deal with them another time.' His cloak became his shroud and he was buried under the road on the night of 13 July. George Washington conducted the simple funeral in guttering torchlight then ordered that the retreating forces march over the grave to ensure that no Indian or Frenchman could find the corpse and defile it.

Braddock, hidebound by concepts of military tradition and discipline, had fought bravely, but in the end, his arrogance was his downfall. The bodies of the men he had led to their deaths lay where they had fallen, just a few miles from their destination. They were scalped and plundered and left as a feast for wild animals. In time, the elements bleached their bones and they became part of the land for which they had fought and died.

News of Major General Braddock's defeat on the Monongahela naturally sent shock waves throughout the Colonies. The hasty retreat of the survivors through the back-country all the way to Philadelphia did not fill the colonists with confidence. 'This whole transaction gave us Americans the first suspicion that our exalted ideas of the prowess of British Regulars had not been well founded,' noted Benjamin Franklin wryly.

The rout also emboldened the Indian warriors, who stepped up their frontier attacks, thereby increasing the flow of refugee settlers from farms and plantations.

Braddock's death left Governor William Shirley as overall commander of the British forces. Shirley, though, was grieving for his son, who had been with Braddock's forces and died with a French musket ball in his head. This was a period of war, however, and there was little time for mourning. 'You will doubtless resolve upon some measures to retrieve the blow that has been given to us,' wrote Pennsylvania's governor Robert Morris to the newly appointed commander, 'which I am in hopes the season will yet allow you time to do.'

Shirley still favoured an attack on the French at Niagara. However, his proposed offensive had hit a snag: among the papers seized at Wilderness were the British plans for the campaign. But Shirley's regiment, Peter Williamson included, was already on its way to Lake Ontario before Braddock met his end in the Pennsylvanian backwoods. Williamson said they marched from Boston by way of the New England townships of Cambridge, Northampton and Hadfield, arriving at Albany, in New York, on 21 July. News would almost certainly have reached them of the Wilderness disaster during the journey to Oswego – and left them in despair about the future. As Williamson later wrote, 'General Braddock's defeat greatly increased the gloom which sat on the countenances of the Americans.'

Nevertheless, they embarked on the 300-mile journey to Oswego, reaching Schenectady, on the mouth of the Mohawk River. A 1,700-strong herd of cattle had earlier left Albany to make an overland journey to the trading post, slowly moving up the Mohawk Valley and along the banks of the Oneida Lake. However, the men those cows were destined to feed lingered for a time in Schenectady to await the arrival of bateaux, small, flat-bottomed boats, which would carry them and their supplies closer to the lakeside fort. Williamson stated that each bateau was capable of carrying six barrels of pork, or equivalent, plus two men, who used 'strong scutting poles, with iron at the ends, to prevent their being too soon destroyed by the stones in the river'. The Mohawk River, he said, was at places so shallow that the men had to climb out and wade upstream, dragging their bateaux behind them. Waterfalls and cataracts also forced them to drag the boats from the water to be carried beyond them. This meant that the army made slow progress towards their immediate destination, which was the Great Carrying Place, where the present-day city of Rome, New York, stands. Here the boats had again to be unloaded and dragged on sledges across country for two or three miles, until they came to Wood Creek, a narrow waterway that cut through the dense forests to Lake Oneida, the Oswego River and on to Oswego itself. There was as much chopping as there was rowing on the creek, for fallen boughs clogged the way ahead and the forest crowded in on its banks like an army preparing to attack. The trees reached up and over the water, blocking out the sunlight and lending the creek a sinister, oppressive atmosphere. The men alternately poling, rowing and hacking their way through this perpetually overcast world could easily have imagined a malevolent Indian behind every trunk and lurking in every shadow. It was with relief that they pushed out of the dark waterway and into the brilliant sunshine of Lake Oneida. Twenty days after leaving Schenectady, Williamson and his comrades saw Fort Oswego for the first time.

Along with Albany, Oswego had long been a major trading centre for the British. In May of each year, the Indians would bring the all-important furs and pelts to this point on Lake Ontario and trade them for trinkets, liquor and guns. In July, the opposite route took the fur goods back to the Mohawk and Hudson Rivers via the Great Carrying Place and then on to ports on the Atlantic. The British built their first fort here in 1727, but in 1754 the old fort was slightly strengthened and construction on a second one began. It was these rough fortifications that the advance party under the direct command of Lieutenant Colonel John Bradstreet, who arrived on 27 May, proceeded to reinforce as hostilities heightened. Oswego was of vital strategic importance, especially in the wake of Braddock's ignominious defeat further south. It was the only British presence on Lake Ontario and, as such, the only point from which they could aim a dagger directly at the heart of French Canada. The French were painfully aware of this military toehold and knew the threat it posed to their strongholds at Niagara and Frontenac.

On his arrival, Williamson spoke to some of the men who had been based in Oswego since the previous year and learned of the 'phoney war' that they had experienced. There had only been one hundred soldiers manning the fort, he said, 'and how it was Fort Oswego was not taken in the spring of 1755 . . . my penetration will not enable me to discuss'. But the French did not attack the undermanned fort at this time, although the soldiers were aware of a military build-up on the lake.

Williamson wrote:

> In May 1755 . . . thirty French batteaux were seen to pass, and two days later, eleven more; each batteau (being much larger

than ours) containing fifteen men; so this fleet consisted of near 600 men. A force, which with a single mortar, might soon have taken possession of the place.

With the British plan to launch an offensive on Niagara and Frontenac finally agreed, it was decided not only to strengthen the fort but also to establish a military presence on the actual waters of the lake. According to Williamson, shipwrights arrived in June from Boston (before he reached the fort) and proceeded to build a forty-foot schooner with space for fourteen oars and twelve swivel guns. By September, he said, four other vessels were ready. However, still no attack was launched from the French side, nor did the new vessels see any action.

Despite the herd of cattle and the food carried on the bateaux, Williamson related that provisions grew very scarce in the weeks following their arrival:

> The provincial stores were soon exhausted, and we were in danger of being soon famished, being on less than half allowance. The men being likewise fatigued with the long march they had suffered, and being without rum (or allowed none at least) and other proper nutriment, many fell sick of the flux [dysentery] and died; so that our regiment was greatly reduced in six weeks time.

He also said that unwary soldiers who were caught outside the fort or away from sentries often fell prey to ambush by Indians and were in danger of being scalped or murdered:

> To prevent consequences like these, a Captain's guard of sixty men, with two lieutenants, two sergeants, two corporals and one drum, beside two flanking guards of a sergeant, corporal,

and twelve men in each, were daily mounted, and did duty as
well as able. Scouting parties were likewise sent out every day;
but the sickness still continuing, and having 300 men at work,
we were obliged to lessen our guards, till Colonel Pepperell's
regiment joined us.

Here there seems to be some chronological confusion in Williamson's
narrative. He appears to have been with the main force heading to
Oswego, commanded personally by Shirley. Bradstreet had arrived at
the end of May, Shirley not until August. Pepperell's Jersey Blues,
under the command of Colonel Philip Schuyler, reached Oswego in
July, so they were already there when Williamson arrived. It would
seem clear that in this section of his narrative, he is either guilty of not
letting the facts get in the way of a good story, or of taking what he had
been told by the soldiers already stationed at the fort and grafting it
onto his own experiences.

The year was waning. It was by now autumn, and both sides knew
that the winter months were not the time to be launching any sort of
offensive. According to Williamson, plans had been made to attack
Niagara and Frontenac before the storms and snows arrived. The plans
were abandoned at the eleventh hour, but not before a small fleet of
nine bateaux had been dispatched with soldiers aboard. One of these
men, he claimed, was Williamson himself.

> The men being weak, and in low spirits, with continual
> harassing and low feeding, rendered our progress very slow
> and difficult; add to this the places we had to pass and ascend;
> for, in many parts, the cataracts, or falls of water, which
> descended near the head of the river Onondaga (in some
> places near one hundred feet, perpendicular), rendered it
> almost impossible for us to proceed; for the current running
> from the bottom, was so rapid, that the efforts of twenty men

were sometimes required to drag the boats along, and especially to get them up hills or cataracts, which we were forced to do with ropes; sometimes a quarter of a mile, before we came to any water.

The four men manning one of the bateaux found themselves in difficulty. The other eight had been hauled over a set of waterfalls, but the flagging troopers operating the rear boat were too weary to drag it out of the water. Williamson said he and two men were sent back to help them haul it out. It was while he was sitting in the boat, fastening ropes, as the other six men were pulling it up the land to avoid the waterfall, that he claims to have found his life in peril. The ropes snapped and the boat slid backwards into 'a very rapid and boisterous stream' – and Peter with it.

Williamson tried desperately but unsuccessfully to steer the boat away from the rocks, but the flimsy, flat-bottomed vessel crashed into the unforgiving boulders and smashed to pieces, pitching him headlong into the violent waters. For the second time in his life, he was completely at the mercy of the elements – he had faced death on the *Planter* as it broke apart on the sandbank, now he was caught in a swirling maelstrom, his body battered from side to side against the rocks.

'Never was my life in greater danger than in this situation,' he wrote, looking back. He was swept downstream before being tossed, beaten and half-drowned, onto the bank. He lay there all night, most of his clothes having been wrenched off by the force of the water, until the search party found him. He was 'in a wretched condition, quite benumbed and almost dead with the cold'.

A fire was built but, said Williamson, it only made matters worse: 'My flesh swelled all over my body and limbs, and caused such a deprivation of my sense, that I fainted, and was thought by all to be dead.' However, he soon recovered, and the weary troops decided to return to Oswego, where they learned that the planned attack had been abandoned. Governor Shirley had decided against any further attempts on Niagara until at least the following spring. Despite attempts by the navy on the eastern seaboard to prevent supplies and reinforcements from entering the St Lawrence River, and thus reaching Frontenac and Niagara, French ships had got through. The small fleet of new vessels based in Oswego had also been unsuccessful in making a dent on the supply fleets. At the end of September 1755, Shirley led the bulk of his forces from Oswego back to Albany, leaving some 700 men to defend the forts. Williamson, following his near-drowning, along with several others who were sick with dysentery, went with him. They left behind, according to Williamson, a garrison of men 'still living in perpetual terror, on the brink of famine, and become mutinous for want of their pay; which, in the hurry of military business, during a year that was crowned with great events, had been forgotten; for, from my first enlisting to the time I was laid up at Albany, I never had received above six weeks pay'. (A soldier received around eight pence a day in pay, but much of that was deducted to pay for his subsistence and uniform.)

The Niagara campaign had been more of a whimper than a bang. The British had more success in their attack on the French military interlopers in Nova Scotia. In June, the French had surrendered besieged Fort Beausejour (later renamed Fort Cumberland) on the Bay of Fundy to Colonel Robert Monckton and Colonel John Winslow. Monckton went on to capture Fort Gaspereau on Bay Verte in Acadia.

For years, the French-speaking and Roman Catholic Acadians had been tolerated under British rule of Nova Scotia. Now the British decreed that any French-speaking residents who refused to swear full allegiance to King George would be forcibly deported and scattered throughout the Colonies. The British ruthlessly moved to deport the masses of French settlers, mostly farmers and fishermen, from the province. Some escaped and joined the Indians to help harass the

British Army. In return, the British burned homes and villages, and rounded up even more Acadians for transportation. They were not welcome in the British colonies, and thousands eventually made their way south to the French colony of Louisiana. They settled in the city first founded in 1718, La Nouvelle Orleans, and also in the Atchafalaya Swamp lands. The name Acadian was contracted to Cajun, and the colonists contributed greatly to the new culture of that southern land. Back in Nova Scotia, New Englanders appropriated the lands that had been their homes.

The fourth prong of the British war strategy, the attack on Fort St Frédéric at Crown Point on Lake Champlain's western shore, was, like the Duquesne and Niagara campaigns, a failure, although the British forces did gain some ground and give the French a bloody nose. This campaign, under the generalship of Sir William Johnson, a strong friend of the Iroquois, started off promisingly with a victory over the French commanded by Baron Ludwig August de Dieskau. He had decided to attack the newly built Fort Edward on Lake George. Johnson sent 1,000 men, including a force of Mohawks led by the ageing sachem Thoyanoguen, known to the English as Chief Hendrick and related by marriage to Sir William. The warrior chief was not convinced a fight was the wisest course for his people. 'If they are to fight, they are too few,' he said. 'If they are to be killed, they are too many.' But fight they did. And die they did.

In September, the French and their Indian allies encountered the British militia and their Indian allies at Rocky Brook on Lake George. Both the British commander, Colonel Ephraim Williams, and Thoyanoguen were killed early in the battle. The British forces retreated to Fort William Henry, which was as yet unfinished, pursued by the French. There Johnson was waiting with his artillery and many of the attackers were cut to pieces. Bitter hand-to-hand fighting followed during which the French were routed and fled back the way they had come. They met with a second British force coming from Fort

Edward and, in gathering darkness, fell under heavy musket fire and stabbing bayonets. Around 400 French and their Indian allies died on that bloody afternoon and evening, while the British lost 262 and 38 Indians. Baron de Dieskau was wounded and taken hostage at Fort William Henry.

Johnson, who had also been wounded during the battle, was urged by General Shirley and colonial politicians to press forward with the plans to take Fort St Frédéric, but he first hesitated, then resigned his generalship. Perhaps his wounds had debilitated him. Perhaps he mourned the death of his friend Thoyanoguen and his Mohawk brothers. Perhaps his duties as superintendent of Indian Affairs called him elsewhere. Or perhaps, as has been suggested, he was influenced by New York businessmen who were illegally trading with the French in Montreal.

Whatever the reason, the attack on Crown Point did not materialise. Williamson lays the blame squarely on colonial politicians:

> The undertaking of the eastern provinces, to reduce the fort at Crown Point, met that fate which the jarring councils of a divided people commonly meet with; for though the plan was concerted in the winter of 1754, it was August before these petty governments could bring together their troops. In short, it must be owned by all that delays were the banes of our undertakings, except in the Bay of Fundy in Nova Scotia, where secrecy and expeditions were rewarded with success, and that province reduced.

And so, with the coming of the winter snows, the war in North America, as yet undeclared, ground to a halt. The British commanders, hamstrung by incompetence, political in-fighting and commercial interests, were pulling back, their plans in tatters. In Williamson's home colony of Pennsylvania, the Quakers continued to refuse to be involved in any form of armed resistance, while the proprietors finagled their way out of footing any bill.

And Peter Williamson was in Albany, recovering from the injuries he received during his descent down the rapids. He left New York and returned to Pennsylvania where, he claimed, he was involved in further adventures against the Indians. By the time he returned to Oswego the following year, the French would have a new commander in chief. His name was Louis-Joseph, Marquis de Montcalm Gezan de Saint Véran — and he would lead his forces to further glory at the expense of Britain.

NINE

You Can't Live in the Woods and Remain Neutral

Peter Williamson arrived in New York by way of the Hudson River; there he discovered that William Shirley's son John had died in the Wilderness battle. 'He was a very promising, worthy, young gentleman, and universally regretted.' The dead man had been a captain in his regiment, Williamson said, and his command had fallen to Major James Kinnair, who ordered that the colonial men in the militia be allowed to visit their families, or remain in the garrison at New York. Williamson, although impressed with the city, had no desire to stay there and so applied for a furlough, which was granted.

On arriving at Philadelphia, he found that the terror of Indian attacks had grown considerably since Braddock's defeat. Most of the troops who had survived the battle had been redeployed to the northern campaigns, leaving only a handful of soldiers and volunteers behind. The colonists feared the new road cut by Braddock's axemen could be used by the enemy to bring even greater numbers of raids down on their heads. They deplored the delays by their political and

Quaker rulers in creating any form of organised defence. Meanwhile, many tribes who had professed friendship with the English had fled to the French side since the Battle of the Wilderness, believing it to be the stronger. According to Williamson, they 'committed great ravages on the back parts of the province, destroying and massacring men, women and children, and everything that unhappily lay in their way'.

He wrote in *French and Indian Cruelty* that in the middle of October:

> A large body of Indians, chiefly Shawonoese [Shawnee], Delawares &c fell upon this province from several quarters, almost at the same instant, murdering, burning, and laying waste all wherever they came, so that in the five counties of Cumberland, York, Lancaster, Berks and Northampton, which compose more than half the province, nothing but scenes of destruction and desolation were to be seen . . . Men, women, children, and brute beasts shared one common destruction: and where they were not burnt to ashes, their mangled limbs were found promiscuously thrown on the ground; those appertaining to the human form scarce distinguished from the brute!

Many of these attacks may have been exaggerated, or even fabricated (and not necessarily by Williamson), in order to demonise the enemy. However, these were hard and brutal times, and vicious bloodletting was not unknown. Despite his oft-repeated sympathy for the Indians who had been cheated and abused by the white man, Williamson was prone in his writing to detail stories of Indian atrocities while glossing over, or failing to mention, those meted out by whites.

On his return to Pennsylvania, he heard of a number of attacks, but, he later wrote:

> Of all the instances of the barbarities I heard of in these parts, I could not help being most affected with the following.

One family, consisting of the husband, his wife and a child only a few hours old, were all found murdered and scalped in this manner: the mother stretched on the bed, with her new-born child horribly mangled and put under her head for a pillow, while the husband lay on the ground hard by, with his belly ript up, and his bowels laid open.

In another place, a woman, with her sucking child, finding that she had fallen into the hands of the enemy, fell flat on her face, prompted by the strong call of nature to cover and shelter her innocent child with her own body. The accursed savage rushed from his lurking place, struck her on the head with his tomahawk, tore off her scalp, and scoured back into the woods, without observing the child, being apprehensive that he was discovered. The child was found some time afterwards under the body of its mother and was then alive.

He noted that the Indians carried many women off into captivity, which was true: women were seen as valuable for breeding purposes. Williamson, again despite his professed respect for the Native Americans, reflects the attitude of the times by observing that the women were 'reserved perhaps for a worse fate than those who suffered death in all its horrid shapes; and no wonder, since they were reserved by savages, whose tender mercies might be counted more cruel than their very cruelty itself'. It has to be pointed out, though, that many of the female and child captives who had been adopted into tribal life were unwilling to give it up.

But, despite all this, the colonial government in Pennsylvania refused to mount a defence. Williamson recalled:

Bound by non-resisting principles from exerting her strength, and involved in disputes with the proprietors, they stood still, vainly hoping the French would be so moderate as to be content with their victory of Braddock, or at least confine their attacks to Virginia.

Not all Indians defected to the French side. The Oneida chief Scarouady remained faithful to British interests and often spoke on their behalf at Iroquois congresses. Knowing that the League of the Hodenosaunee wished to remain non-partisan during the war, Scarouady had plainly told its elders that, 'You can't live in the woods and remain neutral.' He believed the alliance with Britain was the only way for his people to survive. He thought the British would support the sovereignty claims of the Hodenosaunee over the western lands. He was wrong, but he continually showed the courage of his convictions. He had been one of the eight Native Americans who had remained with Braddock's force, and he had seen his son die on that ill-fated expedition when, during a scouting expedition, a nervous British sentry mistook the young Indian for a hostile and gunned him down. The Oneida warrior had little time for Braddock, saying he 'was a bad man when he was alive; he looked upon us as dogs, and would never hear anything what was said to him. We often endeavoured to advise him of the danger he was in with his soldiers; but he never appeared pleased with us.'

Despite this, Scarouady's support never wavered, and in November 1755, he arrived in Philadelphia with two other Indian chiefs and their interpreter, Colonel Conrad Weiser, to plead with the Assembly to show the same kind of support. Williamson was in Philadelphia at the time and in *French and Indian Cruelty*, he reproduced word for word what he claims is a printed copy of the old warrior's speech.

The Indian chief stood before the bewigged and smartly clothed gentlemen of the Assembly and spoke, as he always did, from his heart:

> Brethren, we are once more come among you, and sincerely condole with you on account of the late bloodshed, and the awful cloud that hangs over you and over us.

Brethren, you may be undoubtedly assured that these horrid actions were committed by none of those nations that have any fellowship with us, but by certain false-hearted and treacherous brethren. It grieves us more than all our other misfortunes, that any of our good friends, the English, should suspect us of having false hearts.

Brethren, if you were not an infatuated people, we are 300 warriors firm to your interest; and if you are so unjust to us as to retain any doubts of our sincerity, we offer to put our wives, our children, and all we have into your hands, to deal with them as seemeth good to you, if we are found in the least to swerve from you. But brethren, you must support and assist us, for we are not able to fight alone against the powerful nations who are coming against you; and you must this moment resolve, and give us an explicit answer what you will do. For these nations have sent to desire us, as old friends, either to join them, or get out of the way, and shift for ourselves. Alas! Brethren, we are sorry to leave you! We remember the many tokens of your friendship to us. But what shall we do? We cannot stand alone, and you will not stand with us!

Brethren, the time is precious. While we are here consulting with you, we know not what may be the fate of our brethren at home. We do, therefore, once more invite and request you to act like men, and be no longer as women, pursuing weak measures that render your names despicable. If you will put the hatchet into your hands and send out a number of your young men in conjunction with our warriors, and provide the necessary arms, ammunition and provisions; and likewise build some strong houses for the protection of our old men, women and children while we are absent in war, we shall wipe the tears from your eyes, and make these false-

133

hearted brethren repent their treachery and baseness towards you and towards us.

Then, tears welling in his own eyes, he delivered his final words, a careful balance between plea and threat:

> But we must at the same time solemnly assure you that if you delay any longer to act in conjunction with us, or think to put us off, as usual, with uncertain hopes, you must not expect to see our faces under this roof any more. We must shift for our own safety, and leave you to the mercy of our enemies, as an infatuated people, upon whom we can have no longer dependence.

However, despite these emotional words, the Assembly and the governor still could not agree on raising a militia. Both sides wanted one, although the Quakers continued to object, but the Assembly would not countenance any taxes which omitted the hereditary proprietors, while Governor Morris would not support a bill which saw his superiors putting their hands in their pockets. Benjamin Franklin gives the example of the governor's proposed amendment to a bill: 'The Bill express'd that all Estates real and personal were to be taxed, those of the Proprietaries *not* excepted. His Amendement was for *not* read *only*. A small but very material alteration.'

This was explained to the no doubt bemused Scarouady, who agreed to return to the Ohio country to see the lie of the land while the political in-fighting continued. Finally, with pressure mounting both in the colony and in London, the proprietors gave in and agreed to put up money for the raising of a militia. According to Franklin, the sum, £5,000, was accepted in lieu of their share of a general tax, and the new bill, with an agreed clause exempting them from paying anything further, was agreed.

'The Philadelphians were, at last, permitted to raise and arm themselves in their own defence,' wrote Williamson. He said the men of the province could form themselves into companies and, this being the American colonies, choose their own officers by way of ballot; these would then be commissioned by the governor who, of course, retained the right of veto. Naturally, it was not all plain sailing, for the gentlemen of the Assembly were soon complaining that the recruiting officers were trawling through the thousands of indentured servants for fighting men. They wanted their families and land to be defended, but they didn't want to do without their servants or labourers as a result.

Meanwhile, the Franco-friendly Indians continued their raids on the back-country. And in the same month that Scarouady made his emotional plea to the white man, the tribes he was warning them about launched an attack on a religious community in Northampton County. The ferocity of the attack, and the fact that the religious order concerned had generally shown friendship and kindness to the Native Americans, helped spur the Philadelphia politicians into action.

Like the Quakers, the Moravians were a pacifist Protestant sect. They originated in Germany and were attracted to Pennsylvania by its promise of religious freedom and tolerance. They had converted a number of local Indians to their faith, including members of the Lenape and Mahicans who had found themselves dispersed to this country by the encroachment of the white man and the edicts of the powerful Hodenosaunee. In 1745, the Moravian brethren purchased 120 acres of land on the northern bank of the Mahoning Creek near to the Lehigh River. Here they built a town that was to be a sanctuary to converted Indian and Moravian white man alike. They called it Gnadenhutten, which means 'mercy huts'. A church was built and a burial ground established. There was need of the latter in 1755.

By that year, the settlement had crossed the river to a site now occupied by the town of Weissport. Many of the Indian converts had deserted, intimidated by the raiding along the frontier, but those who remained lived in the new settlement at New Gnadenhutten. The old mission house and surrounding buildings on Mahoning Creek remained home to a few Moravian families. On 24 November 1755, the place would become a funeral pyre.

They came at suppertime, Williamson related, 'muffled in the shades of night, dark and horrid as the infernal purposes of their diabolical souls'. It was the barking of dogs that alerted the families. One man was sent out to see what was upsetting them and was shot. The others were surprised by the appearance of the armed Indians at their door, releasing a volley of gunfire. One man, Martin Nitschman, was cut down immediately; the others, some wounded, managed to escape to the second floor, where they barricaded the doors with heavy bedsteads. Another two men threw themselves from rear windows and made their escape into the woods. From there, all they could do was watch as the war party did their worst. The raiders, tiring of trying to batter their way through the strengthened bedroom door, resorted to setting fire to the house. A young boy climbed out onto the roof, one side of his face burned, the other grazed by a musket ball, and leaped to safety. The wife of one of the men who had earlier saved themselves took heart from the boy's escape and followed his example. Another man tried, too, but was not so lucky – as he landed, two lead balls found their mark and brought him down. Two Indian marksmen finished him by slicing off his scalp. No one else escaped, and the survivors, watching from the tree line, could do nothing but look on as their homes and loved ones went up in flames. One saw his wife at a window, her arms folded across her chest, calling out, ''Tis all well, dear Saviour – I expect nothing else.' Then the flames enveloped her and she disappeared from view in the raging fire and the smoke.

Eleven people died in the attack, and the Indians followed it up with the customary slaughter of the livestock.

The converted Indians in New Gnadenhutten across the Lehigh River heard the shots and saw the glow of the fire in the sky. At first, they wanted to launch their own attack, but the Moravian minister would not hear of it and advised them to clear the town and take refuge in the forest. News of the massacre reached first the main Moravian settlement at Bethlehem and then Philadelphia, where plans were being made to build a series of defensive forts around the frontier. Benjamin Franklin had been given command of the north-western frontier and was to supervise the building of the stockades. Coincidentally, Gnadenhutten had been identified as one suitable site.

The Pennsylvanian Volunteers were going to make their first foray against the enemy. And Peter Williamson, then already a veteran, claimed that he was among them. It would not be long before he was seeing more action.

A Captain Davis, who knew of Peter's experience with Shirley's regiment and wished him to 'instruct the irregulars in their discipline', had recruited him to the local forces as a lieutenant, Williamson claimed. However, he told Davis that he would not go unless Governor Morris issued a certificate 'indemnifying me from any punishment which might be adjudged by the regiment to which I already belonged'. Permissions were duly given and on 24 December 1755, Williamson wrote, he was on the march once more against the Indian foe, this time among a company of one hundred Pennsylvanians who were 'resolving to show as little quarter to the savages as they had to many of us'.

According to Williamson's account, it would be a black Christmas for some of those men.

It took two days' hard march to reach Bethlehem, where 'we were kindly received by the Moravians'. There they loaded six wagons with provisions and proceeded north-west to the Blue Mountains, through the Lehigh Gap to New Gnadenhutten. (In his books, Williamson for some reason calls the site of Fort Allen, which we know to have been

New Gnaddenhutten, Kennorton-head). Half of the company, including Peter, was ordered to march ahead to find out how much, if any, of the town remained standing.

They were within five miles of the town when they were ambushed.

It was the men to the rear of the column, as they marched four abreast along an uneven road, who spotted the enemy warriors first and fired off a salvo. The Indians returned fire and an ensign, the lowest-ranking commissioned officer, was killed outright along with ten other men. The Indians, having blasted their muskets, swept whooping down on the column with their lethal tomahawks in their hands and Williamson, recognising this as a full-blown attack, ordered the remainder of the Pennsylvanians to make for the town. The colonists kept up a running fire all the way, the warriors screaming as they set upon stragglers and felled them with a single blow of their tomahawks. The soldiers ran hard, trying to load their single-shot muskets as they moved and firing back at the shrieking horde on their tail. The town loomed up ahead – but on the other side of the river. They launched themselves into the freezing waters, the cold making their breath catch in their chests, and began to wade across, the Indians hard on their heels. Their clothes freezing to their flesh, the Volunteers dragged themselves out of the water and onto dry land, barely taking a breath as they sprinted across to the comparative safety of the church. The bodies of twenty-seven men littered the road and riverbank, but at least now the Volunteers had a stronghold to defend.

Williamson wrote:

> We made as good preparations for our defence as possibly we could, making a great fire of the benches and seats, and what we could find therein, to dry our clothes; not esteeming it the least sacrilege or crime, upon such an emergency.

The Indian war party took up position around the church, picking off as many of the soldiers as they could. The militia held them off, their long rifles proving just as deadly as the enemy's. But as the day burned itself away and night began to darken the sky, their ammunition ran out. Williamson and his men knew they could not keep the Indians from either firing the church around them or pushing their way in. Once they were inside, there would be desperate hand-to-hand fighting, but they knew it would be a last-ditch effort. Their numbers were dwindling, while the enemy's seemed to be increasing, and they could not hope to overcome the odds. So, when they saw the night sky turn red with the glow of the town burning around them, they decided that a dash through the night was their best hope.

'Dreading the consequences of being detained there, [we] resolved to make one bold effort, and push ourselves through the savage forces,' said Williamson.

The attacking braves fired on the Volunteers as they ran from the church, cutting many of them down, but also hitting a few of their own in the crossfire. Only five of the militia managed to escape, while the rest were left where they fell, dead or dying, to be scalped or tortured by the Indians. Williamson recalled that another two men froze to death before they reached a house in the Lehigh Gap at four the following morning. Here they found Captain Davis with the remainder of the column and the wagons.

The much-depleted company waited at the house for reinforcements to arrive, busying themselves with building a makeshift fort in case they were attacked. On 9 January 1756, Benjamin Franklin, now General Franklin, having been placed in charge of building the line of forts on the north-west frontier, arrived with the main force. They proceeded to the burned-out town and there found that wild hogs had feasted on the bodies of the dead soldiers. All that was left to bury were the bones that were strewn across the remains of the streets.

'We there built a fort in the place where the old church had stood,' claimed Williamson, 'and gave it the name Fort Allen.'

It is an exciting part of Williamson's tale, but a troubling one. To begin with, I can find no trace of a town called Kennorton-head. Fort Allen was, indeed, built – but at New Gnadenhutten. Also, I can find no record of a Captain Davis commanding a company, although there is mention of a Lieutenant Davis. A detachment of militia from the Irish settlements, under a Captain Hays, was sent to New Gnadenhutten and was, in fact, ambushed, but not in the way Williamson described. The river was frozen solid and on 1 January, a number of them had been amusing themselves skating on the ice when they spotted two Indian braves downstream. The soldiers grabbed their weapons and pursued the two warriors, only to find they had been tricked. The Indians were decoys, and they led the troops straight to the muskets of their waiting comrades. The soldiers were slaughtered and the remainder of the company, watching from the town, deserted, leaving it to be burned by the raiding party.

Perhaps Williamson, if he was there at all, decided to massage the story to make it more exciting and heroic. Perhaps he was ashamed of the militiamen being duped so easily and of their subsequent desertion, so he invented a township and improved the behaviour of the troops in battle but retained the name of the real-life fort.

Benjamin Franklin did arrive personally to supervise the building of Fort Allen at Gnadenhutten, although the first job, he wrote in his autobiography, was to 'bury the dead we found there, who had been half interr'd by the country people'. Williamson said it took six days to complete the fort, which is true, although Franklin said, 'It rained so hard every other day the men could not work.' The rain caused him worry, for should the Indians known to be rampaging through the countryside attack them at that point there was a very real danger that the soldiers' rifles would not fire, the gunlocks and powder being soaked and therefore unusable. Franklin, a historian and politician, would have known what happened to Washington's small army at Great Meadows and would not have wished such ignominy to fall on his own command. The tribesmen did not, it seems, have such problems with their weapons. 'The Indians are dextrous in contrivances for that purpose, which we had not,' Franklin wrote.

To reinforce his argument, he told a story of eleven farmers he met while at Bethlehem. They had been run off their plantations by attacking war parties and asked him, as the military representative, for weapons to allow them to return to their homes and retrieve what livestock they could. Franklin gave them guns and ammunition, and the eleven men left the town in the pouring rain. While Franklin and his men huddled together for warmth and shelter in a barn on the way to Gnaddenhutten, the eleven farmers were attacked by Indians and all but one were killed. They did not have a prayer, it seems, for the survivor reported that 'his and his companions' guns would not go off, the priming being wet with the rain'. Franklin was thankful he and his men had not suffered the same fate. 'It was as well we were not attack'd in our march, for our arms were of the most ordinary sort and our men could not keep their gunlocks dry.'

Even Franklin admitted the fort was not much to look at, writing 'such a magnificent name . . . given to so miserable a stockade'. To build it, first the considerable tree-felling skills of the settlers were used. Seventy axemen were set the task of providing the timber for the palisades (a series of wooden stakes dug into the ground). Franklin was amazed by the speed with which these men could bring down a tree and took the opportunity to time two men working on a tall pine: 'In 6 minutes they had it on the ground; and I found it of 14 inches diameter.' Each pine, he said, made three palisades of eighteen feet long, sharpened to a point at the end. The stakes were secured in a three-foot-deep trench, and an army of carpenters constructed a six-foot-high platform behind the defensive palisades on which the troops could stand and blast away at attacking forces. Swivel guns – artillery pieces mounted on revolving platforms – were placed at two of the corners and both were fired almost immediately on being wheeled into place, 'to let the Indians know, if any were within hearing, that we had such pieces', said Franklin.

'Miserable' stockade it may have been, but Williamson said Fort Allen was strong enough 'that 100 men would make great resistance against a much greater number of Indians'. Franklin himself said, 'This kind of fort, however contemptible, is a sufficient defence against Indians who have no cannon.'

Although no Indians attacked at this time, with or without cannon, the white men knew they were in the area. Franklin said that patrols found signs of their encampments in the hills, from which they had watched the work below. 'There was an art in their contrivance of those places that seems worth mention,' he said:

> It being winter, a fire was necessary for them. But a common fire on the surface of the ground would by its light have discover'd their position at a distance. They had therefore dug holes in the ground about three feet diameter, and somewhat deeper. We saw where they had with their hatchets cut off the charcoal from the sides of burnt logs lying in the woods. With these coals they had made small fires in the bottom of the holes, and we observ'd among the weeds and grass the prints of their bodies made by their laying all round with their legs hanging down in the holes to keep their feet warm, which with them is an essential point. This kind of fire, so manag'd, could not discover them either by its light, flame, sparks or even smoke.

The men were happy when working, but when the torrential rain kept them idle they became 'mutinous and quarrelsome', finding fault with everything. They also neglected their devotions, causing the regimental chaplain to complain to Franklin that 'the men did not generally attend his prayers and exhortations'. Franklin, ever the pragmatist, hit on a novel way of ensuring the men received their daily dose of religion. As part of their pay, the men were to be given a gill of rum a day, half in the morning and half at night. 'It is perhaps below the dignity of your profession to act as Steward of the rum,' he said to the Presbyterian minister, 'but if you were to deal it out, and only just after prayers, you would have them all about you.' The minister agreed to the idea and enlisted the help of some of the more devout men to help measure out the daily liquor ration. 'Never were prayers more generally and more punctually attended,' noted Franklin with some delight.

Williamson, though, mentioned none of this. He did say, however, that around 18 January, he was among a detachment of troops ordered to build another fort, Fort Norris, about fifteen miles eastward. The Indians may have felt the force at Fort Allen too strong to attack, but they had by no means given up their struggle. On the way, he said, they found six men dead and scalped. 'By what we could discern, they had made a vigorous defence, the barrels of their guns being broke to pieces and themselves cut and mangled in terrible manner.' Reports were reaching the troops daily of attacks on farms and plantations, and Williamson claims they encountered a raiding party of about fourteen braves and slaughtered them all. He also claims that after building Fort Norris, he was ordered with others to build a third stockade, to be named Fort Franklin. However, as the site of this latter fort was fifteen miles to the west of Fort Allen, this seems unlikely, as Benjamin Franklin seems to have sent separate detachments to build these defensive positions.

Finally, Williamson recalled, it was time for him to return to his own regiment. Taking his leave of the Pennsylvania militia, he returned to New York where he awaited his orders. It was now 1756 and the war was heating up, in the Old World as well as the New. On 16

January, Great Britain signed a treaty with Prussia against France and her allies, who would come to include Russia, Austria, Sweden and Saxony. Meanwhile, the British Navy harassed French vessels in the Caribbean and on the eastern seaboard of North America. Even though the French complained about this piracy, they did not make a formal declaration of war. They did, however, retaliate by attacking and ultimately capturing the Mediterranean island of Minorca, then in British hands. The British government, itching by this time for war, formally declared it on 15 May. The French followed suit in June. Finally, after two years of struggle for possession of territory in North America, the delicate peace in the homelands had also been breached. The French and Indian War had become part of an even greater struggle – the Seven Years War.

TEN

I Have Laid Oswego to Ashes

There were by this time three forts at Oswego – the original trading post known as Old Oswego or Fort Pepperell, the recently built Fort Ontario and a new fortification, Fort George, so badly constructed that it was known as 'Fort Rascal'. The old fort, Williamson said, had a 'weak stone wall, about two feet thick, so ill-cemented, that it could not resist the force of a four pound ball'. The square wooden stockade that was Fort Ontario stood across the river, on the east side, and was situated on the top of a bluff. Pitiful Fort Rascal was further up river. Williamson said that the construction of these glorified stockades made them 'defensible against musketry, and cannon of three or four pound only, the time not allowing works of a stronger nature to be then undertaken'. It was this lack of forethought that would lead to yet another British disgrace in the early part of the conflict.

In order to keep supplies flowing from British-held lands to their stronghold on Lake Ontario, other forts had been constructed. Fort Williams was established at the Great Carrying Place, present-day Rome, on the Mohawk River, while a smaller blockhouse was built on

Wood Creek. The British presence at Oswego was a danger not only to the French emplacements at Niagara and Frontenac, present-day Kingston, but perhaps also to Quebec itself. The French high command knew that if the triple forts were to fall, it would be necessary to cut off the supply lines from New York. In early 1756, when the snow still lay thick on the ground, a 362-strong force of regular French troops, Canadian trappers and over 100 Indians left Montreal and followed the icebound St Lawrence River as far as the point called La Presentation by the French and Oswegatchie by the Indians (present-day Ogdensburg). There, their faces turned southwards and inland. Between them and their destination was an ice and snow-covered landscape, interspersed with freezing and raging rivers.

The British knew of this mobilisation, for Sir William Johnson's considerable network of Indian spies had warned him of the column's progress down the St Lawrence. However, it was thought the force would wait until the thaw to launch any offensive. They did not reckon on the determination and hardy spirits of the French Canadians and their Indian allies. They marched, waded and swam for fifteen days until they reached Fort Bull on Wood Creek, managing to surprise the small garrison at the stockade. The British soldiers were barely able to close the gate against the sudden surge of uniformed Frenchmen, fur-clad Canadians and a few howling Indians.

The attacking force fired through the loopholes cut in the wooden walls, while some of their number hacked at the gate with their axes. The fort was little more than a storage space and had no defensive cannon, although it did have a plentiful supply of grenades, which were lobbed over the eighteen-foot walls. It took about an hour to cut through the gate, and, with a triumphant cry, the French were inside. The resulting massacre was short and bloody. With the exception of a handful of soldiers and one woman, the entire complement of around sixty was shot or bayoneted to death. What supplies and ammunition they could not carry, they destroyed, blowing up the small fort in the process. The French force retreated, leaving a gaping hole in the British supply lines, which were to be continually harried by their Indian allies.

With the soldiers at Oswego starving, it was decided that Lieutenant Colonel John Bradstreet would take command of an army of boatmen to push much-needed supplies through to the forts. Williamson, having been ordered to rejoin his regiment at Oswego, met up with Bradstreet's command at Albany with some other recruits. However, at the Great Carrying Place, he claimed, he was involved in a skirmish with the enemy and received a wound to his left hand 'which entirely disabled my third and fourth fingers'. His wound was 'dressed in a wretched manner' and he was sent back by boat to Albany for treatment.

Bradstreet's convoy of 350 boatmen continued through to Oswego and relieved the garrison. Williamson had his wound treated and was shortly heading back along the Mohawk from Albany, arriving in Oswego in July. In *French and Indian Cruelty,* he related that he was again with Bradstreet's supply train when, on the river, about nine miles from Oswego, a murderous volley of gunfire erupted from the thick forest around them. The boatmen and British troops tumbled dead into the water, and the main body began to pull back. The French ambushers pushed forward to press their advantage. Bradstreet, amazingly with only eight men, kept them occupied with covering fire until reinforcements came up from behind. Finally, they had the French troops cornered in a pine wood and each side blasted away at the other with a withering barrage of musket fire. Bradstreet ordered his troops to attack, and the French, mostly trappers and Indians, were so surprised by the audacity of the move that they retreated into the river. The British forces took their time and picked them off one by one. Although an accurate number of enemy dead could not be calculated, Williamson later claimed that the French lost

130 men, with many more wounded or taken prisoner. The British lost 74 men, mostly in the initial ambush. 'Had we known of their lying in the bush, or of their intent to attack us,' he wrote, 'the victory would have been more complete on our side, as the troops Colonel Broadstreet [*sic*] commanded were regular, well disciplined, and in tolerable health.'

Williamson's account of this period – his leaving New York for Oswego, his wounding and his eventual arrival at the forts – is, once again, chronologically confusing. It is unclear whether he actually reached Oswego after being wounded before he was sent back to Albany. Also, the attack on Colonel Bradstreet's forces took place on 3 July 1756 as they were returning from Oswego and not on the way there, as Williamson stated. Certainly troops rushed from the fort to give aid and maybe Williamson was among them. Again, perhaps, he was guilty of placing himself in the middle of the action when he was, in fact, more at the periphery.

It seems, though, that he was now back in Oswego, which was about to face its greatest threat. For there had been changes in command on both sides of the war.

The French commander was now Louis-Joseph, Marquis de Montcalm Gezan de Saint Véran, a regular soldier who was unhappy with his posting to this godforsaken land. He planned to end this troublesome little war in the New World as swiftly as he could, and his first targets were the British forts on Lake Ontario. He had sent the French forces, commanded by Louis Coulon de Villiers, to the area to harass the British as much as possible. It was a detachment of this force that attacked Bradstreet's flotilla of bateaux. The French also received intelligence that the British were planning to strengthen their fort at Ticonderoga, near Crown Point. Montcalm established his base at Montreal and began to build a considerable force to launch an offensive against Oswego. This would, he hoped, force the British to siphon off troops from Ticonderoga and dispatch them to Lake Ontario.

On his return to Albany, Colonel Bradstreet tried to convince the British command that it was imperative to support the Oswego positions. But John Bradstreet was a colonial and therefore beneath the disdain of the men commanding His Majesty's forces. What was worse, he was of mixed blood, his father being a British Army officer and his mother a French-speaking Acadian. Perhaps if Sir William Shirley had still been in overall command, things would have been different, for he, too, was a colonial and therefore not so deeply in thrall to the inherent prejudices of the class-ridden army hierarchy. Unfortunately, there had been a change at the top. The Massachusetts governor's handling of the war so far had not been successful and he was replaced, first by Major-General Daniel Webb, then by James Abercromby and finally, in July, by John Campbell, Earl of Loudoun. Williamson said that the men at Oswego expected Bradstreet to return with reinforcements:

> in order to take Fort Frontenac, and the other French forts on the Lake Ontario. But alas! As schemes for building castles in the air always prove abortive, for want of proper architecture and foundation, so did this scheme of ours, for want of a due knowledge of our situation!

While Bradstreet cooled his heels in Albany and Schenectady, Montcalm built up a force of between four and five thousand regulars, Canadians and Indians. Smaller forces carried out some probing – Williamson tells of an attack soon after he arrived in Oswego that led to a skirmish in the woods. Sneak attacks were also common, and British sentries and patrols had to be forever on their guard, for if they let it down for even an instant, it could mean their life. Or at least their scalp.

Williamson tells of an Irish soldier named Moglasky, a trooper in the 50th Regiment, who was ordered to stand guard over a newly arrived supply of all-important rum: 'Being curious to know its goodness, [he] pierced the cask, and drank till he was quite intoxicated.' The soldier left his post and found himself a comfortable spot to sleep off the effects of the strong liquor.

He was found the following morning, still asleep but minus his scalp. The sergeant who found him, seeing the oozing, bloody mass that was his head, assumed the trooper was actually dead and not just dead drunk. But as he was raised up, the 'dead' man came to life and asked the sergeant what it was he wanted. 'The sergeant advised him to prepare for death,' related Williamson, 'not having many hours to live, as he had lost his scalp.'

According to Williamson's account, the Irishman did not believe that he had, in fact, been scalped – until he touched the raw flesh where his hair had once been and felt the blood seeping from a deep slash from his mouth to his ear. No one could believe the man had survived the attack, least of all the commanding officer who said, when Moglasky vowed never to steal rum again, that 'it was very probable he never would, as he was now no better than a dead man'. However, after receiving treatment at Albany, the soldier survived and, 'to the great surprise of everybody, was living when I left the country,' claimed Williamson.

Such diversions aside, short-sighted commanders and political one-upmanship in the high command kept much-needed artillery, ammunition and reinforcements from the three forts at Oswego.

And across the lake, at Frontenac, Montcalm was ready to strike.

The garrison at Oswego numbered just under 1,200 men, plus civilians and a small army of sailors and labourers for the fleet of vessels that had been constructed the year before. They had some artillery but were awaiting delivery of a number of six-pounders, which Bradstreet was to have brought on his next trip, along with reinforcements under the command of Major-General Daniel Webb. Williamson still expected the British to make a move against Niagara and Frontenac. 'Had [Bradstreet] returned in time with the cannon and batteau-men under his command,' he believed, 'the French would not have dared to have appeared on the lake.' But Bradstreet, through no fault of his own, did not return in time. And the French did indeed dare to appear on the lake.

On 4 August 1756, Montcalm, his huge force now at Frontenac, where the St Lawrence River feeds into Lake Ontario, began to advance towards Oswego, landing first on Wolfe Island, then moving across Lake Ontario to land within half a league of the British emplacements. It was nearly midnight on 10 August, and the Siege of Oswego was about to begin.

Williamson recalled:

> This day and the next, the enemy were employed in making gabions [cylinders of metal or wicker, filled with earth and used to build fortifications], faucissons and fascines [long faggots for lining trenches and batteries] and in cutting a road across the woods, from the place of landing, to the place where the trenches were to be opened.

In the early hours of 11 August, the French began to erect their battery, which included, Williamson said, '32 pieces of cannon, from 12 to 18 pounders, besides several large brass mortars'. Among the weaponry ranged against the British were, somewhat embarrassingly, some of the pieces abandoned by Braddock's troops after the Battle of the Wilderness. The French front line was only about 180 yards from the British emplacements and the rain of fire unleashed from the cannon and the muskets would have been deafening – and deadly. Two of the British ships were launched onto the lake with orders to fire on the enemy placements, but their comparatively weak fire-power was more an irritant than a danger, and they were easily outgunned. Fort Ontario, on the east side of the Oswego River, suffered the brunt of the attack at this stage. This was one of the newer forts and the 370 men stationed there huddled behind the wooden palisades and attempted to hold off the might of the French force. Although they had only a few small-calibre artillery pieces with which to yap back at the barking French guns, they fought hard against tremendous odds.

Across the river, engineers and soldiers worked feverishly to strengthen the defences at Old Oswego. Lieutenant Colonel James Mercer, commanding officer for all three forts, had established his command centre there, and throughout the two days the roar of the cannon and the rattle of the muskets from the opposite bank became familiar sounds. He was, however, convinced that a second front would be opened from the west or south and concentrated much of his defensive efforts in those directions. When Fort Ontario's few cannon fell silent, Mercer knew the defenders had run out of ammunition. Despite the close range, the French barrage had failed to make a serious breach in the wooden palisades, but, without its own artillery defence, the fort would not hold out much longer. Mercer sent orders across the river that the stockade should be abandoned and the soldiers fall back to the old fort. The fleeing troops spiked their cannon – it was bad enough that Braddock's artillery was being used against them without their own armaments falling into enemy hands – and managed to cross the Oswego River to the relative safety of the old fort.

Montcalm's forces took possession of Fort Ontario, using the gabions to strengthen the wooden walls and hauling up their own cannon. By the morning of 13 August, they were ready to turn their attention to Old Oswego, deeming Fort Rascal to be undermanned, under-gunned and too far away along the river to be of any great consequence to them. The thunder of cannon fire and the rumble of exploding masonry came as a rude awakening to Lieutenant Colonel

Mercer, who still, for some reason, believed an attack would be launched from the landward side. The French cannon made easy work of the crumbling stone of the old fort and ripped through the hastily created defences with ease. As the enemy troops streamed over the river, Williamson said, Mercer ordered his troops to engage them on the riverbank. However, before that order could be followed, a cannonball crashed through a wall and sliced the British commander in half. 'The resolution of this valiant Colonel seemed to be determined to oppose the French to the last extremity,' recalled Williamson, solemnly, 'and to maintain his ground at Oswego, but his final doom came on so unexpectedly, that his loss was universally regretted.'

With their commander dead, one fort lost to the French, another 'scarce in a condition to defend itself against small arms' and the old fort battered by cannon fire and about to be overrun by French troops and Indians, the British lost heart. Command fell to Lieutenant Colonel John Littlehales, who convened a council of war with his officers and engineers. The situation, they decided, was hopeless, and the best they could do was request terms from the French.

And so the regimental drummers beat out the surrender, and the firing ceased. On the walls of Fort Ontario the French artillery fell silent and the infantry held their fire. Two officers were sent to Montcalm to ask what terms he would offer and he replied 'that they might expect whatever terms were consistent with the service of His Most Christian Majesty'. Montcalm, though, was unimpressed by the ease with which the garrison had fallen after Mercer's death. He would offer terms but they would not include the regiment being granted its liberty with its colours. Instead, the soldiers would become prisoners of war.

According to Williamson, those terms were:

Article one – The garrison shall surrender prisoners of war, and shall be conducted from hence to Montreal, where they shall be treated with humanity, and every one shall have treatment agreeably to their respective ranks, according to the custom of war.

Article two – Officers, soldiers, and individuals, shall have their baggage and clothes; and they shall be allowed to carry them along with them.

Article three – They shall remain prisoners of war, until they are exchanged.

At 10 a.m. on 14 August 1756, as the drummers beat a solemn tattoo, Lieutenant Colonel Littlehales formally surrendered the Oswego garrisons to Montcalm. He fully expected the French commander and aristocrat to keep his word regarding the treatment of his officers and men. Montcalm, disgusted though he may have been by the seeming cowardice of the officers, fully intended to keep his word. His Indian allies, however, had different ideas. The regular soldier's way of surrender and safe passage was not their way. They wanted blood, they wanted scalps and they wanted revenge on the British for the deceptions and outrages of the past. So, against Montcalm's orders, they stormed the surrendered fort and slaughtered whomever they found. Williamson described the massacre thus:

> They all behaved more like infernal beings than creatures in human shapes . . . They scalped and killed all the sick and wounded in the hospitals; mangling, butchering, cutting, and chopping off their heads, arms, legs &c with spades, hatchets, and other such diabolical instruments.

Between thirty and one hundred soldiers, as well as a number of civilians, were murdered before the bloodletting ceased. Lieutenant Colonel Littlehales found himself on the receiving end of 'Indian cruelty' when he reached Montreal, for there he was seized by a gang of angry Abenaki Indians and for an hour was dragged along the city walls, being beaten with sticks and called, according to one witness, 'a son of a bitch, a dog and a scoundrel'. He had turned coward during the siege, and that was something Indians would not accept.

But other officers, at least in Williamson's opinion, had behaved honourably:

> Every one of them I had an opportunity of observing during the siege, [behaved] with the utmost courage and intrepidity. Nor . . . can I omit particularly naming Colonel James Campbell and Captain Archibald Hamilton, who assisted with the greatest spirit and alacrity the private men at the great guns.

But no matter how gallant individual officers and men might have been, Oswego's fall was a foregone conclusion. The garrison consisted of a handful of men compared to the vast force deployed by Montcalm, while the defensive installations were pitifully weak.

While the British troops were being transported as prisoners of war, the French set about destroying the forts. They took possession of a vast amount of powder and shot, for, as Williamson observed, 'the quantity of stores and ammunition we then had in the three forts is almost incredible. But of what avail are powder and balls if walls and ramparts are defenceless, and men [in]sufficient to make use of them?' The French also now had possession of the little fleet that had proved so ineffectual, as well as the various cannon and mortars left unspiked.

The fall of Oswego left the French the undisputed masters of Lake Ontario. The triple forts were no longer a dagger aimed at the heart of New France. Their collapse was yet another disgrace to the British Army in North America. British settlers on the western frontier were being harried and driven from their homes by Indian raiders, and those in the north-east, close to Canada, would soon be in a similar situation. Braddock's army had been ignominiously defeated at the Battle of the Wilderness. Certainly, the British had taken Nova Scotia, but they had reached an impasse at Lake Champlain.

With Oswego gone and Fort Bull a smoking ruin, Wood Creek was blocked with logs to prevent French forces from striking deep into New York colony. Other forts were abandoned and destroyed to prevent them from falling into enemy hands as the army retreated east. Indian tribes loyal to the British saw this panic-filled retreat and began to wonder if they had backed the wrong horse. Even the Iroquois sent a delegation to Montreal to hear what the French had to say. Pierre François de Rigaud, Marquis de Vaudreuil, was the governor of New France and he told them, 'I have laid Oswego to ashes and the English quail before me. Why do you nourish serpents in your bosom? They mean only to enslave you.' Delegates at the council threw medals they had received from the British to the ground and hailed the triumphant Vaudreuil as 'the Devourer of Villages'. The French were winning most of the Indian tribes to their side. Only the Mohawks remained faithful to the British, thanks to their relationship with Sir William Johnson. But that, too, was uncertain.

Meanwhile, Peter Williamson was beginning his third period of captivity. First there had been the Aberdeen kidnappers, then the Lenape, now the French. He and the other British prisoners of war were herded onto boats at Oswego and carried across Lake Ontario. The British soldiers were finally going to enter Canada, but not in the way they had dreamed.

ELEVEN

Now We Shall Have Scalps Enough

Although the French Crown laid claim to most of Canada, very little of it was actually settled. The French, as already noted, were never as interested in colonisation as the British, tending to see the vast lands as a natural resource to be milked for profit. It was the Italian Christopher Columbus, working for the Spanish Crown, who first officially made landfall in what was to become known as the New World, but it was John Cabot who first laid claim to part of the continent's north-eastern territories for England. He sailed in May 1497 from Bristol with instructions from Henry VII to 'discover, and find, whatsoever isles, countries, regions or provinces of the heathen or infidels' which until then had been 'unknown to all Christians'. Cabot was actually looking for the North-west Passage to India and China. What he discovered after a fifty-three-day voyage across the Atlantic was a 'new found land', which he claimed on behalf of the English king. It turned out to be a vast island guarding what would later become the Gulf of St Lawrence.

The first French expedition, captained by Italian Giovanni da

Verrazano, was also a search for the fabled North-west Passage. Verrazano sailed up the eastern seaboard of what would become America, discovering Manhattan and the mighty river behind it that Henry Hudson would find again over eighty years later, and also exploring the Newfoundland coastline. However, France did not exploit the detailed charts he had made until a home-grown sailor, Jacques Cartier, discovered the St Lawrence River in 1535 and followed it until ferocious rapids at the juncture of what would be named the Ottawa River forced him onto dry land. Here, he found the Huron village of Hochelaga at the foot of a small mountain. Cartier named the mountain Mont Réal, or Mount Royal. It was Cartier who discovered the name of this new country. The Huron told him they called it *Kanata,* which meant 'village'. Although the country was to be termed New France for many decades, it would eventually become known by a corruption of the Huron word — Canada.

The real French father of Canada was Samuel de Champlain. From 1603, he made a series of expeditions and in 1608 founded the city of Quebec on the site of the village of Stadacona, in what was then Huron country, on a spit of land jutting into the St Lawrence and bounded on one side by the St Charles River. His explorations opened up the St Lawrence as far as Lake Ontario and along the Ottawa River, and beyond to the eastern edge of Lake Huron. But still the French showed little interest in colonisation, although in 1627, Louis XIII did decree that any settlers must be Roman Catholic. This meant that fledgling Canada lost the skills and grit of the French Huguenots, the Protestant sect who fled persecution — like so many other New World settlers — and proceeded to plant roots in the American colonies. Quebec was still little more than a handful of structures when Champlain died in 1635, while further south the English were making inroads into the wilderness. In 1754, the colonist population of New France was a mere 55,009 while that of the Thirteen Colonies was well over one million.

On the coast of Newfoundland and Nova Scotia, enterprising fisherman were casting their nets and making a life for themselves. In Nova Scotia, they would evolve into the Acadians, the French-speaking Catholics who were tolerated by the British only until war and land-hungry New Englanders created the impetus to expel them. The interior, meanwhile, was more or less the province of two different types of white trader – the man who dealt in furs and the man who dealt in souls. For, while the French Canadian trappers were busy learning the ways of the forest from the Indians, the Jesuit missionaries were just as busy trying to teach those same Indians the ways of the Lord. For many Indians of the great interior, their first encounter with the white man was with either a fur-clad trapper or a black-robed priest. It was the former who won the greater victory. The Jesuits learned, despite some successes, that the average Indian just was not interested in a religion in which the greatest reward was a heaven where there was no hunting, war or sex and which was filled with white men.

The real heroes of Canada's early colonial history were the wood runners, the *coureurs de bois* – the trappers. They were mainly young Frenchmen who seized the chance to make their way – and a profit – in the vast uncharted backwoods of the continent. They defied French authority by trapping without licences, forged strong friendships with Indian tribes and married into Indian families. They learned to hunt, eat and live like the Indians, for that was the only way to survive in that unforgiving land. They discarded European clothes and fashions to don buckskin and moccasins, and allowed their hair and beards to grow. They explored quiet streams and raging rivers in their birch-bark canoes. They developed portage routes along the waterways of the interior; they had to carry both canoe and trade goods past foaming white water and thundering waterfalls. It was a hard life and a dangerous one, and the land was peppered with the graves of men who had fallen prey to the elements, wildlife or hostile Indians.

Meanwhile, the French authorities instituted all kinds of punishments for trapping without a licence. Backs were flayed and flesh branded; men could be lashed to the oars of prison galleys. This daring army of young men developed into the *voyageurs*, trappers of all nationalities working for the big companies set up by both Britain and France to plunder the land of its riches. They moved in larger bodies and pushed the limits of the trading lands ever further west. By the early eighteenth century, they had established posts in the valleys of the Mississippi and Ohio. Although Britain recognised the value of the fur trade, New France, with its closer ties to the remote tribes and its regiment of hardy trappers, was at the time exporting almost twenty times more pelts. British traders were catching up, though, and it was, as we have seen, rivalry in the lands beyond the Alleghenies that was the spark that blazed into war. And it was the tough, Indian-fighting French-Canadian trappers who would become Britain's most implacable enemy in the war. The regular French soldier fought because he was trained or ordered to do so, and even the Indian could switch sides if the going got too tough. But the French-Canadian was defending what had become his land.

It was the Jesuits who established a mission on the island of Montreal. The village encountered by Cartier was long since gone, and in 1642, the missionaries established the Villa Marie de Montréal. Although the pursuit of fur was all-important, the French Crown did want to see some colonisation of New France and established governors to rule it. Women were always in short supply and orphaned girls, almost always peasants, were shipped from the mother country to the new colonies in Montreal and Quebec. Settlers' families that numbered more than ten were given cash as a reward. And so the settlement grew until it was the centre of the French fur trade and the main stepping-off point for journeys to the west and south-west.

It was to Montreal on the St Lawrence that the prisoners from Oswego were brought first, and here that Lieutenant Colonel

Littlehales was abused by the Abenaki, whose forefathers had moved to Canada from their Maine homeland after their disastrous defeat in King Philip's War almost one hundred years before. Williamson said the prisoners arrived in the Canadian town on 28 August and were secured in the fort. Meanwhile, their captured colours from Oswego were hung up for all to see, and in churches, choirs sang hymns of praise to God for Montcalm's victory. Littlehales and the other officers had felt surrender was the only sensible solution, but in admitting defeat, they had, at least in Montcalm's eyes, disgraced themselves. If they had mounted some form of defence, then perhaps he would have allowed them to march home with their colours and honour intact, in return for a promise that they would not take up arms against him for a specified time. But now they were in chains and their regimental honours paraded in a New French city to be jeered and spat upon.

'The French used various methods to win some of our troops over to their interest, or, at least, to do their work in the fields, which many refused, among whom was myself,' Williamson wrote. Those who refused to help were loaded onto another ship and taken even further up the St Lawrence, this time to the colonial capital at Quebec, 'where, on arriving, the fifth of September, we were lodged in a gaol, and kept there for the space of one month'.

Once again, Williamson found himself in a prison. It must have seemed like he had come full circle – he had been placed in the tollbooth in Aberdeen and now, a grown man, he was in another prison in the New World. He does not say if he went with other prisoners when they were given the chance to get out into the open air and work, but no one could blame him if he did. However, those drafted workers were soon back in the gaol again:

> During this our captivity, many of our men rather than lie in a prison, went out to work and assist the French in getting their harvest; they having then scarce any people left in that country

but old men, women and children, so that the corn was continually falling into the stubble, for want of hands to reap it; but those who did go out, in two or three days, chose confinement again, rather than liberty on such terms, being almost starved, having nothing in that country to live on but dry bread, whereas we in prison were each of us allowed 2lbs of bread, and half a pound of meat a day, and otherwise treated with a good deal of humanity.

The prisoners were guarded by only eighteen French soldiers, who constantly watched for any sign of their captives rising up against them, 'which had we had any arms,' boasted Williamson, 'we might easily have done, and ravaged the country round, as it was then entirely defenceless'. With the majority of Montcalm's troops elsewhere, the Quebec community would have been right to view the presence of a large number of British fighting men in their midst with some anxiety. Although Williamson's claim that they could have 'ravaged the country' was exaggerated, it is certainly true that a few dedicated, not to mention desperate, men determined to get home could have done some damage. But the 1,600 veterans of Oswego were tired and demoralised. As far as they knew, their leaders in Albany, whose seeming timidity had delivered the triple forts into enemy hands, had deserted them. Now they were lying in a French-Canadian gaol, while the war in the Colonies to the south was not going well. Patriotism is all very well, but most of these men were British soldiers far from home, and they had no allegiance to this vast unknown land.

For Williamson and his companions the war was over.

Further south, meanwhile, the British had been forced to retreat, stung by a series of setbacks. Many of their Indian allies, disgusted by their acting 'like women', had gone over to the French, whose way of thinking they found more to their liking: Governor Vaudreuil promised them blood and treasure; Montcalm, although never certain of their loyalty or convinced of their efficiency in battle, joined in their dances and songs. The British were not generally willing to participate in such displays of solidarity. Most of the officers were like Braddock — disdainful, disrespectful and disinclined to allow their noses to come down from the air long enough to show brotherhood. Of the six nations in the League of the Hodenosaunee, only the Mohawk remained faithful.

Montcalm, never happy in this backward frontier country and eager to return to Europe where the real war was being fought, decided to press his advantage and launch an offensive directly on the British Colonies. Fort William Henry, at the head of Lake George, seemed the ideal target. And so, in the blistering heat of July 1757, he led his army, strengthened by his new-found Indian allies, to Lake Champlain and on to the French-held Fort Carillon, or Ticonderoga (a corruption of the Indian word Cheonderoga, which means 'sounding waters').

At the time, Lieutenant Colonel George Monro commanded the British fort. He was a fierce Scot made famous in the novel *The Last of the Mohicans* by James Fenimore Cooper and its film adaptations. He had 500 men under his command in the outpost and a further 1,700 in a camp outside it. A few miles away, Major-General Daniel Webb, who had lingered at Schenectady while Oswego fell, had based himself in Fort Edward on the Hudson River. Montcalm, at Ticonderoga, had 6,000 French regulars and Canadian militia plus almost 2,000 Indians. Monro fully expected Webb to send more men from Fort Edward. But the reinforcements never came.

The siege began on 4 August. As artillery and marksmen battered the fort, another column set up an ambuscade on the road south to prevent any aid reaching Monro and to stop any dispatches getting out. Inside Fort William Henry, as the casualties grew and the ammunition dwindled, morale slumped. Every day, Monro expected to see Webb and his men appear on the road, but every day he was disappointed. Then Montcalm sent word that he had intercepted a runner from Fort

Edward. Webb, fearing that to send more men would leave the road to the Colonies open, had bluntly said that no aid would be coming, and the best Monro could do was sue for terms. Monro consulted with his officers, just as Littlehales had done the year before in Oswego, and a flag of truce fluttered to the top of the fort's flagpole.

This time, the British defence had impressed Montcalm. His terms were simple – the entire garrison could march to safety, complete with colours, so long as they agreed not to bear arms against France for a total of eighteen months. The fort, of course, was forfeit and would be put to the flame. And so, with drums sounding and fifes blowing, the British troops marched out of Fort William Henry, leaving behind around seventy sick and wounded comrades to be tended by the French. Again, the Indians were not satisfied with the way the siege had ended. They moved into the fort and slaughtered some of the sick before French troops could stop them.

But the Indians were not finished. They had been promised plunder, but the French had allowed the British to leave with their baggage. There was only one way they could have what they had been promised – they attacked the unarmed British column. Some accounts claimed that 1,500 men were killed in just three hours, the Indians, drunk on rum they had found in the fort, attacking from the rear, their war whoop echoing through the hot summer air. One eyewitness said they first singled out 'the negroes, mulattos and Indians and dragged them away'. Reports claimed that they then attacked the whites, killing the men, raping the women and dashing the brains of young children against stones and trees. These reports, however, were exaggerated. Colonel Monro himself said that only 129 men were killed or wounded in the siege and the attack on the road to Fort Edward combined. The Indians were after treasure, and anyone who resisted would be summarily dealt with, but the final death toll was certainly no more than 180. In the end, Montcalm and his officers put their own lives at risk by interceding to stop the killing.

The dead would have their revenge, though. There had been an outbreak of smallpox at the fort, and the infection had passed to the blankets and goods the Indians took away with them. The disease subsequently spread uncontrollably through the native villages, decimating the population – warriors, women, children. Even in defeat, the white man had won.

The loss at Fort William Henry was yet another black day for the British forces, but in Williamson's home colony, Pennsylvania, matters had in fact taken a turn for the better. Having been plagued by bloody Indian raids for a number of years and debilitated by the Assembly's inability to reach an agreement with the governor and the proprietors over taxation, the colony was, while Williamson and his comrades faced the might of the French at Oswego, setting out to strike a blow against the raiders. In April 1756, Governor Morris had done what Scarouady had asked and formally declared war on the Lenape. He declared that:

> The said Delaware Indians, and all others who, in conjunction with them, have committed hostilities against His Majesty's subjects within this province, [are] enemies, rebels and traitors to his Most Sacred Majesty; and [we] do hereby require all His Majesty's subjects of this province, and earnestly invite those of the neighbouring provinces, to embrace all opportunities of pursuing, taking, killing, and destroying the said Delaware Indians and all others confederated with them in committing hostilities, incursions, murders, or ravages upon this province.

The Pennsylvanians had decided enough was enough, especially when a French-sponsored Lenape force attacked Fort Granville and seized a number of prisoners. For too long, the white settlers had watched their elected representatives sitting on their hands while their friends and relations were being murdered or driven from their homes. Now, with a new decisiveness in the air in Philadelphia, it was time to take the fight to the enemy. In August 1756, Colonel John Armstrong, a tough Scots-Irishman who had been born in County Fermanagh in Ulster but settled in Cumberland County, rallied a force of 300 men at Fort Shirley on the Juniata River. He planned to launch an attack on the major Indian village of Kittanning, on the Allegheny River and within the sound of French cannon fire at Fort Duquesne. Kittanning was the home of Lenape chief Captain Jacobs and sometimes of Shingas, the Lenape warrior who had been so insulted by General Braddock that he left his camp. The Pennsylvania Assembly had placed a price on both their heads.

The army of settlers followed the beating of the Lenape drums and the sound of their war chants to the camp. They arrived while the moon was still high and waited in a cornfield until the sun broke through the night on 9 September 1756. They watched as the Indians set a number of fires, not to warm themselves, for the air was mild, but to ward off the blood-sucking gnats. At first light, the shooting began. Captain Jacobs called his warriors to him, saying, 'The whites are come at last. Now we shall have scalps enough.' This day, though, was not to be theirs. The Pennsylvanian settlers were determined to have vengeance for the atrocities of the recent past and to send a clear message to the rest of the Indian nations that they were no longer sitting targets. Captain Jacobs' warriors fought hard and fought well, but their wooden homes were vulnerable to fire. One hut turned out to be a powder store, and the resulting explosion was heard in Fort Duquesne. Jacobs tried to escape by leaping from a window, but he was shot as he ran for cover and scalped, along with many of his fallen braves. Prisoners were shown the scalp and recognised it as his, 'as no other Indians there wore their hair in the same manner', Colonel Armstrong told Governor Morris. Although the chief had sent the women and children to the safety of the woods when the raid began, it seems clear that they were not safe from the attacking whites, for

Armstrong said the freed prisoners 'knew [Captain Jacob's] squaw's scalp by a particular bob; and also knew the scalp of a young Indian called the King's Son'. (At the time, the white man regularly called Indian leaders 'kings' or 'half kings'.)

Armstrong had been wounded in the shoulder, but he recovered, and in January the following year, he was decorated by the province. He later bought much of the land on which Kittanning lay and the county was renamed Armstrong County in his honour. He was not, however, finished with the war.

Although the expedition had managed to remove the threat of Captain Jacobs, the other Lenape war chief, Shingas, was not in the camp that day. He went on to harass the British, having gained the sobriquet 'Shingas the Terrible', but the raid had the effect the colonists had hoped for, as other warrior bands agreed to cease hostilities.

For the British Army and settlers, the Kittanning raid was a rare victory in two years of disasters. Although Williamson mentions it in his book, he must have picked up the details from other published sources. For, while Colonel Armstrong was marching across the mountains towards the village, Williamson was in his Quebec gaol, wondering what was to become of him and his comrades. Finally, it was decided that he and 1,500 other prisoners would be transported from Quebec to be exchanged for French prisoners of war.

Peter Williamson was going home.

TWELVE

We Will Save This Colony or Perish

Peter Williamson, on his way back across the vast ocean he had crossed just thirteen years before, had, by his own account, been active in the French and Indian War for just two years. The struggle for empire was part of a global conflict, and Britain, France and their respective allies were at war not only in North America and the West Indies but also in Europe, the Indian sub-continent and the Philippines. This war, officially begun in 1756, did not end until 1763 and became known as the Seven Years War. In the American colonies, though, it had begun two years earlier.

Although Williamson was out of it, he would always take an interest in what occurred in the Colonies, and in his subsequent writings commented on the successes and failures of the government there. He, along with other Britons, was eager for news regarding the conflict.

By 1758, Britain's secretary of state (effectively prime minister at that time) William Pitt the Elder was tired of his army's disgraces in the northern colonies. Major-General Daniel Webb had proved singularly ineffective, not to say cowardly, in his actions over Oswego and Fort William Henry. The supreme commander, John Campbell, Earl of Loudoun, a middle-aged Scottish Lord with all the arrogance and prejudices of his breed, had been, to say the least, a disappointment. He arrived in 1756 with his servants, furniture, personal surgeon, horses and a special coach – as well as two mistresses – and had seemed on occasion more intent on establishing Royal control over the somewhat unruly colonials than on striking a blow against the French. He reserved great disdain for the colonists, civilians and militia. His main victory was the forced billeting of regular army personnel in the houses of settlers, an issue he seemed to regard as more important than actively defending the Provinces against the enemy. Benjamin Franklin, by then out of military service and awaiting passage to England to fight the Pennsylvanian cause at Parliament, commented that indecision was one of His Lordship's strongest features. As someone remarked to Franklin, the commander was 'always on horseback but never rides on'. Loudoun planned to besiege the French-held stronghold at Louisburg on Cape Breton, the northern promontory of Nova Scotia. The British had won this from the French in 1745, but it had been returned to them as part of the peace treaty of Aix-la-Chapelle in 1748. Heavily fortified, the port was seen as the gateway to the Canadian interior, guarding as it did the straits between Nova Scotia and Newfoundland leading to the Gulf of St Lawrence and the St Lawrence itself. French warships took refuge here between attacks on British naval and commercial shipping on the eastern seaboard and in the West Indies. Taking Louisburg back was of the utmost importance if the Canadian troops were to be broken. Loudoun led his troops to Halifax, Nova Scotia, where he spent his time in parades and war games before deciding against an attack on the French stronghold and returning to New York. He had heard the French had reinforced the garrison, and as a result, he had taken fright. Although this was good news for his demoralised, tired and disease-ridden men, Loudoun's campaign of 1757 was, according to Benjamin

Franklin, 'frivolous, expensive and disgraceful to our nation beyond conception'. He believed that General Shirley would have made a better commander, had he been kept in place, saying:

> For tho' Shirley was not a bred soldier, he was sensible and
> sagacious in himself, and attentive to good advice from others,
> capable of forming judicious plans, quick and active in
> carrying them into execution. Loudoun, instead of defending
> the Colonies with his great army, left them totally expos'd
> while he paraded it idly at Halifax.

Whether Shirley would have made a better fist of the campaign is open to doubt, as his own military record was far from exemplary.

It was while Loudoun preened and paraded at Halifax that Fort William Henry fell, and it has been argued that one of the reasons the timid Major-General Webb did not send reinforcements for its relief was that he had no reinforcements to send – they were all in Nova Scotia playing war games with the commander in chief.

At home, William Pitt was furious. 'Nothing is done. Nothing is attempted,' he thundered. 'We have lost all the waters. There is not a boat on the lakes. Every door is open to France.' Loudoun was recalled at last in 1758, and Pitt sent men he could trust to take control, including Lord George Howe, who was to support General Abercromby, and James Wolfe, a young, tubercular officer who was later to become the hero of Quebec. Overall command of the army fell to Lord Jeffrey Amherst.

A three-pronged attack plan was formulated. Fort Duquesne was to be taken. The French bases at Ticonderoga and nearby Crown Point were to be attacked. And Louisburg was to be besieged. If all three campaigns succeeded, the British would have begun a new phase in colonial warfare. By taking and holding Duquesne, they would be breaking the hold the French had on the profitable Ohio Valley. By grasping Ticonderoga, they removed the threat of invasion from the north. By snatching Louisburg, they would control the seas and prevent much-needed provisions and reinforcements from reaching the interior. The British did not merely want to regain lost ground and seize control of the disputed lands of the Ohio Valley; they meant to drive the French completely from the northern continent.

Louisburg was the first target. A fleet of over 100 ships picked up 14,000 troops at Halifax on 28 May 1758. Lord Amherst and General Wolfe were in personal command. The siege began on 8 June and lasted until 26 July. The French fought bravely, but in the end, sheer force of numbers brought them to their knees. The British proceeded to harry French emplacements across Cape Breton and made inroads on the St Lawrence River. Across the Atlantic, news of the first real victory in the Americas was greeted with the peal of church bells and bonfires in London. The captured French colours were conveyed by ship to be proudly displayed in St Paul's Cathedral.

News of the victory made up for yet another defeat that month.

General James Abercromby was preparing his attack on Ticonderoga. Abercromby had not seen great success with his previous exploits, but he had under him a number of able officers, including Pitt's friend Lord Howe, seen by many as the real commander of the force. The colonial forces were also well represented, by Lieutenant Colonel John Bradstreet, Sir William Johnson with 400 Indian allies, and Major Robert Rogers, a hard-drinking, hard-fighting New Englander whose famed Rangers, a group of volunteer colonial fighters, had already caused a great deal of trouble for the French throughout the war.

It was the Rangers, all experienced woodsmen, who led the advance through the forests that surrounded the fort at Ticonderoga. Montcalm, though, was waiting for them. On 8 July, the British forces made their first assault on the fort, sited on a spit of land jutting out into Lake Champlain. Wave after wave of British forces tried to break

171

through Montcalm's defences but were cut down by a hail of musket fire and grapeshot or, in the case of the Scots Highlanders, met with the flashing steel of French bayonets. French-Canadians sniped at the attackers from the trees, and by the end of the day, almost 2,000 men were dead, dying or taken prisoner. Included in the death roll was Lord Howe. 'The noblest Englishman that has appeared in my time,' said James Wolfe, 'and the best soldier in the British army.' The French, by comparison, had lost only 377 men.

With many of the French troops from Fort Frontenac, on Lake Ontario, having been sent to defend Ticonderoga, the British seized the opportunity to launch an offensive there. Lieutenant Colonel John Bradstreet had long wanted to strike back at the French in this area but had been prevented by the high command. However, his new commanders were of a different stripe and were keen to make up for the defeat at Ticonderoga, so he was ordered to lead the assault. He took 3,000 men, including Oneida Indians. Along the way they had to clear Wood Creek of the timber with which Major-General Webb had clogged it during his hasty retreat following the fall of Oswego. On 25 August, he was at Frontenac and within three days the undermanned garrison surrendered. With the fort and its small fleet of warships in British hands, Lake Ontario was now theirs and the French outposts in the Ohio Valley were cut off from New France.

The year was now drawing to an end, and the British still had Fort Duquesne to deal with. In June, the fiery Scots general John Forbes had set out through Pennsylvania with six to seven thousand men, made up of Highlanders, colonial militia and warriors from the Iroquois, Catawba and Cherokee nations, cutting a new road over the mountains and into the Ohio Valley. Among his officers were George Washington and John Armstrong, who led the British at Kittanning. Delays in starting out, skirmishes and battles along the way, disagreements between officers and illness all served to hold the campaign back, and by November, the huge force still had not reached

Duquesne. A reconnoitring force of over 800 Highlanders, under Major James Grant, was sent ahead to check out the lie of the land. They reached the fort and decided to march a column down to the gates. The ensuing battle left many of the British troops and officers dead or captured. The weather was changing and the first snows were beginning to fall. A seriously ill Forbes was about to call off the attack and return over the mountains to winter quarters when he received intelligence that the fort was severely undermanned. France's Indian allies had left to rejoin their families for the winter, and many of the Canadian militia had deserted due to lack of provisions thanks to Bradstreet's victory at Frontenac. By the time the British reached the fort on 24 November, the French had blown it up and completely withdrawn. General Forbes returned to Philadelphia, but his illness worsened, and he died in March 1759.

The French had been having it all their own way until 1758. Now, with success in Cape Breton, Lake Ontario and the Ohio Valley, British fortunes had reversed. In the year to come, they planned to build on those successes and make the northern continent theirs.

As ever, the need for Indian support was pressing. Various tribes met at Easton, Pennsylvania, in the autumn of 1758, and promises of mutual support were made. Among these nations were the Seneca, who had been allied with the French but had grown tired of war. Their spokesman, Tagashta, said:

> We now remove the hatchet out of your heads that was struck
> into them by our cousins, the Delawares . . . We take it out of
> your heads and bury it under the ground, where it shall always
> rest and never be taken up again.

At a great council in April 1759, Sir William Johnson rallied Native American support. A campaign was planned to take Fort Niagara and among the fighting force were braves of the Six Nations of the Hodenosaunee. The army moved by way of the Great Carrying Place, where a new fort, Fort Stanwix, had been built, to Oswego, which was already undergoing reconstruction. By 7 July, the British force was at Niagara and demanding its surrender. The French refused and the British began cannon bombardment a few days later. On 20 July, the British commander General John Prideaux was killed by cannon fire and Sir William Johnson, who some believed would have been in command all along if the old British prejudice against colonial officers had not held sway, took command. Five days later, the French capitulated.

The following day, Ticonderoga fell to General Amherst.

Quebec was surrounded. The British at Cape Breton had cut off its access to the sea and the mother country. Its western frontiers were now in colonial hands. Its people were tiring of war. For the second year in succession, the harvest failed and provisions were running short, although a convoy did manage to snake up the St Lawrence in the spring of 1759. The Canadian governor, Vaudreuil, and his military commander, Montcalm, had never seen eye to eye. Vaudreuil was Canadian-born and he did not like Montcalm's disdain for his country and people. He believed that guerrilla-style tactics were the way forward; Montcalm preferred the traditional way of fighting, believing it to be more honourable. Montcalm had grown weary of what he saw as his banishment to a country he viewed as inherently corrupt, thanks to government officials growing rich through the war. He was, however, a professional soldier and he would not shirk his duty. 'We will save this colony or perish,' he vowed. 'But what a country, where all the knaves grow rich and honest men are ruined.'

The siege of New France's capital began on 12 July. General Wolfe adopted ruthless tactics, burning villages and killing civilian settlers, in a bid to goad Montcalm to come out and fight, but the French forces resolutely kept to their fort 300 feet up on the cliffs above the river.

As time went on, Wolfe realised that he needed a full set-piece battle to settle the siege and satisfy his pride. Canadian militia and Indians still loyal to the French did attack British troops, but the colonial fighters and New England Rangers, with regular troops who had learned a thing or two since Braddock's defeat, were able to repulse them. The siege lasted through July and August into September. One assault failed in a bloody manner. Skirmishes at the rear of the British lines with Indians and Canadians whittled at their numbers. Wolfe fell ill and recovered. The city was bombarded by artillery fire. And still Montcalm refused to come out and fight.

Finally, Wolfe decided on a daring strategy. He and an attack force would scale the cliffs on the northern shore and lure the French out for one final, vainglorious struggle. Wolfe's tuberculosis was worsening; he knew he was dying by inches and his record thus far had not been as shining as he might have wished. He would take Quebec or he would die trying. The pale-faced, stick-thin young general had his eye on posterity as he formulated what was a kind of highly dramatic suicide bid. Four thousand men followed him up the steep cliffs by way of a very narrow track and onto the Plains of Abraham to the west of the city. By the time they reached the plateau, night had given way to a grey and drizzly day. Montcalm was alerted and he rode out to see a line of red stretched in the fine mist on the plain. He deployed his forces and the two armies prepared to face death on the rain-sodden plain.

The French fired first, and Wolfe himself was among those hit, although the ball passed through his wrist, so he wrapped a handkerchief round the wound to stem the blood and continued directing operations. Then the British let loose, the line of muskets firing in unison, smoke puffing from their flintlocks, the lead balls singing through the damp air towards the French troops. The blue-coated soldiers fell as the balls found their marks, blood spraying onto the grass. The line held and Montcalm himself was there, like his

British counterpart, rallying his men, bolstering their courage. The British reloaded and let loose another volley before charging screaming across the ground, bayonets raised, swords waving, leaping over the bodies of the fallen to get at the living. There were Highlanders among them, and their famed charge was as much a shock as the withering gunfire of the line. This blood-red line of death proved too much for the French forces, and they broke and ran. Wolfe was among the advancing troops, and as he raced towards the city a sharp-eyed marksman's musket ball found him, piercing his groin. A second ball entered his lungs, and he was brought down. He was carried to the rear of the lines where he found his longed-for hero's death after being assured of victory, saying, 'God be praised, I now die in peace.'

Montcalm was still on his horse trying to rally his troops when he too was shot. He made it back into the city, where he died early the following morning and was buried under the floor of a convent. Five days later, the city surrendered and the seat of New France's government moved to Montreal down the river. But the French interest on the continent was now very much on the wane, and the war here lasted only a further year, until on 8 September 1760, the French colonial government signed a document of capitulation.

Although the war in Europe and India raged on for a further three years, France had lost all its territories in North America. But the land had never really been theirs to begin with. It had always belonged to the Indian peoples, despite what the white man may have said or done.

Peter Williamson, writing in far-off Britain before the end of the war, recognised the need for friendship between the British and the Native Americans: 'If the Indians are not satisfied with the conclusion of a peace between us and the French as to America, I mean, unless they are fairly dealt with, we shall gain but little by all our conquests.'

However, the white man always had trouble dealing fairly with the

Indians. For every tale of Indians attacking settlers, there were others of settlers committing atrocities against Indians. Some of the warriors might have thought that they would have been rewarded for siding with the British, but that was not to be the case. The Lenape petitioned for the notorious Walking Purchase to be declared illegal, but political manoeuvring by the Penns, Sir William Johnson and the Iroquois – who also benefited from the land fraud – blocked any such move. Certainly the Crown established laws ostensibly to protect native interests but, as always, the white man's interest was given priority at every turn. Sir Jeffrey Amherst, the British commander, was dismissive of the tribes. 'The only true method of treating the savages,' he said, 'is to keep them in proper subjugation and punish, without exception, the transgressors.'

His policies helped lead to an uprising in 1762, which in turn led to the British government declaring that everything west of the Appalachians was to be viewed as Indian land. No tracts were to be sold to white settlers without the agreement of the Indians and any settlers currently living there were to return to the east. It was an unenforceable law, and whites ignored it to stream through the newly discovered Cumberland Gap into the Ohio Valley. The League of the Hodenosaunee tried to intervene, but its influence was waning. Wars erupted, fresh atrocities were committed, and in the end, the Indians lost. They always lost. Since the coming of the white man, they had been forced westwards or wiped out.

A later chief, Tecumseh of the Shawnee, said:

> Where today are the Pequot? Where are the Narragansett, the Mohican, the Pokanoket, and many other once powerful tribes of our people? They have vanished before the avarice and the oppression of the white man, as snow before a summer sun.

Over a century after the French and Indian War, Red Cloud of the Oglala Sioux summed up 300 years of history when he said, 'The white man made us many promises, more than I can remember, but they never kept but one; they promised to take our land, and they took it.'

THIRTEEN

This Scurrilous and Infamous Libel

The children were fascinated by him. He was a tall man, but that was not what attracted them. He had a curious stiffness in his left hand, but such deformities – and much worse – were commonplace at a time when Britain was rarely at peace. What was unusual was a man in the streets of their villages and towns dressed in a curious deerskin concoction. The fact that he was also painted and decorated like a savage made him truly enthralling. But there he was, in squares and greens the length of the country, whooping and gyrating, leaping in the air and spinning around, brandishing a curious-looking axe and generally acting in a manner more befitting a lunatic in Bedlam than a denizen of the quiet corners of rural England.

There was, though, no fear of this strange visitor, for the citizens and their children knew this was all for show. And anyone who had any doubt was soon put at ease as his hat was passed round for contributions. The man was simply an entertainer, a strolling player, plying his trade and earning a few pennies.

But then he would begin to tell his tale: of how he was snatched in childhood from his home and transported thousands of miles across the vast ocean to a land peopled by savages; of how he was captured by those same savages and suffered at their hands 'the most severe hardships'; of how he witnessed 'many instances of diabolical cruelty, perpetrated by those savages on the persons of several of the inhabitants of the back-settlements' of that far-off land. He told them of how he escaped from his captors 'almost in a miraculous manner' before volunteering to fight in His Majesty's service against the Indians and their masters, the French, and wreak vengeance on his oppressors. He told them of death and loss in the great silent forests and of a place called Oswego where brave men fell, but the enemy reigned supreme. Finally, he told them of being sent back to England in a prisoner-of-war ship and exchanged for French captives.

He told them all this, and the hat was passed round again. He told them all this, and with each telling the tale grew. He told them all this and came to believe some of the exaggerations and fabrications, until even he could not separate fact from fiction. The tale was the thing, and he told it well.

And when he was finished, he packed up his costume and his weapons, and he set off again. He travelled north. Always north.

Peter Williamson said that he and 500 other men were loaded onto the French packet-boat (a mail boat) *La Rénomée*, commanded by Captain Dennis Vitrée, in Quebec in late September 1756. The vessel sailed up the St Lawrence and across the Atlantic bearing a flag of truce. He and the others were treated well during the six-week voyage, he said, 'yet we were almost starved for want of provisions. One biscuit, and two ounces of pork a day, being all our allowance.' He and his comrades were also 'half dead with cold' through lack of clothing. He claimed that, the ship being small, many of them had to remain on deck in all weathers — and with the autumn gales blowing up on the Atlantic, that could not have been a comfortable experience. On 6 November, the ship hove into view of Plymouth Harbour, and the British soldiers on board gave a mighty cheer at being in sight of home. 'But these our troubles and hardships were not, as we expected, put to a period for some time,' said Williamson. The French and British had agreed no cartel (a written agreement regarding exchange of prisoners), so they had to remain on board ship as it bobbed at anchor off the coast. They could see the houses and fields of home. If they listened, they could hear English voices. But they were still on French territory, albeit in English waters, and still prisoners. Williamson said the situation remained thus for a further week before the Lords of the Admiralty reached agreement with their opposite numbers in Paris so that the ship was allowed to sail into port and the men could disembark.

The men were billeted in towns and villages across Devon, including Totnes, Newton Abbot and Newton Bushell. Williamson himself was sent to Kingsbridge, a fishing port, where for the first time in many months he was able to relax, secure in the knowledge that he was not under any immediate threat of death from an Indian tomahawk or French musket ball. 'I was happy being quartered in Kingsbridge,' he said, 'where I met with such civility and entertainment as I had for a long time been a stranger to.'

Able-bodied exchanged prisoners of war were generally reunited with their regiments or seconded to others before being sent back to whichever front the generals deemed fit. Captain Archibald Hamilton and Major James Campbell (who was not a Colonel, despite the rank Williamson gave him in his book when he picked out these two men for particular praise over their conduct at Oswego) later confirmed that Williamson was:

> a soldier in General Shirley's Regiment of Foot, which was raised in Philadelphia, New York, New England, America, has been with us in several expeditions against the Indians in the year 1755 and 1756 in one of which he was wounded.

They went on to state that:

> he was with us at the siege of Oswego where we were later
> taken prisoner by the French and sent to Canada and that he
> always behaved faithfully and honestly and after our arrival in
> England that he was draughted [*sic*] into a Regiment commend
> [*sic*] by General Sinclair from which we know he was
> honourably discharged on account of his wound at Plymouth
> April 1757.

Once having been declared incapable of further service, some soldiers were sent to Chelsea Hospital for wounded ex-servicemen, but, Williamson said, as he 'had only served in a provincial regiment, not in one upon the British establishment [raised in Britain]', he could not be provided for there. So, in April 1757, Peter Williamson, having been handed the princely sum of six shillings and thanked for his loyal service to the Crown, stood a free man in Plymouth and turned his face north.

Six shillings (thirty pence in modern terms) was a considerable sum in those days, but not enough to get him home to Aberdeen. During his time in Devon, and perhaps even before that, Williamson had kept himself occupied by writing an account of his adventures. The storytelling he honed in towns and villages during his long, 800-mile walk back to Scotland. For he had returned from the Colonies with a deerskin costume as well as an Indian tomahawk, knife and pipe, and he supplemented his funds by giving impromptu performances to the residents of the places he travelled through. His storytelling and energetic performances got him as far as York, where he found himself penniless. He threw himself on the sympathy of 'the honourable gentlemen of the city' for support and told them his story, showing them his now completed manuscript. These charitable gentlemen decided to pay for the printing of the work for Williamson's benefit.

We know that in later years Williamson was an active Freemason and may have been part of the Brotherhood when he returned from the Colonies. It may be that he used Masonic connections to obtain the aid of those York businessmen in printing his book. In the wordy style of the times, the volume was entitled *French and Indian Cruelty Exemplified in the Life and Various Vicissitudes of Fortune, of Peter Williamson, a Disbanded Soldier*. With certain incidents no doubt manipulated to make them more sensational – for Williamson may not have been highly educated but he knew his reading public – the book was an instant bestseller. Within three weeks of it hitting the booksellers of York, it had sold 1,000 copies, while in Newcastle it moved 650 in 2 weeks. Williamson's profit on every 1,000 books sold was £30, more than enough to get him home to Aberdeen without having to resort to walking.

But there was trouble awaiting him in Aberdeen. He might no longer be under threat of death, but he was to find that in the land of his birth, there were men just as ruthless as any backwoods native. They did not carry muskets and knives but complaints and writs. They did not hide behind trees and bushes but lurked behind laws and respectability. Peter Williamson's new battlefields would be the courtrooms of his native Scotland.

The Scotland to which Peter returned in 1758 was different from the one he had left fifteen years before. The Jacobite Rebellion begun in 1745 had ended one year later, and the government, determined that no such defiance should ever rear up again, resolved to dismantle the way of life that had helped spawn it. The bloody repercussions had begun even as the sound of musketry and cannon echoed across the bleak moorland of Culloden, when an order was handed down that no quarter was to be given. Although many were taken prisoner, dying Highlanders were shot or bayoneted where they lay, their blood seeping into the heather and moss beneath them, their groans carried away by the sleet-filled wind. The army, composed not just of English troops but also of many Lowland and Highland Scots, then spread out across the mountains and glens of the north, intent on stamping out the clan system. Suspected Jacobites were hunted and killed or captured to be transported to English gaols or prison hulks rotting on the Thames. Those found guilty were executed or exported as slaves to the Colonies. Their homes were looted and burned. Highlanders were not allowed to carry arms, which was understandable, but the playing of bagpipes was also banned, as was the wearing of tartan. The north country was ravaged by the men commanded by the King's fat son, the Duke of Cumberland – 'Butcher' Cumberland as he became known. Among his officers was James Wolfe, later the hero of Quebec, who had fought at Culloden and had refused to finish off a wounded Jacobite when ordered to do so.

While the north underwent the turmoil of rebellion and counter-rebellion, the east and south of the country prospered. The cities expanded, and the merchants and tradesmen grew rich and powerful on colonial trade in sugar, tobacco and slaves.

The country was a centre of invention, medicine, art and education. The Scottish Age of Enlightenment brought to notice some of the finest minds of the day: philosophers like David Hume and Adam Smith; doctors like James Lind, who tackled scurvy with citrus fruits and typhus with wood smoke, and pioneering surgeon brothers William and John Hunter; explorers such as James Bruce of Abyssinia, and Alexander Mackenzie, who would travel extensively in Canada and America. James Small, working in England, devised the iron plough that would be in use all over the world for 150 years. James Watt, studying under Scottish professor Joseph Black, who first discovered latent heat, went on to develop the separate condenser and improved the efficiency of the steam engine. William Murdoch invented gas lighting. John MacAdam revolutionised road-building, Thomas Telford bridge-building. The list went on and on, all eighteenth-century men with forward-thinking minds, all Scots.

Aberdeen had grown, too. It had remained loyal to the Crown during the rebellion, but, even so, Jacobite gentry had fled there after Culloden intent on taking ship for the Continent, and there were merchants in the city more than willing to take their money. Cumberland's dragoons swept up retreating Highlanders and crammed them in the tollbooth. By the time Peter Williamson returned, Aberdeen's textile-manufacturing industry had expanded, and the city had its first newspaper, the weekly *Aberdeen Journal*. Its population had grown to around 15,600, and a great number of new houses had been built, many from the granite quarried nearby. It was a burgeoning, prosperous town that was changing as the world around it changed.

Peter would find, though, that the more things changed, the more they stayed the same.

When he arrived in Aberdeen in June 1758, he immediately tried to trace his parents but found that his father, James, had died a few years before. He was told that James had moved from Hirnley following the death of his wife shortly after Peter's disappearance to 'a town in the land of Auchinhowe' and later to Dalvair. This was the second time Williamson had returned from a forced absence to find that loved ones had died in the interval, and he was no doubt hit hard by this sad and unexpected news. Peter did manage to trace some of his relations, and they presumably enjoyed an emotional reunion, although he gives no details of this in any of his writings.

He had carried with him a number of copies of his book and he began to hawk these around the streets of Aberdeen, showing an entrepreneurial spirit that would remain with him throughout his life. The book sold well; he was, after all, a local lad with an exciting tale to tell. However, not everyone was pleased to read of his adventures. In Aberdeen's great merchant houses and council chambers, men pored over the pages of what they termed 'a pamphlet', and their faces first paled then turned red with rage. Although they were not named, some recognised their hand in the kidnapping trade. Word was issued – silence this troublesome upstart, this libellous adventurer who had besmirched their good name. And Alexander Cushnie, procurator fiscal of the burgh court of Aberdeen, was the man who heard these words and acted on them.

At the instigation of the men who felt their reputations were damaged by Williamson's writings, Cushnie lodged a complaint with the Aberdeen provost and magistrates, saying:

> that by this scurrilous and infamous libel . . . the corporation
> of the City of Aberdeen, and whole members whereof, were
> highly hurt and prejudged; and therefore that the Pursuer
> [Williamson] ought to be exemplary punished in his person
> and goods; and that the said pamphlet, and whole copies
> thereof, ought to be seized and publicly burnt.

Unsurprisingly, considering that some of them may have been the men who had complained to Cushnie in the first place, the magistrates agreed that this was a case to be investigated and issued a warrant for Williamson's arrest. He was seized at his lodgings by a town officer and brought before the magistrates at the courthouse. Standing before the local baillies, as magistrates were known, Peter Williamson admitted he was the author of the book, which had been published at York. He was then, he said, 'concussed into a declaration of a very extraordinary tenor'.

He had to agree to 'make such satisfaction and reparation as the magistrates might think proper' after admitting that 'he had no ground for advancing and uttering the calumnies therein mentioned against the merchants of Aberdeen'. His claims, they wanted him to admit, were simply 'the fancy he took in his younger years, which stuck on his memory, (and) though he does not find he had reason to do so, he believes these things to be true'. However, he had to say he was 'willing to contradict in a public manner what he so advanced in the foresaid pamphlet concerning the merchants of Aberdeen'.

In the meantime, until he agreed to do everything they ordered, he was to be imprisoned and the remaining 350 copies of *French and Indian Cruelty* seized from his lodgings and kept in the clerk's chambers. For the second time in his life, Peter Williamson was locked up in the Aberdeen tollbooth. And for the second time in his life, it was done at the instigation of 'honourable' merchants. This time, though, he was not in the damp and dingy surroundings long, for his landlord, local vintner George Mackie, stood bail and Peter was released to his custody.

The following day, Williamson was summoned back to appear before the magistrates and was told that he had been found guilty of 'causing print, and of publishing and dispersing the foresaid calumnious and injurious pamphlet, reflecting greatly upon the characters and reputations of the merchants of Aberdeen, and on the town in general, without any ground or reason'. The good baillies ordered that the pages of the book which contained 'any scandalous reflections against the merchants and town of Aberdeen' were to be 'cut out at the sight of the Dean of Guild and Town Clerk; and when these leaves are so cut out, appointed the same to be publicly burnt at the market cross, by the hands of the common hangman'.

But it did not end there. The guilty man was also to lodge a document with the court confessing that his book contained 'several false and calumnious aspersions . . . without any just grounds or foundation'. He was then to beg the pardon of both the offended merchants and the magistrates 'in the most submissive manner'. This recantation was to be published locally as well as in York and anywhere else in the British Isles that the court thought proper.

Peter complained that the entire proceedings were unfair and unjust. He refused to sign any document that the six magistrates placed before him. He had been through many hardships, thanks to the greed of the town's merchants. He had lost his family and he had lost his wife. He had faced death at the hands of raiding Indians and in the King's service. He had been wounded fighting for this country's interests abroad, for goodness sake. He deserved better. He would not sign. He would not back down. He would not give in.

The magistrates said that he left them with only one alternative – Peter Williamson would be imprisoned. The thought of yet another period of incarceration terrified him. Standing in that courtroom, alone, friendless, with no lawyer to speak for him, Peter Williamson surrendered. Just as he knew he was beaten when the Lenape snatched him, he knew now he was outgunned and outmatched in this Scottish court. He agreed to sign the document and paid his ten shilling fine, for this was Scotland, and some money had to be made from the matter. He was also ordered to leave the town. Later, the Aberdeen town drummer rattled out an alert to the people that sentence was about to be carried out. Amid great ceremony, watched by the dean of guild, the town clerk, the procurator fiscal and the baillies, the libellous pages were sliced from Williamson's 350 books and burned at Aberdeen's Market Cross by the town 'hangie'. The remaining pages were never returned. Nor were the 350 copies of another pamphlet written by Williamson and published at York which had also been taken into custody, entitled *Some Considerations on the present State of Affairs, wherein the defenceless Situation of Great-Britain is pointed out, and an easy rational and just Scheme for its Security at this dangerous Crisis proposed, in a Militia*. That treatise did not attack the merchants, but nevertheless Williamson's copies were lost.

Seething with anger, Williamson left Aberdeen. He had expected more from his homeland. He had written only what he knew to be the truth: he had been kidnapped and sold as a servant, and there were merchants in the town who had profited from the trade. Perhaps that trade was no longer practised, but it had reached its end only a handful of years before. 'It is inconceivable,' he later wrote, 'that, of a whole bench of magistrates . . . not one was of an age capable of recollecting what had happened only 14 years before.'

Although the baillie court had sentenced him, and the procurator fiscal had preferred the charge, Williamson knew that at least some of the men who had been guilty of the trade in 1743 were behind the legal moves against him. He had also been told that some of them were baillies themselves, making them his accusers, witnesses against him and his condemners.

He had been forced by his own fears, corrupt officials and a legal system more interested in protecting its own than upholding justice to deny what he knew to be the truth. Now he was banished from the town he thought of as home.

As he left behind the spires, the houses and the harbours of Aberdeen, his face and his heart hardened, just as they had three years and a lifetime ago over his wife's grave in the snow-flecked fields of Pennsylvania. He had vowed then to have revenge on the men who had destroyed his life. He made that vow once again.

The baillies and merchants of Aberdeen had not heard the last of Peter Williamson.

FOURTEEN

He Can Fell Twa Dugs wi' Ae Bane

From the Edinburgh *Evening Courant*, 7 October 1758:

> Lately arrived from North America and lodges at Mrs John
> Mitchells in the uppermost entry James Court, Edinburgh,
> Peter Williamson, who was taken from his home in the back
> settlement of Pennsylvania by a party of Indians who
> carried him to their home town where he resided a
> considerable time, and afterwards attended them in several
> of their excursions before he had the opportunity of making
> his escape. By residing so long among them he has acquired
> a particular knowledge of their customs, manners, and
> dress; and as he brought over with him a compleat dress, he
> has already exhibited to the publick with a general
> satisfaction.

Armed with a fresh supply of his *French and Indian Cruelty*, Williamson
was announcing his presence in the Scottish capital. He was back to

performing his costumed war dance and anyone who bought a copy of the book at one shilling was entitled to see the display for free. The advertisement went on to explain why he was up to his old tricks again:

> The unhappy sufferer who is reduced by his misfortunes, has been advised to take this method to raise a little money to carry him back to America. He would therefore humbly hope for the encouragement of the publick, which though he cannot pretend to deserve yet he will gratefully acknowledge. He is to be seen at his lodging above mentioned from five till nine at night, and as the going through the different ceremonies and manners of the savages is very laborious, he would humbly beg that as many as possible would attend at a time; as he cannot propose to exhibit unless six at least be present. As he intends to leave the town the latter end of next week he hopes those who intend to favour him with their company will do so betwixt [now] and that time.

But Peter had no intention of returning to America. He had scores to settle with the baillies of Aberdeen and the men behind them – the merchants. He had consulted with a lawyer, and 'on a fair relation of my grievances,' Williamson said:

> the injuries I had suffered, appeared to him so flagrant that he did not hesitate to declare his opinion that I was not only entitled to ample damages . . . but that the Court of Session would find no difficulty to award these, with full cost of my suit.

Williamson also had another plan. While he had been making legal inquiries around Old Parliament Close, where the courts were situated, he had noticed that court and commerce worked there cheek by jowl. He resolved to place a foot in both camps.

The Edinburgh that Williamson found in 1758 was not the sprawling city of today. It snaked up the hill from Holyrood Palace to the castle on its volcanic eyrie in a series of close-packed tall buildings made of wood and stone, known as lands, and narrow alleys, known as wynds. The New Town, later built on the other side of the drained Nor' Loch, was in 1758 not even a gleam in the eye of an enterprising provost. So the great and the good rubbed shoulders with the humble and the horrible. They walked the cobbled streets and stepped over gutters filled with filth and excrement, or dodged the not-so-fresh supplies of the same as they were thrown from high windows.

In his time in Aberdeen, Philadelphia, Boston and New York, Williamson would have grown used to the jostle and rush of city streets. He would have had some experience of the press of people as they walked and talked and lounged in doorways and stairways, of merchants hawking their goods and workers plying their trade, of the fishwives, chimney-sweeps and salesmen all bawling their wares. There seemed to be hundreds of them in the streets every day, and it was well known how prone the people of Edinburgh were to mob and riot in the name of religion, to right a wrong or simply because it was something to do. In Williamson's time, the unelected leader of the Edinburgh mob was a hunchbacked Cowgate cobbler named General Joe Smith. The rank was honorary, but no less commanding for that – it is said that local magistrates often consulted with him before making a decision, lest their judgment bring the rage of the streets on their heads.

The men responsible for keeping the peace were the town guards, or the 'town rats' as they were called, because of their faded red uniforms. They patrolled the streets, singly or in pairs, old Highland soldiers mainly, sporting cocked hats and hefting the vicious-looking

Lochaber axe, part hook, part hatchet. Legend had it that the town guard had existed even before the Romans conquered this far north and had joined the invaders in their attempts to pacify the ancient Scots.

Then there were the caddies, the street-runners, who thronged the area round the Cross in the High Street. This army of ragged rascals knew everything about the city: they were its tourist information, courier and newspaper services in one. Their cousins, the chairmen, were the taxi drivers of the day, transporting the dainty and the well-dressed above the murky streets in sedan chairs.

Williamson would have been used to the sight of aristocrats with black servants following at their heels, and that of pigs rooting about unchecked in the detritus on the streets. But the smell would have shocked him, the overpowering stench of the ancient, overcrowded city that, in a few years' time, would be instrumental in deciding those who could afford it to transport themselves across the new bridges to the wide streets and squares of the New Town. There they could enjoy fresher, cleaner air. There they could breathe.

Then there was the weather. Perched as it is among hills and on a salty spit on the wide waters of the firth of Forth, Edinburgh suffered then, as it still does, from exposure to the elements. Writing over one hundred years after Peter's arrival, Robert Louis Stevenson noted about the city:

> She is liable to be beaten upon by all the winds that blow, to be drenched with rain, to be buried in cold sea fogs out of the east, and powdered with the snow as it comes flying southward from the Highland hills. The weather is raw and boisterous in winter, shifty and ungenial in summer and a downright meteorological purgatory in spring.

But the architecture and the ambience of the place were unique. There was the glory of Holyrood Palace and the martial presence of the Castle. The long walk between the two passed noble buildings and squalid slums. There was the gothic splendour of St Giles Cathedral and the crumbling black heart of the Tollbooth, the town jail, the site of which is marked today by an array of stones in the pavement in the shape of a heart. And behind these two was Parliament House, the building that had once been the seat of government but was, by 1758, the centre of the city's principal industry.

It was in the area around these three landmarks that Peter Williamson found not just his livelihood and his home, but also his means of revenge on the magistrates and merchants of Aberdeen.

The Great Hall in Parliament House is an impressive room. Its high, vaulted, oak-beamed ceiling has witnessed many dramas since it was completed in 1639. Then, it was the home of the Scottish parliament, known as the 'Three Estaites' for its mixture of religious leaders, gentry and lay members. The parliament governed until 25 March 1707, when it dissolved itself to merge with Westminster following the Act of Union. The Great Hall then became the Court of Session, the main outlet for Scottish civil justice. Justice in Scotland, though, often leaned towards the person who was richer or stronger. One or two centuries before, it was not uncommon for accused lords to appear with miniature armies at their backs and the presence of these hard-faced, battle-scarred warriors bristling with weaponry was enough to have the charges against their masters dismissed. Bribery, too, was not unusual, with judges accepting money from lawyers in return for favourable decisions. On occasion, judges who were disinclined to accept such inducements failed to appear in court, having been forcibly detained by agents of one party or another.

Such blatant abuses had been stamped out by the mid- to late eighteenth century, but courts, as we have already seen in the example of the baillie court in Aberdeen, could still be guilty of showing prejudice or partiality.

The curious thing about court cases when Williamson arrived in Edinburgh was the apparent bedlam that surrounded them. The Great Hall is a wide open space today, where bewigged and black-robed advocates walk and consult with clients and fellow lawyers. It is a place of calm, of sanctuary. But in the eighteenth century, the Great Hall was a smoky, noisy babel, filled with lawyers shouting their cases, judges yelling them down and men milling about listening to whatever case took their fancy. And if the cases on offer did not spark their interest, or if the advocates needed something to wet their thrapple after a particularly passionate period of pleading, the Great Hall could supply that, too. At the northern end of the hall, cut off from the legal machinations by means of a screen, were a number of stalls, selling books, hats, hardware – and drink.

Peter's plan was to open a coffee house there and serve throat-lubricating liquids – and not just coffee – to the thirsty lawyers, students and hangers-on who daily thronged the hall. Indian Peter's Coffee House was made up of three or four small compartments, giving the impression of privacy. However, anyone wishing to discuss important matters with their lawyer in confidence would have been disappointed, for the walls of the compartments were made of very flimsy material – some simply of brown paper. Despite this, Indian Peter's Coffee House became a firm favourite with lawyers and the literati of the day; Williamson, slowly learning the intricacies of Scots law and, spurred on by the success of *French and Indian Cruelty*, ambitious to write more, was delighted.

One young poet who frequented the coffee house was Robert Fergusson, who had worked as a lowly clerk in an Edinburgh legal office. In his poem *The Rising of the Session*, about the annual vacation of the court in March, Fergusson wrote:

This vacance is a heavy doom
On Indian Peter's coffee-room,
For a' his china pigs are toom;
Nor do we see
In wine the sucker biskets soom
As light's a flee.

But stop, my Muse, nor mak' a main,
Pate disna fend on that alane;
He can fell twa dugs wi' ae bane,
While ither fock
Maun rest themselves content wi' ane,
Nor farer trock.

('China Pigs' were bottles, 'toom' meant empty, a 'sucker biskst' was a sugar biscuit and 'soom' meant swim.)

Robert Burns admired Fergusson's verse a great deal, although the young Edinburgh poet did not live to enjoy the Ayrshire Bard's adulation. He died in 1774, aged only twenty-four, in Edinburgh's lunatic asylum, Darien House, following a severe illness and a fall. When Burns, another Scottish poet destined to die young, visited Edinburgh twelve years later, he acknowledged Fergusson's influence on his own work by seeing to it that a stone was erected on his grave in Canongate Kirkyard.

Williamson thrived in Edinburgh. His bookselling adventures between York and Aberdeen, despite the hurdles thrown in his way by the magistrates, seemed to have sparked in him a flair for business which would help him through the legal battles that lay ahead. He had written two books and would soon have finished more. His coffee house was popular and he opened another tavern in Old Parliament Close. The sign there read 'Peter Williamson, Vintner from the Other

World', and customers were enticed inside by a wooden Indian – a carved statue of Peter in full native dress. This tavern, too, became a regular haunt for lawyers, judges, poets and writers.

These were the days of public executions – it was believed that justice must not only be done to malefactors, but also be seen to be done – and many men, women and children publicly went to their deaths in Edinburgh, either in the Grassmarket or on a raised platform adjacent to the notorious Old Tollbooth, also known as the 'Heart of Midlothian', which loomed beside St Giles Cathedral in the High Street. Depending on the notoriety of the case, the public attendance at these hangings could number just a few dozen or many hundreds and even thousands. Among the regular attendants were the city's baillies and judges, whose custom it was to have a dinner after the drop. This dinner, called the 'deid-chack', was often held at Peter Williamson's Old Parliament Close establishment.

But even as his business interests grew, he had not forgotten his Aberdeen prosecutors and persecutors. In 1760, an action was raised in the Court of Session by 'Poor Peter Williamson, late of the Province of Pennsylvania in North America, Planter, now residenter in Edinburgh, Pursuer against Alexander Cushnie, late Dean of Guild and Procurator fiscal of the burgh Court of Aberdeen, and others'. ('Poor' means that, despite his successful book and his blossoming coffee house, Peter had managed to finagle an early version of legal aid). The Court of Session was told by Williamson's 'doer' (his lawyer) that the Aberdeen procedure and judgment against him was 'most iniquous [sic] and oppressive' and called on the court to reverse the sentence and, in addition, award the pursuer damages and expenses. The court allowed a Proof before Answer (a hearing of evidence) and in September 1760, Williamson was back in Aberdeen making inquiries.

And so began the courtroom battles of Peter Williamson. By the time he was finished – and it would take years – the men behind the kidnapping trade would wish their agents had never lifted that ragged boy from the quayside or, failing that, that they had let him continue selling his book in 1758. For during his inquiries, Peter uncovered a number of secrets – none of which the merchants wished to be made public.

First, though, he had to settle his original score by having the 'iniquous and oppressive' judgment reversed. Their Lordships finally decided in February 1762 that Peter's claim was well founded and ordered the defenders to pay him personally one hundred pounds in damages, as well as making them liable for all costs. It was no mean amount and the defenders – procurator fiscal Cushnie and baillies William Davidson and James Jopp – lodged an appeal, claiming the award was excessive. But the court stuck by its original decision.

However, the magistrates wriggled over payment. In a letter dated 4 February 1764, they were still arguing over the instruction that the cash was to come from their personal fortunes. The letter is addressed to Walter Scott, father of novelist Sir Walter Scott, Writer to the Signet (a judicial officer), and it says:

> We are very sorry to find by yours of the 30th past that there was a sentence pronounced against us in Williamson's process, whereby we are deemed to pay him a very large sum out of our own private pockets.

The Baillies insisted they had acted properly throughout the proceedings in 1758 and claimed they did not know that 'men or boys were ever transported from Aberdeen to America contrary to the law'. When Williamson first appeared in Aberdeen, selling his book in the streets, they claimed:

> [He] had the appearance of an idle stroller, and could give no good account of himself; and had procured this pamphlet to be composed for him of such shocking circumstances, in order

the more easily to impose upon, and draw money from the credulously vulgar.

They went on to say that they took the action against him purely 'to vindicate the character of those we believed to be innocent, and were unjustly reflected upon'. Their verdict was, they insisted, born from 'an error of judgement and not from any sinister design'. They concluded:

> Under the circumstances, you will easily perceive how much
> we were surprised on reading yours, giving an account of the
> sentence against us; and how hard a thing it is to be decerned
> to pay a sum of money, or a fine, for doing what we considered
> to be our duty.

So there it was: the Aberdeen magistrates had arrested and convicted a man without a proper hearing, seized and destroyed his property to protect the good name of men who were most likely their friends, all in the name of duty. Now they were peeved because the Establishment had not stood by them and was forcing them to put their hands in their own pockets. In the end, they managed to wriggle off that particular hook, thanks to the connivance of the Earl of Findlater, Aberdeen's patron, who contrived to help them siphon the money from a fund designed for the common good which was raised by the sale of wrecks off the coastline. Clearly, whatever was good for the magistrates was good for the common people.

The case against Cushnie and the others had opened up a can of worms. Williamson's victory had awakened in him a taste for litigation. But more importantly, his investigations had revealed the names of the businessmen who were behind his kidnapping. And they were his next targets.

Peter Williamson was going back to war.

FIFTEEN

He May Be an Indian King or Any Other Great Man

Patrick Baron was a wright, or carpenter, in Aberdeen, and it was his desire to export to the Colonies some wooden furniture he had made that saw him sucked into the shadowy world of the indentured servant trade.

Being a respected artisan in the town, he knew many of the local dignitaries and merchants, and in April 1743, he was asked by Captain Robert Ragg to help fit out a ship recently arrived from London that was destined for a transatlantic voyage. The ship was the *Planter* and, according to Mr Baron's later deposition:

> [He] happened to have a good deal of wright work on hand, such as chairs, tables, etc. He asked Captain Ragg if he could get these carried to America in said ship and sold there for his behalf. Mr Ragg informed him that he could as the ship was outward bound and not loaded with any heavy cargo.

The carpenter found out that there was a partnership of local worthies, some related to Captain Ragg, involved in sharing the profits of this venture. The men were named as Walter Cochran of Dumbreck, who was at the time town clerk depute of Aberdeen, Baillie William Fordyce, Baillie William Smith, Baillie Alexander Mitchell of Colpna, Captain Ragg himself and Alexander Gordon of Gight, who were each to have a full share. The seventh share was to be split between merchants James Black and John Elphinston. In a letter to lawyer Walter Scott, one of the agents employed to defend the merchants against Williamson, Baron wrote:

> As soon as the ship was purchased, they resolved to send her to North America and as they had no freight outward it seemed it was agreed that they should engage servants, which was a current trade at that time, and they accordingly employed James Smith for that purpose.

Baron, though, had no interest in the ship or its contents, apart from his fitting-out contract and the possibility of sending his tables and chairs for sale in the New World. At the time, he knew nothing, he said, of the engagement of Aberdeen saddler James Smith to procure a cargo of indentured servants. It was not until 29 April that he took a more active interest in the fortunes of the commercial adventure. For it was then that Alexander Gordon of Gight, one of the original partners, dropped out and a full seventh share became available. The other partners wanted him to put up the cash for the missing seventh share and applied pressure. At first, Baron said, he declined the offer 'having no proper knowledge of trade or commerce which was carried on by the other partners', even though they were his 'good friends and intimate acquaintances'. However, Messrs Cochran, Fordyce et al. were not to be dissuaded. Captain Ragg pointed out to Baron that if he took up the offer, he would not have to pay the cost of freight on the outward voyage and would, furthermore, share in the sale of the servants' papers and the tobacco cargo they planned to bring back. The lure of profit proved too strong for the Aberdeen carpenter and he agreed to invest. But, he later insisted:

> Although I took a share of the ship and adventure then, I could not suspect there had been any neglect or informality in the attesting or indenting of the servants as they were all gentlemen of superior knowledge in business to myself.

Thanks to his earlier investigations, Williamson already knew the identities of some of those 'gentlemen of superior knowledge'. They were all local merchants and, in the cases of Cochran and Fordyce, undeniably influential in both local government and local law. He did not know about Patrick Baron and the other men until Cochran and Fordyce very kindly informed him. He had already raised his action when the merchants' doer, John Taylor, wrote to Williamson's, trying to avoid a protracted legal battle. Mr Taylor wrote that he:

> understood from Mr Cochran, one of the Defenders, that they rather chused to end the matter in an amicable way than enter into a Process. I cannot omit writing to you, to let you know this much, that you may converse [with] Williamson . . . and learn what the lowest demand will be for a total discharge without any Process.

Williamson, though, was not to be fobbed off with a paltry amount. The action he had lodged claimed for damages to the then incredible sum of £1,000 plus £200 costs. If he had proved anything in his still short life, it was that he was a fighter. He would not settle. He would have his day in court.

The defenders may have already known the manner of man he was, because in the same letter their lawyer wrote:

> I humbly suggest, that if the summons must be executed, there may be also included in it Alexander Mitchell of Colpna, William Black, son and heir and executor to the deceased James Black, late Baillie here, and Patrick Baron of Woodside, then Wright here, who were all part of this company.

Williamson had no doubts about what the good gentlemen were trying to do. 'The plain meaning . . . was that these gentlemen laid their account with being found liable in very high damages and therefore wanted the number of defenders to be increased, that the proportion of each might be lessened.'

So, a new summons was raised, this time also naming Alexander Mitchell of Colpna and Patrick Baron of Woodside. It was decided not to burden James Black's heirs with the legal battle. According to court papers, by the time the action was settled, only Cochran and Baron were still alive, although the other men's heirs were deemed liable for any share of the damages.

Cochran and Fordyce, directing operations, wished the net to be cast even wider. They admitted that they owned a share of the ship but pointed out that it had made only one voyage before it was lost on the way to Philadelphia. They also admitted 'that there were sundry servants sent out on board the said ship to America' but insisted that 'all these servants were above the years of pupillarity, voluntarily engaged and regularly indented'. They did not believe Williamson was ever taken on board the *Planter* in the manner he claimed, but added that 'if he was, it was done without their knowledge'. They then went on to name more names, and one of them was Captain Robert Ragg, who was a cousin to Cochran and related by marriage to Fordyce. Ragg, along with merchant John Elphinston and baillie William Smith, they claimed, 'had the sole direction of the servants, the defenders not taking anything to do with that branch of the trade'. They insisted that no proceedings could be taken against them unless these three men were 'brought into the field'. Scenting a scandal brewing, the good men of Aberdeen were pointing their fingers in all directions in a bid to deflect the full glare of public and official scrutiny. They had been guilty of supporting and profiting from misery, and now they were facing a very public fall from grace. However, they had resolved that, if they did fall, they would not do so alone.

Cochran claimed he took a share in the ship only to help his relation, Captain Ragg. It was Ragg, he said, who had proposed they take on a cargo of servants. He said:

> It was proposed and thought expedient by the Master and
> some of the owners, in order to defray a part of the outwards
> expense, that servants should be indented and engaged to go
> to America, and their indentures regularly attested, as was
> usual in most of the sea ports of Scotland at that time.

There was, however, no written contract made regarding this agreement, so no one could say exactly which of the owners it was who agreed with Captain Ragg to embark on this commercial adventure.

Cochran confirmed that Aberdeen saddler James Smith was employed to 'engage and indent as many servants as he could procure'. However, he went on to insist that the intention had been for this to be carried out 'in a legal and ordinary way of engaging such, by getting them duly attested and their consents obtained to go to America'. Some of the people engaged by James Smith deserted, Cochran claimed, while others were dispensed with on application. As far as he was concerned, everything was legal and above board. All the servants who embarked on the *Planter* had, as far as he was aware, done so willingly.

Here, then, was the crux of the merchants' defence. The servants on the *Planter* had willingly agreed to go and had been duly attested before a magistrate. It was certainly the case that many of the servants aboard the ship had indeed chosen to make the trip, but that was not Williamson's point. It did not matter how many of his former shipmates were on board out of choice, the point under debate was whether he had been abducted and taken against his will to America. He insisted that he had been; the defenders insisted that he had not. Walter Cochran said that details of the trade in Philadelphia were documented in account books, that these were brought back to Scotland by Robert Ragg and that nowhere in the lists was a lad named Williamson, Williams or McWilliam. Captain Ragg, then living in Chatham, agreed. In a letter from Robert Ragg to Cochran, dated 6 October 1762, it seems clear that the old sailor had no idea that his cousin was in the process of implicating him in the case, for he signs it 'I am, dear sir, your most obliged and affectionate brother, Robert Ragg'. The letter reads:

> I am favoured with yours of 20th of September and am sorry you are out to trouble . . . on Williamson. I do not remember any of that name that went out in the Planter and am certain if he is not mentioned in the account of what was got for the servants indentured (if ever he was indented) he must have run away at Aberdeen or Cape May where the ship was lost and I am sure there was no servant on that ship but what was legalie attested before they went from Aberdeen. I cannot tell if any register is kept at Philadelphia of the sale of servants but I imagine not and shall write Mr Elliot and John Elphinston at Philadelphia to inquire into this affair. Please my compliments to Mrs Cochran . . .'

Patrick Baron, meanwhile, was very unhappy with being implicated by the men he thought of as friends. He thought it 'extremely hard that he should be called as a defender in a summons of this kind' and tried desperately to distance himself from the case, in order that his good name not be splashed by the legal mud about to be thrown in their direction. He applied to the courts to be allowed to:

> state his defence to your Lordships separately from the other defenders who were merchants in the town of Aberdeen and as such had the more immediate management of that particular adventure in which he came to have a very late and innocent share.

Pointing out that Williamson had said he had been kept prisoner since January 1743, Baron emphasised that he had only become involved in the business at the end of April, just prior to the *Planter* setting sail. He wrote:

> I had no concern until the month of April even verbally and till the 29th of April, which is the date of my vendition, it is not possible I could be guilty of the alleged crime of kidnapping him prior to the 8th of January, which is the time he condescends the experience was laid out on him.

He instructed Walter Scott:

> not to make up or settle that affair for me in any manner but either by arbitration or before the proper judges so as I may have an opportunity of laying before them the singularity of my case.

He was supported by evidence from James Smith, who swore that:

> The defender Patrick Baron never spoke to him nor gave him any directions whatsoever about indenting servants to go to

America . . . neither did he know or was informed that the said
Patrick Baron was an owner of the said ship till sometime after
she sailed from the port of Aberdeen.

Walter Scott was of the opinion at this stage that Baron had a case, and
that it was unlikely he would be found liable. He said that it appeared
that any wrong had been done before the carpenter had any
involvement in the business. However, he later changed his opinion,
and Baron's attempt to distance himself from his erstwhile partners
appears to have failed, for his name continued to be linked with those
of Cochran and the others.

They had tried to prevent the action from being raised in the first
place. They had tried to settle out of court. They had tried, and
succeeded, in spreading the blame. Now all that was left to the
defenders was to somehow influence the court.

Williamson, meanwhile, was building up a more complete picture
of the kidnapping trade. And while the defenders continued to insist
there was no documentary evidence of his ever being on the *Planter,* he
knew different. Cochran had claimed Williamson's name did not
appear in any of the books brought back from America, which may
well have been true. He did not mention a book that had never left
Scotland.

Williamson continued to bring forward witnesses to give evidence of
the atrocious trade. Local man Alexander Grigerson said that when he
was a young boy, he was walking with another boy near a birch wood
close to the Kirk of Crathie on Deeside when three men on horseback
approached them. Grigerson stated the men 'said kind words to them'
and offered to 'clothe them like gentlemen' if they came along with
them. But the witness had heard tales of young lads being carried away
and refused to go. The smiles slid from the faces of the men then, and
the honeyed tones left their voices as they threatened that if the boys

would not come willingly, they would take them by force. The two boys ran off and, knowing the area better than the riders, managed to evade capture. From their hiding-place, they saw the men hunt for them for a period, then give up and leave. If there were plenty of other fish in the sea, then it was also true that there were other boys and girls in the country waiting to be reeled in.

Twelve-year-old James Ingram was snatched while running an errand to Aberdeen from the village of Loanhead, about half a mile distant. His mother, Margaret Ross, also provided a deposition, saying she had heard he had been taken by a merchant called Alexander Gray in order to be sold to the plantations and went to visit the man in his shop. She said he took her by the shoulder and threw her out. Eight days later, she attended chapel in Aberdeen's Gallowgate and saw James there. Delighted and relieved to have her son back in her care, she took him home.

A few nights later, as she and her husband lay sleeping, four men came for the boy, who was lying at their feet in the bed. The men insisted the boy had been legally indentured and took the weeping child away from them. Mr Ingram followed them, and he claimed that they took the lad to the home of Alexander Gray. The family went to a magistrate and managed to obtain an order for the boy's return. They found him naked and shivering in Gray's house and the mother carried him away 'covered in her plaid'. She had never consented for her son to be taken, 'even though provisions were very dear and scarce, and many were difficulted to get their bread'.

Later, her son did sell his indentures, this time with her blessing, and after spending several weeks in the tollbooth, finally set sail for the Colonies.

John Kemp, father of the boy Peter Kemp who had been taken at around the same time as Williamson, attested that he knew nothing of any illegal methods being used to induce his son. However, he said that while the *Planter* lay at anchor at Torry, the boy returned to him and was unwilling to go back. Mr Kemp claimed that Captain Ragg and others involved in the trade spoke with him repeatedly in the street, warning him that if he did not send his son back they would come and take him. They also threatened to have Mr Kemp thrown into the tollbooth. As we know, Peter Kemp did return and sailed on the *Planter*. He never claimed that any undue means were brought against him and insisted he received no ill-treatment. At the time of the court case, he recalled a boy named Peter Williamson being on board, but he could not say for certain if the adult male bringing the court action was the same person, although he said he had 'some faint remembrance of his likeness by his eye'. However, he went on to state that he 'neither can nor will swear that he is not the man or that he is the man'.

Sailor William Wilson, though, was certain he was the same person. He had met up with Peter Williamson again quite by chance. Wilson's mother-in-law kept an inn in Leith, and in 1758, he had arrived there to find a man discussing with some gentlemen a voyage from Aberdeen to Philadelphia. The 'particular account given by him of the transactions of that voyage' – including the name of the ship's master and first mate, as well as the death of the young woman and the Highlander on his knees saying a prayer over her body – led the sailor to ask the man his name and he told him it was Peter Williamson. The sailor recalled the 'stout, well-set boy' who used to 'run up the ship's shrouds and come down the ship's stays'.

Alexander Middleton had been apprenticed to Patrick Baron in 1743 and had been assigned to help build the bunks below decks for the servants. He recalled a boy named Peter Williamson being on board, having heard the name being called from a roll at every meal. He said that 'several of the boys used at sometimes to be crying and seemed dissatisfied with their situation and others satisfied'. However, 'at this distance of time', he could not recollect 'whether the pursuer [Williamson] was satisfied or dissatisfied with his situation'. He said that he had 'many times heard many different people in Aberdeen and about that place complaining of the merchants in Aberdeen for transporting poor people's children in the way they did'. He said he had 'heard these people cursing the merchants for these purposes'. Middleton had known of many boys being sent away from the town but said he did 'not know whether they were kidnapped, taken away by force or in what way they were taken off'. He had seen many boys and girls 'confined in barns before they were sent away and he has likewise seen others of them coming out of the prison of Aberdeen to be sent away'. Among those who sailed with the *Planter,* he said, 'there were several of them about the pursuer's age, some of them younger, some of them very young.' However, at the time, 'the victual was dear' and he believed it was 'owing to this and the scarceness of provision that made several go abroad'.

This had been a point raised by the magistrates during *Williamson* v. *Cushnie* and others. They had insisted that if Williamson had in fact been on the ship, he had gone willingly for 'there was a great scarcity in the country' and that he, along with several other boys, 'was obliged to leave his father's house for mere want of bread'. This was disputed by Williamson, who said that 1743 was not a year of famine, while other witnesses said that James Williamson, Peter's father, not only had 'a plough going in Hirnley', but he also had one in Upper Balnacraig. They insisted that Williamson Snr 'was in such circumstances as to keep his children and his family without their being obliged to beg their bread'.

Middleton went on to say that in 1758, he saw Williamson in the streets of Aberdeen selling his book. He believed that he was the same boy he had seen on the *Planter.* The book, he said, was about his travels in America, 'which book,' he went on, 'was quarrelled or found fault with by the then Magistrates of Aberdeen'. Middleton said he had heard that 'by a sentence of these magistrates [the book was] burned by the hands of the common hangman' and also that 'the pursuer was imprisoned and banished the liberties of the city of Aberdeen for publishing and selling the said book'.

Andrew Wilson was employed at the Custom House in Aberdeen in 1758 when he was sent by Baillie Osburn with a shilling to buy a copy of Peter Williamson's book. In the street, he said, he met with local man Thomas Jeffrey and asked him if he had seen the man Williamson who was selling 'a pamphlet' about his adventures in America. Jeffrey wondered if this was the same Peter Williamson that he had under his care some years before. The men found him in Castle Street, and Wilson duly bought his copy then returned to the Custom House to deliver it to the baillie, leaving Williamson and Jeffrey together. Later, he returned to Castle Street to find the men and was told by a cobbler that they had gone to Wylie's tavern but had left word for him to meet them there. He went to Wylie's and found Williamson and Jeffrey together in a room, deep in conversation. He heard Jeffrey declare:

> he knew Peter Williamson to be the same person who he some time ago had under his care in a barn in the Green of Aberdeen, from which barn he was afterwards removed to the Tollbooth of Aberdeen, where Jeffrey also had care of him and where there he had often held him up upon an iron door.

Jeffrey also said that Peter Williamson was taken from the tollbooth and carried to Torry and there put on board Captain Ragg's ship for America. Jeffrey admitted to Wilson that he had been hired by James Smith 'from whom he had got money to take up boys for America'.

The depositions and testimony of witnesses were telling. It was known that the trade in indentured servants existed, for it was a legal enterprise. What was either not known, or not acknowledged, were the lengths to which the merchants and their agents were willing to go to fill the holds. Williamson and his legal advisers produced witness after witness with their own story to tell, or who could corroborate part of their case. The defenders, however, could do little but first deny that Williamson was ever on board the ship and then, when it was proved he was, insist that he went there willingly. That being shown not to be the case, by friends of Peter's father, they resorted to the ancient defence of 'It wasn't me, it was him'.

The most damning piece of evidence against them was the so-called 'kidnapping book', which Walter Cochran had been forced under oath to produce during Williamson's case against Cushnie and others. This was a statement of account between the partners and their agent James Smith that detailed every item of expenditure in regard to the obtaining of the servants and their upkeep until the ship sailed. With regard specifically to Williamson, there were a number of entries: 'Jan 8th one thousand seven hundred and fifty three – To one pair of stockings to Peter Williamson, six-pence; To five days of diet, one shilling and three-pence.' On 17 January there was an entry, 'To the man that brought Williamson, one shilling and six-pence.' And finally, 'To Making two shirts for Williamson, four-pence.' The entire account showed that for the year until May 1743, Smith received over £160 from the partners in respect of his labours. And the entire balance was signed off by none other than Walter Cochran, town clerk depute of Aberdeen.

Smith himself admitted signing the book and also that either John Elphinston or Walter Cochran had approached him with regard to indenting servants for the *Planter*. He was, naturally, adamant that neither of them ever suggested that under-age boys or girls be indentured – nor, of course, was there any mention of kidnapping. He did admit that some of the ungrateful servants, having been fed and clothed at his expense, would try to desert. When caught, he said, the older ones would be confined in prison and the younger people in workhouses or 'poor's hospitals' until their ship sailed. After all, a contract was a contract.

He did not remember who brought Peter Williamson to him, saying that 'the drum was sent through the town of Aberdeen inviting all persons who were disposed to engage as servants to go to America to apply to him'. As a consequence, he believed, both Williamson and Peter Kemp were brought to him. He confirmed that Peter was lodged with Helen Law. However, although he could state categorically that the Kemp boy was engaged with the consent of his father, he could not say the same for Peter Williamson. By the time of the court hearings, twenty years later, he could not tell whether the adult Peter Williamson before him was the same person as the boy from 1743, commenting that as far as he knew 'he may be an Indian King or any other great man'.

The curious thing about the kidnapping book, Williamson said, was that 'there is not one article stated for writing or executing any indenture or contract whatsoever'. It detailed every other expenditure, it seems, but nothing related to appearing before a magistrate and signing off the indentures. It did, however, have one very curious entry, detailing how a John Smith spent one shilling 'with three whores at the Windmill'. As Williamson later said, 'unless it was laid out for the purpose of filling them drunk and then decoying them shipboard' it is not easy to see just what advantage that particular excursion had to the partners. Perhaps, though, the sporting women had been hired to help lure unsuspecting young men into the trade by using their womanly wiles to entice them into drunkenness – and then into pledging their indentures. Or perhaps John Smith had an evening's entertainment on the company expense sheet.

Despite the existence of the account book, it had not been easy to convince some of the witnesses to speak. Williamson claimed that somehow representatives of the defenders had managed to convince his Aberdeen landlord to steal his list of witnesses and the questions he planned to put to them. Many of these witnesses, Williamson complained, were 'prevailed upon to disobey the will of the Diligence, and most of those who appeared on consequence of it were greatly intimidated, having been precognosed by Mr Fordyce, the Defender, who was Justice of the Peace'.

It was not the only dirty trick the defenders would pull during the case.

SIXTEEN

Power Will Not Sanctify Oppression

With his witnesses being suborned and intimidated, Williamson agreed that the case should go to arbitration, which would take place in Aberdeen, rather than a full Court of Session process. With the consent of both sides, advocates John Thain and James Petrie were duly appointed arbiters – the former on behalf of Williamson, the latter for the defenders – with Charles Forbes, sheriff-substitute of Aberdeenshire, being made oversman, or judge-arbiter. Depositions running to nearly one hundred pages were taken from the witnesses who appeared. During this period, Williamson claimed, Mr Petrie 'endeavoured to give a favourable turn to everything that was deposed against the Defenders'. The ship's books were not produced at this time, although Cochran and others were allowed to state that there was nothing relating to Williamson in them. Williamson's patience ran out. He complained to the judges at the Court of Session in Edinburgh and it was agreed between the arbiters that he should be awarded damages. The defenders had always been willing to pay something to make this case go away, the only question was how much. It was then decided that the oversman, Mr

Forbes, who had not been present during the deposition stage, should determine the figure payable.

Here the merchants saw an opportunity to make the whole affair disappear without them having to part with any of their hard-earned silver. Charles Forbes had recently lost his beloved mother and, being a man 'very much addicted to liquor', had marked the funeral and subsequent period of mourning by 'a train of drinking for some days'. With two days to go before the entire affair would have to be referred back to the Court of Session, and therefore pass from their influence in Aberdeen, the merchants put in motion a scheme that made a farce of Scots law.

Whether or not he had got wind of what they planned, Peter got in the first blow. He also knew of Mr Forbes' love of the drink and had taken him for a meal at the New Inn in Aberdeen on Friday night, 12 November 1762. During this dinner party, the inebriated oversman had intimated that he was leaning in Williamson's favour, perhaps both figuratively and literally. He remained at the New Inn until one or two on the Saturday morning when two of his maidservants came to help him home and pour him into bed. However, those acting on behalf of the defenders were not to be outdone. Early on the Saturday, the sheriff-substitute, still under the influence of the previous evening's conviviality, was aroused from his bed by a Colonel Finlayson, a friend of the merchants, and enticed out with the promise of further liquid delights. He was taken, or carried, to the howff (a low drinking den) of a vintner named Campbell, where they had rented a room. There he was plied with spirits, wine and punch, all washed down with the occasional draught of porter.

Forbes had stated that he would render his judgment at 3 p.m. on Saturday in a tavern called Mitchell's. When neither he nor the defenders' doer James Petrie showed up for the appointment, Peter Williamson went round to Forbes' home. Servants told him that their master had left before eight that morning with Colonel Finlayson and had not been seen or heard from since. The servants said that he had been out most of the previous night, which Williamson already knew, and also that at six in the morning he had sent one of them to buy a bottle of brandy. Smelling a gin-soaked rat, Williamson hunted the streets of Aberdeen for the missing man, who, having partaken of a liquid lunch, had settled down to a game of ombre (a three-handed card game using only forty cards of the pack, the eights, nines and tens of each suit being discarded). The game was further enlivened with the quaffing of a bottle and a half of wine, a mug of porter, two bottles of claret, and a mutchkin and a half of rum punch.

By this time, Williamson knew something was seriously amiss. His search had failed to turn up the drink-loving lawyer, any of the defenders or their agents. This 'naturally created a suspicion of their practising upon a man intoxicated with liquor'. The thought would not have been too far from his mind because that was exactly what he had been doing the previous evening. Finally, he was told that Mr Forbes was in Campbell's with supporters of the merchants and he immediately rushed round. The defenders had expected this and the landlord had been told not to let Williamson through the door – or anyone else for that matter. Having been rebuffed, Williamson alerted his lawyer, John Thain, who accompanied him back to the howff. Thain told Campbell that he knew Mr Forbes was inside and said he wished to speak with him. Campbell shook his head. Thain said that he was acting under orders from the Court of Session and that he had a very important piece of evidence in his pocket – namely the kidnapping book – which Mr Forbes had to see before he made judgment. The landlord was unimpressed by the authority of the court and not at all interested in how much evidence the lawyer had in his pocket. He had been well paid to keep people away from the drinking session upstairs, and he intended to keep to his contract. He told Thain that he was under no obligation to tell anyone which gentlemen were in his house. Confronted by a publican used to dealing with rowdy drunks and determined not to let him pass, there was little Thain could do. He left the sheriff-substitute to his drinking.

No one knows how long Charles Forbes remained in Campbell's howff or how he managed to survive the superhuman drinking session. He was found the following day in his own bed, not dead but dead drunk. Later, lawyer David Morice read out Forbes' decree finding in favour of the merchants at Aberdeen's Town Cross. Unsurprisingly, the sheriff-substitute himself was not long for this world. He died soon after this incident.

Williamson, outraged at either the disgraceful process or the fact that he had been outdone, knew he had lost the battle. The war, though, was a different matter.

Back in Edinburgh, where the law could not be so readily influenced by the merchants, the baillies or their friends, Williamson lodged a complaint with the Court of Session over the way Forbes' judgment, the Decreet-Arbitral, had been reached. The sheriff-substitute, he said, 'was so much intoxicated with liquor, as rendered him incapable of any judgement at all'. Cochran, Fordyce and the others fell back on a 1695 act which dictated that no Decreet-Arbitral could be reduced on grounds of iniquity, but only for bribery, corruption or falsehood on the part of the judge-arbiter. Williamson's answer was that when an oversman had made his determination to the best of his judgement, however erroneous or unjust that may be, it was true that his decree could not be overturned. However, in this case, Forbes had not heard any witnesses nor viewed any of the evidence. His decision had been taken – and, in fact, the decree actually signed – while representatives of one side of the argument were pouring vast quantities of alcohol down his throat. That decree stated that he had heard both parties, considered the proof, and had God and good conscience before his eyes. He had not seen the kidnapping book nor the ship's books and had not spoken to Williamson or Mr Thain while he was in the clutches of the defenders' friends. If that was not falling into corruption and falsehood, then Williamson did not know what was.

With the case now back before their Lordships at the Court of Session in Edinburgh, the merchants found matters less to their liking. They were determined that the ship's books were not to be scrutinised and could not understand that their word and the word of their doers that there was nothing in them relating to Peter Williamson was not enough. John Fraser acted on their behalf and said he had the 'Book of Accounts and Clearance of the Prices and Expenses of sundry ships, and of the produce of sundry voyages', beginning in March and April 1740 onwards. Among them was an account of a proposed voyage in April 1743 from Aberdeen to Maryland of the ship *Planter,* Robert Ragg, Master. Fraser stated that he had:

> read over the several accounts, clearances with all the other particulars wrote in said book as carefully as he could, but could not discover therein any one word or article relating to Peter Williamson, nor is the name Peter Williamson or any person of the name Williamson or McWilliam insert or wrote in this book, from the beginning to the end of it, as far as the Deponent can discover and that is the truth.

Williamson's doer wanted the books produced in court, but the other side objected to this. They did, however, offer to let any 'proper person' view them and report if there was anything in them relevant to Williamson. It was suggested that Williamson's agent, Alexander Gordon, inspect them, but the defenders said they would rather have his advocate (an agent or doer was the equivalent of a solicitor and could not speak in certain courts) look at them because 'these books contain the secrets of their trade; and as a client can use greater freedom with his agent than his lawyers, he might prevail upon him to be more communicative than they would be'.

By November 1764 – two years after Forbes' Decreet-Arbitral – not one of Williamson's representatives had seen the ship's books. The defenders still insisted they would be of no use to his case, citing their own lawyer's deposition that he could find no mention of him. This was not good enough for Williamson's team, and on 3 November, the court heard that:

> The Petitioner [Williamson] does not, in the least, doubt Mr Fraser's veracity or attention, but yet he would still incline to see the books; for as mention is several times made of the Petitioner in the kidnapping book kept by Smith, and as it has been proved beyond all possibility of contradiction that the Petitioner was one of those transported to America in the ship Planter, it is very surprising that his name should not make its appearance as well as the names of his fellow passengers; and if it is true that he is not mentioned in these books the Petitioner can account for it not otherwise than by supposing that they have undergone a reformation since the commencement of this Process against the Magistrates of Aberdeen. That is, he imagines, that as these Magistrates cut out from his book such leaves as have given them umbrage, so the Defenders, in imitation, have removed from the Ship's books such leaves or pages as they foresaw might be troublesome to them in their cause.

Williamson had been told that his name did appear in these books before his legal war had begun. Now he was being told it did not appear. He wanted the books produced to see if they had been amended in any way. If it appeared that they had been mutilated, then it was clear that the defenders had made false depositions, and the oversman had made his judgment based on false evidence. Again, the merchants were willing to allow any 'proper person' appointed by the court to view the books:

but they can by no means agree that this whole book should be produced which contains the secrets of a variety of transactions carried on by them in the course of trade and it is imagined that the pursuer will not insist on such an unreasonable demand.

Finally, the court appointed Robert Leith, depute clerk of session, to view the ship's books, holding the view that 'secrecy of mercantile transactions after twenty years was not a sufficient reason for withholding them'.

If it was true that Williamson's name did not appear in the ship's accounts, then the question of what the merchants had to hide arises. Was their refusal – which lasted at least six years – merely a legal tactic designed to delay the process for as long as possible? Or was there something in those accounts that they did not want scrutinised, whether relating to Williamson or not? Would the turning over of the books turn over a stone that hid some unpleasant facts about their business? Had there been bribes or some other underhand dealings that the accounts would reveal?

Unfortunately, these questions cannot be answered, as the papers relating to Williamson's case do not contain details of what, if anything, was found in the accounts. Williamson himself never mentions them in his own writings, so it may be safe to assume that the ship's books, if they were ever seen by anyone outside the merchants' inner circle, did not assist him in his case.

He had, though, managed to prove to the satisfaction of their Lordships of the Court of Session that he had been wronged. His parade of witnesses, the skulduggery with Forbes, perhaps the ship's accounts, but certainly the kidnapping book, all combined to convince them that his case was proved. On 3 December 1768, their Lordships recalled the late Sheriff-Substitute Forbes' judgment and awarded Williamson damages of £200 plus 100 guineas (£105) costs.

It fell far short of Williamson's £1,000 claim, but it was still a sizeable amount, and, for Williamson, it was an end to his long battle for justice.

So, twenty-five years after he was first abducted, ten years after he was brought to task by the magistrates of Aberdeen and six years after Sheriff-Substitute Forbes pronounced against him, Peter Williamson had finally had his revenge on the men behind his transportation to America. In a later edition of *French and Indian Cruelty*, he added an account of his legal adventures which ended with a vote of confidence in the Scottish legal system, confidence which, in his case at least, was not ill-founded. The passage was also a stirring call to arms for anyone who felt oppressed by the rich and powerful:

> I shall trouble the reader no farther on the subject, my chief intent in publishing this narrative of my Process being to warn gentlemen in power and station not to abuse them by a lawless exercise of their authority against the poor and innocent – for they may be assured that power will not sanctify oppression, nor will justice be hoodwinked by riches. On the other hand, the weak and friendless need not despair of obtaining redress, though groaning under the yoke of tyranny: let them have but the resolution to apply to the College of Justice; Providence will throw friends in their way, their oppressors shall hide their heads and the cruelties they have committed be retaliated upon them.

It could be argued that by taking him from the streets of Aberdeen as they had in 1743, the merchants and the men who worked for them did Peter Williamson something of a favour. Had he remained in Scotland it was likely that he would have become a farmer like his father. Had he not been a success in that field, he might have moved with his family to a city like Aberdeen, Perth, Glasgow or Edinburgh and gone into trade. He might even have ultimately emigrated from Scotland to the American colonies.

But now, aged thirty-eight, here he was in Scotland's capital. He had suffered, it is true, but he had also capitalised on his life and adventures, both real and imaginary, in print and in court. He had set himself up in business. He had also married for a second time. There is an entry in the Edinburgh records stating that a Peter Williamson, keeper of the American Coffee House, married Jean Colin, daughter of deceased John Colin, farmer, in Old Greyfriars parish, on 7 September 1760. What happened to this woman is unclear, for eleven years later he was married again, this time to a woman who would bear him children but also cause him great hardship. With the closure of the case against the Aberdeen merchants, Peter might have thought himself free of the courts, but he was wrong. He had one more major legal adventure to live through. Before that, he had progress and innovations to make in the commercial world.

SEVENTEEN

Fleet on the Wings of the Penny Post

Poet Robert Fergusson had noted Peter Williamson's ability to 'fell twa dugs wi' ae bane'. This referred to the fact that he did not depend solely on his coffee house within Parliament House for income. He had a writing career that began with the various editions of *French and Indian Cruelty* and continued with the aforementioned *Considerations on the present State of Affairs*. In 1768, he produced *The Travels of Peter Williamson among the different Nations and Tribes of Savage Indians of America*, which was on sale in his coffee house as well as, the title page records, 'R. Fleming, Bookseller at the Cross, and by other booksellers in Great Britain and Ireland'. This ambitious work shows that Williamson was never one to shy away from expressing his views on any subject while also using his experiences, great and small, to their fullest advantage. The book was split into three separate parts, part one detailing his 'Travels among the Indians of America', part two being 'A concise view of the whole world' and the final part, predictably given his recent trials and tribulations, 'Some general observations on Submissions and Decreets-Arbitral'.

The book also contained an illustration of 'Williamson's New Machine for the Reaping of Corns', which became known as the basket scythe. He had devised this in 1762, writing to the *Evening Courant* that the scythe 'in the hands of a single man would cut more oats than six shearers'. In his *Travels* he wrote:

> As I have yet a few of these machines unsold . . . gentlemen may be furnished with them by applying to me at my house in the westermost entry to the Parliament-Close, Edinburgh, where their orders will be thankfully received and punctually observed by their most obedient and humble servant, P. Williamson.

Early on, he realised that the real money was made not just in writing books, but in printing and publishing them as well. His attempts to learn the printing trade were rebuffed by the established tradesmen in the town who, any Masonic connections nothwithstanding, protected the secrets of their business jealously. However, as he had already proved, Peter Williamson was not a man to be so easily discouraged, so in 1769, he bought a portable printing press in London, set it up in his coffee house, and proceeded to teach himself the intricacies of the trade. One of the first works to come off this press was a poem entitled *Mob Contra Mob or The Rabblers Rabbled* by Dundee poet William Meston. On producing the pamphlet, priced sixpence, Williamson could not resist cheekily dedicating it to the printers of Edinburgh:

> It is true I was not bred a printer; but upon trial you will find me as alert a scholar and as forward to learn the business as any in your profession. When I brought down my portable printing presses from London I applied to some of your

geniuses for instruction; but I found you like the priest who could not pray out of his own pulpit. From your backwardness to assist me I was obliged to set my own inventions to work, which a learned lawyer tells me is mighty good; and thus I soon acquired the mystery of printing, to the amaze [*sic*] and astonishment of you all. I find, however, that I cannot be so much benefited by learning the mechanical part of printing as by that mysterious part of the business you have lately discovered, of increasing your news-papers to an enormous size, and yet, as by the art of Leger-de-main, to make them contain less matter than they did before. One of the most valuable branches of the trade is to keep the public as ignorant of the art as possible . . .

He promised that he would obey their rules by not disclosing the secrets of the trade to outsiders, but he could not pass up the opportunity for a further swipe at the overly secretive printing brotherhood: 'For my part I was born in Aberdeenshire, where it is thought a crime to be honest; and I think such precepts the best lesson a printer can get.'

He went on to publish editions of his own writing, books of Psalms, editions of the works of Scots poet Sir David Lindsay of the Mount, a volume by Voltaire and various pamphlets. A curious addition to his publications list is described in an advertisement published in 1773 in which Williamson proudly proclaims that he is selling at his premises in the Luckenbooths:

in packs, or in two books, the Impenetrable Secret, or proverb cards, price six pence, which discovers one's thoughts in a surprising manner, and are extremely useful for enticing youth to read as well as innocent amusement for all ages, being a collection of moral sentiments.

By 1773, he had apparently given up his lucrative coffee house ventures and was concentrating solely on his even more successful printing business. He had, as we have seen, opened premises in the Luckenbooths, the small shops, often little more than stalls, that lined the High Street opposite St Giles Church. Similar stalls were crammed up against the church walls themselves and operated around the dark stones of the Old Tollbooth that formed an island in the High Street very close to the church and Parliament Square.

But, not content with elbowing his way in to existing trades, Peter Williamson began to show a knack for innovation. It was in 1773 that he published *Williamson's Directory for Edinburgh, Canongate, Leith and Suburbs*, the very first Edinburgh directory, which contained not just a list of the magistrates of the College of Justice, but also of those citizens and businesses who had agreed to give their names and addresses, arranged alphabetically and according to occupation. It was in the first edition that he announced that 'he has entirely left off the business of a vintner' and was to devote his time and attention solely to the business of printing and bookselling. He did urge his regulars to remain loyal to his successor, though.

However, within a year, he had broken his promise. Although he did not return to the purveying of coffee and spirits, he did introduce yet another first for the city. While he had been operating his coffee house, he had found that he was regularly called upon to deliver notes and letters to members of the legal profession, eventually employing someone whose sole task it was to deal with these requests. It occurred to him that there was considerable profit to be made by extending this unofficial and limited letter-carrying system to include ordinary businesses and members of the public. Never one to let a money-making opportunity go by, Williamson developed the idea of a penny post for the city.

The notion of a penny post was not a new one in Britain. There had been a public postal service since 1635, when Charles I had realised that cash could be made for his coffers by throwing the existing Royal post service open to the public, although those who took advantage of the service were mainly merchants and aristocrats. However, it was not until 1680 that a London merchant named William Dockwra developed the idea of a cheap service for the capital. In Dockwra's scheme, postage was pre-paid by the sender – and not by the receiver as had previously been the case – and the letters and packets were delivered daily and often within the hour. He established offices across the city to receive and sort the mail, and the basic charge was as low as a penny. He operated his highly successful service for two years before the government realised it could benefit from the business and took it over, giving him a life pension for his trouble.

Williamson would certainly have known about this success in London, although the idea of a penny post had not yet extended to the rest of the country. He planned to introduce such a scheme for Scotland's capital, and in his 1774 *Directory* he proclaimed:

> The Publisher takes this opportunity to acquaint the public that he will always make it his study to dispatch all letters and parcels, not exceeding three pounds in weight, to any place within an English mile to the east, south and west of the Cross of Edinburgh and as far as south and north Leith every hour of the day for one penny each letter or bundle.

Basing his new service in his Luckenbooths premises, Williamson convinced seventeen shopkeepers across Edinburgh to become official receiving stations for letters. These included his own premises in Swan's Close, which acted as the General Post Office, as well as the shop of bookseller John Wilson in front of the Exchange, James Grant's grocer's shop in Halkerstson's Wynd and John Anderson's grocery in Chalmer's Court. Thirteen other businesses in Bristo Street, Cowgate, Grassmarket, Canongate, Calton, St Andrew's

Street, James Court and in Leith all signed on. He also hired six men at a rate of pay of four shillings and sixpence per week, to be full-time porters, or caddies, giving them a hat with the words Penny Post sewn on. He developed a system of stamps for each letter, either 'Penny Post Paid' in red or 'Penny Post Not Paid' in black. The stamps were of a circular design, very similar to modern-day postmarks. The system was immediately popular with lawyers, excise officers and local government officials. Soon, though, the reading and writing general public realised they had an economical and fairly efficient postal service on their doorstep.

Like all good ideas, Williamson's penny post became a target for men whose imagination could not actually come up with such a scheme but could stretch to imitation and even theft. His postmen were lured away to rivals and, it is said, even physically attacked, while customers were poached by less dependable deliverers with promises of a more efficient service and cheaper rates. Williamson was finally forced to urge his customers to ensure they gave their letters and parcels only to his uniformed caddies or authorised agents.

Even though his penny-post business was thriving, Peter did not ignore his publishing interests. In March 1776, he launched *The Scots Spy or Critical Observer*, a weekly newspaper packed with local information and gossip. As a means of thanking the many lawyers who had helped him in his legal battles – and also, it has to be said, by frequenting his coffee houses – he dedicated the first edition to 'Henry Dundas, of Melville, Esquire, Dean of the Faculty of Advocates; and to the other members of that most respected body'. The *Spy* was not the success he might have hoped, however, and ran only until August that year before it disappeared from the streets. The following year, he resurrected the notion and launched it again. This time it lasted only from August to November before it vanished for ever.

By now a tall, portly, prosperous-looking figure, Peter Williamson was one of the best-known men in the city. His penny post was immortalised in Fergusson's poem 'Codicile to Rob Fergusson's Last Will':

> To Williamson and his resetters
> Dispersing of the burial letters
> That they may pass with little cost
> Fleet on the wings of the Penny Post.

Cumbernauld-born James Wilson, a poet and satirist now long forgotten, dedicated his 1766 *Miscellanies in Prose and Verse,* written under the pen name Claudero, to Peter. He wrote:

> To Peter Williamson of the Mohawk nation, alias the Indian King; bookseller in Edinburgh; keeper of the American Coffee House there; Inventor of the Reaping Machine, of the Mariner's Diving-Box etc; author of the book entitled French and Indian Cruelty; Prosecutor of the Aberdeen Kidnappers; planner of the American conquest; exhibitor of the Indian dress; the scalping knife, tomahawk, war dance and death bellow; Trumpeter-General for Free-masons and Jack of all trades in Edinburgh, etc, etc.'

Peter was doing well for himself. His marriage to Jean Colin had ended, either through death or divorce, and on 10 November 1771, while still listed simply as 'vintner in New North parish', he took a third wife, Jean Wilson. She was daughter to the bookseller John Wilson who would agree two years later to be one of the authorised collection points for his penny post. She has been described as 'an energetic woman', who for sixteen years was 'an exemplary wife'. Energetic she certainly was, for she bore Peter nine children, although only four survived, while also pursuing her trade as a mantua-maker (a dressmaker). In an advertisement on the cover of her husband's 1788 *Directory,* it was proclaimed that:

> Mrs Williamson and her daughter at the house, first forestair above the head of Byres Close, engrafts silk, cotton and worsted stockings, makes silk gloves, and every article in the engrafting branch, in the neatest manner and on the most reasonable terms; likewise silk stockings washed in the most approved stile; also Grave Cloaths made on shortest notice.
>
> Orders given in at the General Post Office, Luckenbooths, will be punctually attended to.

By that time, though, Peter had discovered that, energetic though she may have been, she had become far from exemplary in expending some of her energies. And the resulting scandal threatened to deprive him of everything that he had worked so long and so hard to build.

EIGHTEEN

. . . Where She Used to Meet with Lewd and Wicked Men

It is part of popular crime legend that William Brodie, formerly Deacon of the Wrights and town councillor of Edinburgh, and latterly thief, died on a gallows of his own design. But as is the case with most legends, that is some way off the truth. Brodie, a celebrated cabinetmaker, had perhaps been interested, as part of his public work, in improving the system of judicially dispatching felons, but he did not build the new trapdoor gibbet on the platform jutting from the west end of the Tollbooth. He did, though, show a professional interest in how the mechanism worked before he himself put it to the test.

Brodie had been a respected tradesman and politician in the city. He had inherited his cabinetmaking business from his father, as well as a healthy bank balance and some property. When Robert Burns visited the city, he stayed in apartments beside Deacon Brodie's. Without a doubt, Peter Williamson, living in Byres' Close opposite the Tollbooth and just a short stretch of the legs from the Deacon's home in Brodie's Close, would have been acquainted with the thieving worthy. Peter liked a drink or two, a fact that would soon be made very public, as did Deacon Brodie. Peter was also known to enjoy the city's nightlife in the company of low-life adventurers, as did Brodie.

The city streets changed as darkness fell. By day, the High Street was a bustling hive of open trade and industry; by night, it was no less industrious but more furtive. As the 'town rats' banged the ten o'clock drum, the lawyer had already set aside his wig, the merchant his account book, the street trader his stall or barrow and taken to the tavern for his recreation. Meanwhile, the night people took the place of the businesspeople on the cobbles. Robert Fergusson, in his poem *Auld Reekie*, wrote:

> Near some lamp-post, wi' dowy face,
> We' heavy ein, and sour grimace,
> Stands she that beauty lang had kend,
> Whoredom her trade, and vice her end.
> But see wharenow she wuns her bread
> By that which Nature ne'er decreed;
> And sings sad music to the lugs,
> 'Mang burachs o' damn'd whores and rogues . . .

The prostitutes plied their trade in street and tavern and, of course, bawdy-house. In 1763, it appears there were only about five or six such houses of pleasure in Edinburgh, but within twenty years, they had spread to every corner of the city. In 1775, there was even a list drawn up to tell the city's young dandies where they could go for the best professional female companionship. *Ranger's Impartial List of the Ladies of Pleasure in Edinburgh* was a kind of league table of the best practitioners of their art. From it we learn that Betty Clark at Miss Walker's was 'about 21, of the middle size, red hair and very good teeth'. Flame-haired Betty was 'far from disagreeable' but had a 'sulky temper, which sometimes cools the keenest desire even in the height of their mutual embraces'. However, she was known for giving a lover 'the utmost satisfaction, as she understands the power of friction admirably well'.

Short, brown-haired Jenny Stewart also possessed good teeth. This nineteen year old could be found at Mrs Young's and was voted 'the entire mistress of her trade'. Molly Jones was 'about 20, rather short, good complexion, brown hair and very good natured'. Based in the Cowgate Port, she was known to 'give general satisfaction in the Critical Minute'. Miss Fraser at Miss Nairn's establishment was 'as pretty a little filly as ever man clapped leg over'. Little more than sixteen years old, her youth and beauty had already brought her 'a great many admirers and she is of so good a disposition that she does her best to oblige them all'.

In the main, taverns, not to mention brothels, were not well-lit establishments of open aspect to the street. They were found down back wynds and up closes: windowless, airless, dark places where men and women came to drink and debauch. The houses were open to people of all classes, for such places have always been democratic when it comes to making a profit. Here the judge and the lord rubbed shoulders with the criminal and the vagabond. The merchandise on offer ranged from high-quality brandy imported, or smuggled, from France to spirits that were little better than rubbing alcohol. Some of the beer was no less potent – *Chambers Traditions* states that Younger's Edinburgh Ale 'almost glued the lips of the drinker together, and . . . few, therefore, could despatch more than a bottle'. Food was also available, oysters being a favourite among all classes, served by a fat landlady with arms like wings or a thin waif who could be tempted, if the price were right, to pleasure a man in some back room, if the establishment was that way inclined. Meanwhile, the landlord, if one existed, for often it was a woman who owned the house, served the drink, and kept the tally and a watchful eye on the often boisterous clientele. Whether he was an old soldier, proudly displaying his scars and amputations, or a man bred to the trade, the tavern keeper became a well-known figure in the town and the keeper of many a secret.

The literati and legal elite formed themselves into clubs for gaming, drinking and educated debate. The young dandies, known as 'macaronies', got themselves liquored up and took to the streets for fun and frolics. They might find themselves a whore or a game of cards, or perhaps a thrilling cockfight. And as dawn broke, they and the judges and nobles, all drunk as lords, could be found weaving their way home, in Fergusson's words, 'some to porter, some to punch, some to their wives and some their wench'.

Whether Peter was addicted to gambling, in particular the barbaric sport of cockfighting which was then popular, is not known, but the seemingly upright William Brodie most certainly was. He was also something Peter was not – a successful burglar. His luck ran out, however, for on 1 October 1788, having been found guilty of robbing the Excise Office, he was hanged in front of a jeering crowd on the Tollbooth platform.

The event was the talk of the city, Brodie's fall from grace being a very public one. At around the same time, the seeds of another public scandal were being sown. For, according to witnesses in a divorce case heard the following year, it was while Brodie was in the Tollbooth – fashioning a draughts board out of the flagstones of his cell to pass the time until the drop – that Jean Wilson, the wife of Peter Williamson, was proving that her energies had led her far from the marital bed.

It was in the autumn of 1788 that Peter Williamson first brought his divorce suit against the mother of his children before the Commissary Court of Edinburgh, which had had jurisdiction in matrimonial disputes since the Middle Ages. He told the lay members of the divorce court hearing his case that his wife had 'cast off all fear of God and forgetting all her conjugal vows and engagements has for these several years bygone followed a tract of keeping fellowship, company and society with Godless, lewd and abandoned men'. She had also been 'breading, entertaining and conversing with them privately and adulterously alone at bed and board'.

Furthermore, he claimed she had for the past twelve months:

> been in the practice of frequenting different houses of bad fame within this city and neighbourhood where she used to meet with lewd and wicked men to whom she gave the use of her body carnally and in which houses she has often got herself intoxicated with liquor.

Jean's adulterous practices, the suit continued, were also carried on in the family home:

> [She] appointed such lewd and wicked men to call upon her . . . and did there retire with them to a chamber where in there was but one bed and where upon different occasions she has allowed such men to have carnal knowledge of her and did otherways privately, familiarly and adulterously converse with them.

Jean Wilson did not take the accusations lying down. She stated that she had been 'married to the pursuer these seventeen years during which they have had nine children, four of whom are alive, three sons and a daughter'. One of the sons was at the time in the Heriot's Hospital, a boarding school, and the other three children were living with their mother.

She pointed out that since her marriage she had continued her work as a mantua-maker to help provide for her family and 'had the happiness to be countenanced and employed in sundry families of rank and respectability, among many others of a lower station'. Her husband, she claimed, had not been as hard-working. Had he, she said in her statement:

> been disposed to be equally as assiduous and attentive in his business as a printer and master of a penny post office, which he still carries on, besides the profits from his annual publication of his Edinburgh Directory, they might have done very well together.

Peter Williamson, she alleged, had given himself up to:

> tippling and intoxication with mean and low people so that he was generally abroad at night till two or three in the morning and in this dissipated way the profit arising from his occupation was habitually spent and dissipated.

He had also 'contracted the habit of groundless jealousy' against his wife.

Jean Wilson described herself as being 'naturally of an affable and cheerful temper' and her business dealings often meant she had to call into the homes of her customers while some of those clients had occasion to call on her at home. 'This has been unhappily construed into criminality without any ground or foundation whatever,' she asserted. It was her husband's drinking cronies, bearing her ill will, who had convinced him that she was committing adultery.

She challenged Peter to name particular men with whom she had been unfaithful and to submit a list of dates and places when and where the infidelities had taken place. She was entitled to know just who he believed she had been sleeping with, 'otherwise no married woman be she ever so chaste and virtuous can be safe'. Meanwhile, she pointed out, she and her fourteen-year-old daughter were 'reduced to great hardship and distress', so she also wanted the court to order her husband to pay an aliment to allow her to conduct her defence.

Jean had made a number of accusations which, Peter Williamson noted, were 'reflections which in prudence she ought not to have made'. Her problem was that, though it might well be true that Peter enjoyed a dram or two, she could not lodge any proof. As for Jean and her daughter suffering hardship, Peter pointed out that both of the women in his family were accomplished mantua-makers and, as such, were capable of earning more than he – his daughter alone was able to bring in twenty shillings a week, which sum his wife pocketed. In addition, he claimed, far from his drinking away the profits of the penny post, he had lately had them greatly reduced by his wife and her father, who had set up in opposition, entering into an agreement with some of his own caddies to lure business away. She had also accused him of selling the family furniture, but the truth was that she and her father had 'carried off privately everything that was valuable and left not sufficient to pay the rent'.

Peter Williamson claimed he had gone from the condition of a reasonably wealthy businessman to that of a near-pauper. He was now again on the Poor's Roll, the benefits scheme, and had been forced by his wife's action to 'betake himself to strange lodgings, separated from his wife and family, destitute of every necessary of life, and his substance called in question by his creditors'. The court came down on his side and refused to order him to make any payment, but they did reserve the right for Jean Wilson to apply to the Poor's Roll herself for assistance.

The court deemed it necessary to hear witnesses in the suit. Peter Williamson cited nineteen individuals, but only nine were heard. His wife, on the other hand, had none to call. Each of the nine witnesses examined were 'solemnly sworn kneeling with their right hand on the Holy Evangil, purged of malice and partial counsel'. One by one, they painted a far from rosy picture of the Williamson household – and of the woman of the house. In what follows, the pursuer is Williamson, the defender his wife.

Euphan Stewart, aged twenty-two, said he had entered the service of Peter Williamson on the first day of the races at Leith in 1788 and had left it at Martinmas (11 November). He told the court that he remembered 'frequently seeing David Stephen, trunk maker in Edinburgh, come frequently to the pursuer's house and always at times when the pursuer was far from home'. Stewart went on to say that 'on such occasions the defender and David Stephen sometimes went into the dining room by themselves where there was a concealed bed and sometimes into the defender's bedroom, shutting the door behind them'. The former servant said that the couple 'sometimes continued together for two hours'.

He said that the first instance that led him to 'suspect something criminal betwixt David Stephen and the defender' was when she came home one afternoon from her shop and sent him 'to desire David Stephen to come to her'. Stewart was puzzled by the nature of the relationship, however. He said that Jean Wilson used to say that Stephen 'was a bad man and using his wife ill'. The fact that she 'chused to be so much in his company' deepened his suspicions that there was something going on between them, so after he had followed his orders and fetched Stephen, he resolved to do what any self-respecting servant would – he snooped. After the man and woman went into Jean's bedroom, closing the door behind them, he waited for a few minutes then looked through the keyhole. He said he saw them sitting on two chairs and that 'Stephen [was] sitting close to the defender with his hands about her neck and likewise observed him put his hand into her breast'.

Asked when this took place, Euphan Stewart replied that it was at the time of Brodie's execution, October 1788. This occasion, he claimed, was not the only time he had been sent with messages to David Stephen. He was despatched three or four times with letters to the man's shop, and although Stephen was not always there to receive them, he always came to the house quickly.

The couple also met in other places. A Mrs Tait kept a public house in Bell's Wynd, near the Cross in the High Street, which, Stewart believed, 'has the character of being a house of bad fame'. Jean Wilson had received two or three messages to visit Mrs Tait at her house and 'she went accordingly'. Naturally, this could have been in the furtherance of her business – she mentioned the grafting of silk stockings and the altering of one or two gowns – but Euphan Stewart was unconvinced, for there were other such establishments where he believed she was a regular.

At around 6 p.m. on the Monday following Brodie's hanging, Jean Wilson said she was going to visit a Mrs Rigg of Morton at the Meadows. Later, Stewart had to go to Peter Williamson's office in the Luckenbooths with a message and caught sight of his mistress going down Forrester's Wynd and disappearing into a stairway. While he waited in the office for Mr Williamson, he saw David Stephen looking in, then 'up to the windows of the Pursuer's house, which is situated at the upper end of the Luckenbooths on the northside. The office or shop is on the opposite side and farther down the street.' Stephen then went into the same stairway at the end of Forrester's Wynd. At eight that evening, Jean Wilson came into Peter Williamson's office and demanded a shilling. When he refused to give it to her, she sent one of his men to the shop of a Mrs Bowie nearby to borrow it. With the shilling in her hand, she set off again for Forrester's Wynd and did not return until midnight when she was 'much the worse for liquor'.

According to Euphan Stewart, at the first door of the stair at the foot of Forrester's Wynd there was a 'house of bad fame' kept by a Miss Lockhart. Jean Wilson did, in fact, know two families who lived above the bawdy house, but she had not been to see them that night. Euphan Stewart knew this for a fact because he had taken it upon himself to make inquiries. He was convinced that she was not only overly familiar with David Stephen but was also overly fond of the bottle. 'The defender is mostly abroad and very seldom come home before eleven o'clock,' he said, 'and was always the worse for liquor.' She also sometimes sent him out for more drink when she came home.

David Stephen was called as a witness and was circumspect about his involvement, although he did admit to receiving letters and notes from the defender. He also admitted that he knew the woman 'had carnal knowledge of a man different from her husband'. Although he declined to name the man, or confess his own involvement outright, he did state that 'his knowledge of the above circumstance is not derived from the information of others'.

Euphan Stewart's predecessor was Elizabeth Robertson, who was around sixteen years of age when she entered the Williamson's service at the beginning of 1787. She stayed with them until the summer of 1788, before the first race was run at Leith. She confirmed Jean Wilson's habit of going out at night, claiming to be visiting customers, namely Mrs Rigg of Morton's or Mrs Tait in Bell's Wynd. But the young woman said that her mistress 'used ordinarily to come home about eleven or twelve at night and was sometimes the worse for liquor'.

The maidservant recalled one night when Jean Wilson went out 'betwixt eight and nine to Mrs Tait's house to keep her husband's birthday'. At around midnight, Elizabeth called at the Tait establishment to accompany her employer home and was kept standing in the kitchen until between one and two in the morning, during which period she was cursed by a drunk man. The very right and proper young woman decided that this was beyond the call of duty, so she left Bell's Wynd and whatever nocturnal adventures her mistress was getting up to and returned to the Williamsons' house in Byres' Close. The front door was locked, but Peter opened it for her and let her in, no doubt noting that his wife was not with her. The maid went to her bed right away and did not know when Jean Wilson came home.

This witness said that she knew Peter Williamson's patience over his wife's activities snapped and he hit his wife. She said that she sometimes heard the woman crying and that Jean more than once claimed that her husband 'had beat her'. Often at these times she was 'very much the worse for liquor'.

One summer night, Jean Wilson came home drunk and sent the maid for two bottles of beer. However, Elizabeth went no further than the bottom of the stairs for she knew that all the shops were closed. On the stairway, she fell into conversation with two servants of their neighbour Mr McKenzie, a lawyer, 'and was inform'd by them of their finding the Defender lying on the stair with a man and that she was much intoxicated with liquor and that they brought her up and put her in at the Pursuer's door'. They said that 'her cloak was in disarray, the sleeve of her gown loose, her bonnet turned aside and her napkin much disordered'. This could have been the result of the woman taking less care with her appearance while drunk – or of some close-mouth fumblings with the unnamed gentleman. This seems to have been the last straw for young Miss Robertson. The lawyer's servants urged her to leave Jean Wilson's employ, and she duly informed her 'that she would stay no longer in her service'.

Jean Wilson had claimed to her servant that the woman found lying in the stair was not, in fact, her, but a female lodger. In response, Mr McKenzie's daughter told Elizabeth that this was not the first time her mistress had been found in this condition and 'that she need not go to expose herself by telling lies about the matter'. There was no female lodger in the Williamson household, and Elizabeth Robertson, of course, knew this. Jean, in turn, knew that she knew and tried to buy her silence over the matter with the present of a pocket napkin and the promise of a printed gown. The girl, though, had made up her mind. She wanted to leave – and leave she did.

Other witnesses spoke of Jean Wilson's drinking habits. Lewis Murray, servant to Hugh Murray, a porter dealer, said he often enjoyed a drop or two in the establishment run by William Johnston in Writer's Court. The witness freely admitted that Johnston's was 'a publick house which he believed to be a bawdy house or house of bad fame because it was generally by habit and repute seen to be and because [he] has frequently seen women whom he knew to be prostitutes frequenting said house'. He said he saw Jean Wilson there frequently between the hours of seven and nine 'in the company of Mrs Johnston, the mistress of the house, and another woman whose name [he] had forgot, but whom he believes is an English woman and whom he knows carried on business as a milliner in the city'. His employer, Hugh Murray, was also a customer of Johnston's and said he had seen Jean Wilson there 'passing from one room to another'.

During her time in their service, Elizabeth Robertson saw not just evidence of her mistress's drinking, but also of her infidelities. She said that a lawyer named Campbell often came to the house when Mr Williamson was not at home. He went into Jean's bedroom or the dining room and the door was closed behind them. Sometimes, she said, this particular visitor would come at eight and stay until after ten. One winter evening, Peter Williamson returned home unexpectedly while his wife was at supper with Mr Campbell. While Jean kept Peter occupied in the kitchen, Elizabeth was sent to clear the table. Campbell, she said, cowered behind the door. Later, after Peter went to bed, Jean and Campbell sat in the dining room alone for quarter of an hour before she let him out of a side door onto the stairway.

Another of Jean's gentlemen callers was Leith merchant Mr Grant. Once, Elizabeth was sent with a message for Jean's son in Heriot's Hospital to come and see his mother. She thought it strange that she be sent all of a sudden to see the young man, who 'had not been in the house for six or seven weeks prior to this period'. She also thought it strange that she be sent at teatime 'and nobody to bring the kettle'. Jean Wilson may have had more brewing than tea and wanted the house to herself. When Elizabeth Robertson arrived back from her errand, Jean was gone and the house locked.

Jean, it seemed, was no snob when it came to granting her favours and did not confine her dalliances to merchants and lawyers. David Gray, a full-liveried servant to a baker, also called sometimes and went with Jean into the dining room, 'where they remained sometimes an hour and sometimes less and sometimes more by themselves with the door shut'.

Her sexual activities apparently had an effect on her health. She complained of a pain in her side and had sent a servant to fetch Canongate surgeon John Carstairs. This other servant told Elizabeth that the mistress was suffering from a venereal disease. She warned her 'not to allow any of the children to drink or take anything out of the wine cup of the Defender'.

The cause of her malady was no idle below-stairs gossip, for Jean Wilson was indeed poxed. Dr Carstairs confirmed that he had treated Jean Wilson from the latter end of September or beginning of October 1787. He had found sores about her private parts 'which on inspection [he] immediately perceived to be venereal'. He put her on a course of mercury 'in consequence of which in about six weeks the Defender declared . . . she was completely cured'. (Salves of mercury were a commonly prescribed, and often lethal, means of treating sexually transmitted diseases. The poisonous ointment was rubbed into the skin of the sufferer. The room was kept warm, and the patient was left to sweat the disease out.) Dr Carstairs said that she seemed 'exceedingly unwilling to believe that her disorder could possibly be venereal and declared that if it was so she could have got it from no other person but her husband'. She claimed to have seen medicines about his shop and 'observed stained cloaths in his pocket'.

Elizabeth Robertson claimed that the disease and the doctor's visits were kept from Peter Williamson, who always appeared healthy and continued with his business dealings. He seemed unaware of his wife's condition, even though the illness made her 'deaf and hoarse for some time'. Dr Carstairs, however, said the patient had never asked him to conceal his visits from her husband. He said he 'had every reason [to believe] from the Defender's conduct and conversation that the Pursuer was acquainted with the nature of her complaint and knew of the [doctor's] attendance'. His fee, though, came in 'small partial payments', with the remainder being delivered to him partly by 'a little, fresh complexioned girl whom [he] knew to be the Defender's daughter and partly . . . from the serving maid'.

Williamson had built up a damning case against his wife. She had been painted as a drunkard, an adulteress and a liar. Despite her own protestations of innocence, she had been unable to produce any witnesses or evidence on her own behalf. Accordingly, in March 1789, the commissaries found her guilty of adultery and divorced her from 'the Pursuer's fellowship and company and society in all time coming'. Williamson was declared 'at liberty to marry whom and when he pleased as if the said Defender had never been married to him or was now naturally dead'.

Free of his troublesome third wife, and with his children restored to him, Peter Williamson embarked on the final stage of his life.

NINETEEN

He Is Now Arrived Almost at the Seventieth Year of his Age

Apart from the well-publicised details of his own life, little else is known of Peter Williamson's family. We know he had four children who survived but it is only possible to trace the names of the three boys and the birth dates of two of them: James, born 30 September 1778, and William, born 25 October 1781. The third boy was named John, but the name of the daughter who followed her mother into the mantua-making business remains elusive. After his divorce from Jean, Peter married for the fourth and final time on 6 May 1789, to Agnes McGeorge of the New Kirk parish who was described in the records as 'relict [widow] of Jasper Scoular, shoemaker'.

His daughter, it seems, returned to his side. In the 1790 edition of the *Directory,* there is an advertisement addressed 'To the Public':

> P. Williamson solicits the interest of the public in behalf of his
> Daughter, who has been regularly taught the Art of Ingrafting
> Silk Stockings, and making Silk Gloves and Mits in the neatest

manner. Likewise Washes Silk Stockings in the most approved taste. Orders are taken in for her at her Father's General Penny-Post Office, Luckenbooths, where her Employers may depend on their Work being done with Dispatch.

Following the adventures and excitement of his first sixty years, the final decade of Peter's life was relatively uneventful. He remained in the printing business and in 1789, in accordance with his tendency to milk his life for every penny, released an account of his most recent court battle, *The trial of divorce at the instance of Peter Williamson, printer in Edinburgh, against Jean Wilson, daughter of John Wilson bookseller in Edinburgh, his spouse*.

He continued to produce his *Edinburgh Directory* until 1796, missing only one year, when, he said, 'it was inconvenient for him to attend to the publishing of that year's Directory'. Publication was entrusted to a shoemaker named Aitchieson, who promised to give Peter 200 copies 'for his expense and labour', as well as promising to make it clear that the volume was published 'with his permission'. Aitchieson, it seems, made the mistake of failing to hand over the promised copies and Peter again resorted to the law to seek redress. There are few details of this case, and it may be that the suit died with Peter.

His postal system, too, passed from his control. In 1792, the postmaster general of Great Britain decided that his department would operate a new penny-post service in the area. The new scheme would boast four receiving houses in the city to accept mail not only for the new penny post, but also for the general post. The new service was to cover not just Edinburgh, but also Leith, Dalkieth, Musselburgh and Prestonpans. It was proposed there would be two deliveries: letters dropped into the receiving stations at night or before the general carriers left would be delivered that morning, while there would be a second delivery between the hours of two and four in the afternoon. Musselburgh and Prestonpans would be serviced by a rider who would set out in the morning, while another horseman would take the Dalkieth mail from him at Musselburgh and then rush back with return letters. The first rider would return to the city in time to catch the London mail coach.

Of course, Peter could not hope to compete with the capital and organisation of the government-run service. He was, by this time, sixty-two years of age. He was getting tired, and perhaps the stresses and strains of his life were catching up with him. However, he remained able to plead his case skilfully, although he continued to play his old trick of gilding the lily, on this occasion by exaggerating his age. In a 'Memorial' to the postmaster general, dated October 1792, he stated:

> The Memorialist having been lately informed that the long established Penny Post for this city and suburbs, under his direction, is soon to be taken from him and united with that of the General Post Office, humbly submits the following particulars to the consideration of the Postmaster General.
>
> The Memorialist after having experienced for a number of years such various vicissitudes of fortune as are scarcely to be paralleled in history, besides having been wounded in His Majesty's Service in America in the year 1754 from whence he was sent to England where he was discharged without any pension, at last fixed his residence in this city. But having been brought up to [no] particular branch of business he, for a considerable period, struggled hard to obtain even the means of common subsistence.
>
> About twenty-five years ago, with a view to better his situation, he was advised, with the assistance of friends, to set foot on a penny post office for the . . . city and its suburbs; an institution which the negligence and impositions of running stationers, chairmen and porters rendered absolutely necessary.

He accordingly, at considerable expense, commenced and has carried on the necessary arrangements in that department of publick utility. Nothwithstanding violent opposition and frequent interruption from various quarters, his unwavering fidelity and attention however gained him the confidence and encouragement of his fellow citizens and rendered his exertions in their service the only means of subsisting himself and family. He is now arrived almost at the seventieth year of his age and while flattering himself that the fruits of his future industry in the time above mentioned, would have enabled him to enjoy the few remaining years of his existence in comfort and with a suitable provision for his family, he will be rendered by the Establishment proposed to a situation truly distressing. He humbly hopes however that generous British Legislature will view his case with sympathy, and act towards him in a manner similar to which was experienced by the person who first established a Penny Post service in the City of London prior to its junction with the General Post Office Revenues. Or at least they will grant him an annual provision adequate to the loss he may sustain, or an appointment in the new arrangement suitable to his advanced age and ability.

An accompanying letter to the postmaster general from post office official Francis Freeling stated that:

Williamson has conducted himself with propriety and in some years he has got about £50 from his employment. It will be for your Lordships to determine upon such a statement whether it may be proper to allow Williamson a pension for his life as the Revenue is to benefit from the discontinuance of his penny post. I presume from his advanced age he will be incapable of sustaining an appointment in the new arrangement.

The postmaster general took note of the situation and in 1793, awarded Williamson a pension of twenty-five pounds a year. Peter took the cash and returned to his old trade as a vintner, opening a house at the first entry to Gavanlock's Land at the west end of the Luckenbooths on the north side of the road. He remained its landlord until 1797.

The world around him had changed. There were wars, of course, with France and Spain – and those pesky colonists in North America with their notions of freedom and prejudices against taxation and restrictions on trade. Seeds sewn during the French and Indian War burst into life in 1775, when the first shots in the American War of Independence were fired at Lexington. They bloomed the following year when the Patriots produced their Declaration of Independence on 4 July, the twenty-second anniversary of George Washington's retreat from Great Meadows.

Life, though, was catching up with Peter Williamson. Thanks to his writing, his legal adventures and his business dealings, he had become certainly one of the best-known men in the city, if not in Scotland. He was not universally liked – many believed, and probably rightly, that he had exaggerated his adventures. He was famous enough to be caricatured in his lifetime by barber-turned-artist John Kay, who had a print shop in Parliament Square. Some years after his death, Peter figured prominently in another painting. This hangs in the museum of the Grand Lodge of Edinburgh and shows the inauguration of Robert Burns as the poet laureate of the lodge on 1 March 1787. Considerable doubt hangs over whether this ceremony actually took place – there is no mention of it in the Lodge minutes, while it is believed Burns himself was in Anstruther on that date. However, artist and Freemason Stewart Watson depicted the scene in the middle of the nineteenth century, placing many well-known members of the order in his painting. Williamson, a committed Mason, can be found near the centre.

On 19 January 1799, aged sixty-nine, Peter Williamson lost his final battle. He died in his home, attended, it is to be hoped, by his wife and daughter. His obituaries, in newspapers and the *Scots Magazine,* all mentioned his being kidnapped as a child from Aberdeen, his transportation to America and his spending time there with the Indians, although they are wrongly named as Cherokees. They spoke of his 'amusing the public with their manners and customs', of his celebrated war whoop, of his businesses, in particular the institution of the first penny post in Edinburgh and the publishing of the *Directory*.

He appears to have left no will, although there was an advertisement in the Edinburgh *Courant* in September 1799 stating that 'if John and James Williamson, sons of the deceased Peter Williamson, will apply to John M'Gladshan, writer in Edinburgh (agent for his executors) they will hear of something to their advantage'. Over one year later, in December 1800, the advertisement was run again, this time with the addition of the words 'Not to be repeated'. Whether John and James ever found out something to their advantage, we do not know.

Peter was interred in an unmarked grave in Calton Cemetery, in the shadow of the newly built Calton Jail, which would replace the crumbling Heart of Midlothian. He was buried, as per his own instructions, wearing the Indian costume he brought back with him from America. The grave, the plot for which was owned by a Mr John Scott, lies fifteen paces north-east of where the monument to the political martyrs now stands. A memorial on the spot marks the death of an Agnes Williamson, aged sixty, on 7 February 1824. Agnes, though, was not Peter's daughter, for her father was a William Williamson, a clothier from Galashiels, who may well have been a relative.

Peter's work lived on after his death. His *French and Indian Cruelty* was reprinted many times, with particular success in 1812, and continued to sell well. The postal service he founded grew under government sponsorship. His notion of business directories spread across the country. Archibald Constable wrote about him, saying he was 'a great wag, of very jocular manners, and was accustomed to say droll and amusing things to those persons with whom he was in habits of intercourse'. His life is recorded at length in *Chambers Miscellany* and he is mentioned in various nineteenth- and twentieth-century articles and books.

It has been suggested that he was the inspiration for David Balfour in Stevenson's *Kidnapped* and for the 1970 film *A Man Called Horse*, starring Richard Harris. The former may well be true, but the latter is not, as it was inspired by another true-life tale.

Peter Williamson was a man both of and ahead of his time. His experiences in the Colonies brought out a deeply independent streak that only really came to the fore when he returned to his native land and faced seemingly insurmountable odds in his quest for justice – and cash. J.M. Barrie said that there are 'few more impressive sights in the world than a Scotsman on the make', and if that is true, then Peter Williamson must have been most impressive indeed. He was not our greatest writer, rather he plundered his past shamelessly for gain, appropriating details from others where and when he needed them. He was not the most innovative or successful businessman, but he saw ways to break new ground in commerce and he seized them. He was no lawyer, but he haunted the courts and wielded the law like a weapon.

But he is largely forgotten now and his name appears on no plaque or statue to his memory. It remains only on yellowing sheets of paper, is carried on the winds of North America, and echoes through the narrow alleys and wynds of old Edinburgh.

Perhaps his spirit is still with us, in the vast forests and great lakes of North America, in the drab corridors of Edinburgh courtrooms and the bright light of Parliament House. Perhaps it walks the dark streets of the Old Town by night and drinks with Robert Fergusson and

William Brodie, and perhaps even Robert Burns, in howffs long vanished. It is the spirit of adventure, of storytelling and of enterprise.

If he had a memorial, perhaps it would read, with a little help from a later writer, as follows:

Peter Williamson

1730–1799

Abducted as a child, captured by Indians, scourge of Aberdeen magistrates.

Purveyor of books, wines, spirits and tales.

'There was things which he stretched, but mainly he told the truth.' Mark Twain

Bibliography

Anderson, Fred, *The Crucible of War*, Faber and Faber, London, 2000

Anderson, W. Pitcairn, *Silences That Speak*, Alexander Brunten, Edinburgh, 1931

Barbard, Edward S., ed., *Story of the Great American West,* Reader's Digest, New York, 1977

Bradley, A.G., *Wolfe*, Macmillan and Co., London, 1895

Brogan, Hugh, *Longman History of the United States of America*, Longman, New York, 1985

Brown, Dee, *Bury My Heart at Wounded Knee*, Picador, London, 1975

Chambers, Robert, *Traditions of Edinburgh*, W&R Chambers, Edinburgh, 1967

Chambers Miscellany, Vol 1, Chambers, Edinburgh

Coleburn, Lord Henry, *Memorials of his Time*, Robert Grant and Son, Edinburgh, 1946

Colley, Linda, *Captives*, Jonathan Cape, London, 2002

Cooper, James Fenimore, *The Last of the Mohicans*, Wordsworth, London, 1992

Cordingly, David, *Life Among the Pirates*, Little, Brown & Co, London, 1995

Drimmer, Frederick, *Captured by Indians*, Dove Publications, New York, 1961

Goldman, William, *Four Screenplays*, Applause Books, New York, 1997

Goldman, William, *Which Lie Did I Tell?*, Bloomsbury, London, 2001

Hay, William J., *The Book of the Old Edinburgh Club* (Vol. 22), the Old Edinburgh Club, Edinburgh, 1929

Hewitson, Jim, *Tam Blake & Co*, Canongate Books, Edinburgh, 1993

Holmes, Richard, *Redcoat*, HarperCollins, London, 2001

Josephy, Alvin M., Jr, *500 Nations*, Random House, London, 1995

Kiple, Kenneth F., ed., *Plague, Pox and Pestilence*, Weidenfeld & Nicolson, London, 1997

Life in the Age of Exploration, Reader's Digest, London, 1994

Life in Colonial America, Reader's Digest, London, 1997

Lindsay, Maurice, ed., *Scotland: An Anthology*, Robert Hale, London, 1974

McDonnell, Frances, *The Adventures of Peter Williamson*, Frances McDonnell Publications, St Andrews, 1994

Maddocks, Melvin, *The Atlantic Crossing*, Time Life, New York, 1981

Milius, John, *The Life and Times of Judge Roy Bean*, Bantam Books, New York, 1973

Miller, Lee, ed., *From the Heart*, Pimlico, London, 1997

Prebble, John, *Culloden*, Penguin, London, 1996

Robertson, Joseph, *The Book of Bon Accord*, Aberdeen, 1839

Roughead, William, *Rascals Revived*, Cassell and Co., London, 1940

Skelton, Douglas, *Devil's Gallop*, Mainstream Publishing, Edinburgh, 2001

Smith, Robin, *The Making of Scotland*, Canongate Books, Edinburgh, 2001

Stevenson, Robert Louis, *Kidnapped*, Chatham River Press, New York, 1983

Tebbel, John and Keith Jennison, *The American Indian Wars*, Phoenix Press, USA, 1960

Ward, Geoffrey C., *The West*, Weidenfeld & Nicolson, London, 1996

Williamson, Peter, *The Travels of Peter Williamson*, Peter Williamson, Edinburgh, 1768

Williamson, Peter, *French and Indian Cruelty*, Peter Williamson, York, 1758

Williamson, Peter, *Life and Curious Adventures*, Peter Williamson, Aberdeen, 1812

MAGAZINES AND NEWSPAPERS
Blackwoods Magazine
Cornhill Magazine
Edinburgh Courant
Philately in Scotland
Postal History Society Bulletin
Scotland on Sunday
Scots Magazine
Scottish Field

NATIONAL ARCHIVE OF SCOTLAND RECORDS
CS29/10 March 1762 *Peter Williamson* v. *Cushnie & others*
CS226/9407 *Peter Williamson* v. *Fordyce & others*
CC8/5/19 Register of Consistorial Decreets 4 Feb 1788–28 Dec 1789
P01/13
GD248/590/4

USEFUL WEBSITES
www.dep.state.pa.us
www.quaker.org
www.explorepahistory.com
www.motherbedford.com
www.famousamericans.net
www.nysm.nysed.gov
www.pa-roots.com
www.rootsweb.com
www.ushistory.org
www.mohicanpress.com
www.publicbookshelf.com
www.u-s-history.com
www.wingedvictory.com
www.montrealnow.com
www.wikipedia.org
www.scotlandspeople.gov.uk
www.electricscotland.com
www.nas.gov.uk